JOEL & ET... COEN

BLOOD SIBLINGS

EDITED BY PAUL A. WOODS

PLEXUS, LONDON

Published by Plexus Publishing Limited
55a Clapham Common Southside
London SW4 9BX
Tel: 0207 622 2440
Fax: 0207 622 2441
www.plexusbooks.com
First Printing

Joel and Ethan Coen: blood siblings. - 2nd ed. - (Ultra screen
series)
   1. Coen, Joel 2. Coen, Ethan 3. Motion pictures - Reviews
   I. Woods, Paul A.
   791.4'3'75

   ISBN 0 85965 339 0

Printed and bound in Spain by Bookprint S.L., Barcelona
Cover & book design by Phil Gambrill
Cover photograph by Henny Garfunkel/Retna Ltd, USA

Acknowledgements
The following articles appear by courtesy of their respective
copyright holders: 'Introduction' and 'Afterword' by Paul A. Woods
copyright © 2003 by Plexus Publishing Limited. 'The Coen
Brothers Unplugged' by Ian Nathan, from Empire Magazine, June
1996. Copyright © 1996 by Emap Metro. 'Blood Simple' from
Variety, 23 May 1984. Copyright © 1984 by Variety. 'Blood Simple'
by Stephané Braunschweig, from Cahiers du Cinema, July/August
1985. Copyright © 1985 by Cahiers du Cinema. 'Goose Bumps' by
Kim Newman, from City Limits, 25 January 1985. Reprinted by
permission of the author. 'Simply Bloody' by Anne Billson, from
Time Out, 31 January 1985. Reprinted by permission of the author.
'Bloodlines' by Hal Hinson, from Film Comment, March/April
1985. Reprinted by permission of the publisher. 'Joel and Ethan
Coen' by Eric Breitbart, from American Film, May 1985. Reprinted
by permission of the publisher. 'Crimewave' from Variety, 22 May
1985. Copyright © 1985 by Variety. 'Crimewave' by Steve Jenkins,
from Monthly Film Bulletin, April 1986. Reprinted by permission of
the publisher. 'Raising Arizona' from Variety, 4 March 1987.
Copyright © 1987 by Variety. 'Raising Arizona' by Steve Jenkins,
from Monthly Film Bulletin, July 1987. Reprinted by permission of
the publisher. 'Ethan and Joel Coen' by Kevin Sessions, from
Interview, April 1987. Reprinted by permission of the publisher.
'Invasion of the Baby Snatchers' by David Edelstein, from American
Film, April 1987. Reprinted by permission of the author. David
Edelstein is co-author with Christine Vachon of Shooting to Kill.
'Interview with Joel and Ethan Coen' by Michel Ciment and
Hubert Niogret, from Positif, July/August 1987. Reprinted by
permission of the publisher. Copyright © 1987 by Positif. 'Miller's
Crossing' from Variety, 3 September 1990. Copyright © 1990 by
Variety. 'Miller's Crossing' by Steve Jenkins, from Monthly Film
Bulletin, February 1991. Reprinted by permission of the publisher.
'Shot by Shot' by Steven Levy, from Premiere, March 1990.
Reprinted by permission of the publisher. 'Chasing the Hat' by
Richard T. Jameson from Film Comment, September/October 1990.
Reprinted by permission of the author and the publisher. 'The Joel
and Ethan Story' by John H. Richardson, from Premiere (US),
October 1990. Reprinted by permission of the author. 'A Hat
Blown by the Wind' by Jean-Pierre Coursodon, from Positif,
February 1991. Copyright © 1991 by Positif. 'Barton Fink' from
Variety, 27 March 1991. Copyright © 1991 by Variety. 'Barton Fink'
by Steve Jenkins, from Sight and Sound, February 1992. Reprinted

by permission of the publisher. 'A Rock on the Beach: Interview
with Joel and Ethan Coen' by Michel Ciment and Hubert Niogret,
from Positif, September 1991. Copyright © 1991 by Positif. 'Barton
Fink and William Faulkner' by Marie-Jose Lavie, from Positif,
September 1991. Copyright © 1991 by Positif. 'Finking It' by John
Powers, from Sight and Sound, September 1991. By permission of
the publisher. 'Coen Brothers A – Z: The Big Two-Headed Picture'
by Mark Horowitz, from Film Comment, September/October 1991.
Reprinted by permission of the author and publisher. 'The
Hudsucker Proxy' by Todd McCarthy, from Variety, 31 January
1994. Copyright © 1994 by Variety. 'Strange Bedfellows' by John
Clark, from Premiere (US), April 1994. Reprinted by permission of
the author. 'The Sphinx Without a Riddle' by John Harkness, from
Sight and Sound, August 1994. Reprinted by permission of the
publisher. 'Double Vision' by John Naughton, from Premiere (UK),
September 1994. Reprinted by permission of the author. 'Do Not
Miss Fargo' by Graham Fuller, from Interview, March 1996.
Reprinted by permission of the publisher. 'Fargo' by Leonard
Klady, from Variety, 12 February 1996. Copyright © 1996 by
Variety. 'Fargo' by Todd McCarthy, from Premiere (US), March 1996.
Reprinted by permission of the author. 'Joel and Ethan Coen' by
Peter Biskind, from Premiere (US), March 1996. Reprinted by
permission of the author. 'Hell Freezes Over' by Lizzie Francke,
from Sight and Sound, May 1996. Reprinted by permission of the
publisher. 'Closer to Life than the Conventions of Cinema' by
Michel Ciment and Hubert Niogret, from Positif, September 1996.
Copyright © 1996 by Positif. 'The Big Lebowski' by Mike
Goodridge, from Screen International, 30 January 1998. Reprinted by
permission of the publisher. 'The Brothers Grim' by Andy Lowe,
from Total Film, May 1998. Reprinted by permission of the
publisher. 'The Logic of Soft Drugs': Interview with Joel and Ethan
Coen by Michel Ciment and Hubert Niogret, from Positif, May
1998. Copyright © 1998 by Positif. 'The Big Lebowski' by Roger
Ebert, from the Chicago-Sun-Times, 6 March 1998. Copyright ©
1998 by the Chicago-Sun-Times. 'Double Vision' by Jonathan
Romney, from The Guardian, 19 May 2000. Copyright © 2000 by
The Guardian. 'Brothers in Arms' by Jim Ridley, from Nashville
Scene, 22 May 2000. Copyright © 2000 by Nashville Scene. 'Hi
Honey, I'm Homer' by Philip French, from The Observer, 17
September 2000. Copyright © 2000 by The Observer. 'An Interview
with the Coen Brothers and Cast of The Man Who Wasn't There' by
Gerald Peary, from the Boston Phoenix, November 2001. Copyright
© 2001 by the Boston Phoenix. 'Pictures that Do the Talking' by
Andrew Pulver, from The Guardian, 13 October 2001. Copyright ©
2001 by The Guardian. 'The Man Who Wasn't There' by Peter
Bradshaw, from The Guardian, 26 October 2001. Copyright © 2001
The Guardian. 'Intolerable Cruelty' by Jean Oppenheimer, from The
Hollywood Reporter, 5 September 2003. Copyright © 2003 by The
Hollywood Reporter. 'Intolerable Cruelty' by David Rooney, from
Variety, 3 September 2003. Copyright © 2003 by Variety. It has not
been possible in all cases to trace the copyright sources, and the
publisher would be glad to hear from any such unacknowledged
copyright holders.
   We would like to thank the following film companies,
photographers and picture agencies for supplying photographs:
Henny Garfunkel/Retna Ltd, USA; Imagenet; Palace Pictures;
Electric Pictures/London Magazine; Kristine Larsen/Retna; Rank
Film Distribution; bfi Collections; Melinda Sue Gordon/Circle;
Patti Perret/20th Century Fox; National Screen Service; Manifesto
Film Sales; Polygram Filmed Entertainment; Michael
Tackett/Polygram Filmed Entertainment; Paul Smith/All Action;
Merrick Morton/Polygram Filmed Entertainment; E
Source/London Magazine; Armando Gallo/Retna; Universal
Pictures; Working Title Films/USA Films; Working Title
Films/Buena Vista Pictures.

CONTENTS

THE HUDSUCKER PROXY

FARGO

THE BIG LEBOWSKI

O BROTHER, WHERE ART THOU?

THE MAN WHO WASN'T THERE

INTOLERABLE CRUELTY

THE COEN BROTHERS UNPLUGGED

BY IAN NATHAN

The Coen brothers come as a pair. One directs (Joel), the other produces (Ethan), they both write and edit (under the pseudonym Roderick Jaynes). They make the cleverest, most distinctive and most uncategorisable movies in town. On first impression they are a trifle geeky; twitching, twittering and lapsing into lugubrious pauses and mumbles. Yet when it comes to their brilliant movies, they're so laid back they could fall over. And with Hitchcockian candour they'll deny all knowledge of trickery...

BLOOD SIMPLE (1983)

THE PITCH
JOEL: Well, you know, it's funny, we've never pitched a movie in our lives. We've never had to. How would we describe it?

ETHAN: Murder melodrama, Texas, you know.

JOEL: It's a melodrama. Sort of James M. Cain style.

ETHAN: And cheap. That would be a part of the pitch.

THE INSPIRATION
ETHAN: We'd read a lot of James M. Cain. We were certainly steeped in them and to some extent using them, those tightly plotted murder melodramas. We had also read some true crime – there had been some famous passion murders, husband and wife, domestic things.

JOEL: I had been working on very low budget horror independent movies as an assistant editor before we made *Blood Simple*. I'd been influenced by that genre also.

THE TITLE
ETHAN: It's a phrase Dashiell Hammett used in *Red Harvest* to describe what happens to the main character. The narrator, in a sense, goes crazy through his own fault and all these murders that take place through the story. It seemed like an evocative title.

THE CASTING
ETHAN: The only part we wrote for a specific actor was M. Emmet Walsh. Everybody else was just the usual audition process.

JOEL: Emmet had done a movie called *Straight Time* which we thought he was terrific in. That movie was in the back of our minds when we wrote the script.

THE MOVIE
Did you deliberately turn up the background noise for atmospheric effect?

ETHAN: Oh, the ceiling fan?

JOEL: Yeah, I don't know where that came from. The idea originally was some kind of confusion about the phonecall.

ETHAN: Did we do it on things beyond the ceiling fan?

Yes — dogs barking and the incinerator. Virtually to the point where you can only just hear characters speak.

JOEL: That was probably a mistake.

ETHAN: Yeah, that was bad sound. Dan Hedaya doesn't project at all. It's a mistake, you've caught us!

RAISING ARIZONA (1987)

THE PITCH

ETHAN: I guess it is a sort of a frenetic comedy. I wouldn't want to have to pitch it because it is a crazy comedy about people who kidnap a baby. It doesn't sound that appealing.

THE INSPIRATION

ETHAN: That started with thinking about Holly [Hunter] who was a friend of ours. We drew the character in the movie from her. There is a lot of physical comedy but there aren't any specific movie antecedents to it.

JOEL: It was a reaction, to do something much lighter, much more comedic, much faster paced. And, in a weird kind of way, more character driven.

THE TITLE

JOEL: There was a guy in Minnesota who owned a store called Plywood Minnesota.

ETHAN: It was unfinished furniture.

JOEL: We sort of took that and made it into Unfinished . . .

ETHAN: What the hell was the name? Unpainted . . .

JOEL: Unpainted Arizona. The father of the twins was then named Nathan Arizona.

ETHAN: He was the mogul of Unpainted Arizona.

THE CASTING

JOEL: Holly's part was written specifically for her and the part that Fran [Frances McDormand] played was written for Fran.

What did you see in Nicolas Cage?

JOEL: That was a difficult part to cast. As soon as we met Nic we knew he could play it. He just seemed to have the imagination and energy for the role.

THE FILM

Do you have an obsession with roads?

ETHAN: Yeah . . . I tell you, the only movie I remember looking at technically for *Raising Arizona* was the second *Mad Max* movie. We wanted to see how they staged the fight at the end . . . Which isn't really responsive to your question.

JOEL: We do have a thing about the roads, we use them a lot.

ETHAN: I think roads are bullshit. Isn't the first shot in *Blood Simple* on a road? Yeah, we have some roads.

Why do you think **Raising Arizona** *has been your most popular film [up until* **Fargo***]?*

ETHAN: It's a flukey business. It is obvious, for instance, that *Barton Fink* wouldn't be. It is more accessible than something like *Barton Fink*. That obvious thing aside, it is notoriously impossible to predict how movies are going to do.

MILLER'S CROSSING (1990)

THE PITCH

ETHAN: We were both really enthusiastic about Dashiell Hammett's novels. It's really nothing more or less than our attempt to do a Hammett story.

It's not a gangster film?

ETHAN: Not *per se*. We weren't thinking of *Scarface* or *Public Enemy* or what have you. Or Jimmy Cagney or Humphrey Bogart, except in so far as Bogart had done Dashiell Hammett stories. The influence of gangster movies was more indirect.

It seems more a gangster movie than a private eye movie.

JOEL: Definitely.

ETHAN: It's true. Especially with coats and fedoras, but it is sort of structured as this lone character trying to work out what happened while there is chaos all around him, which is the essential Hammett story.

THE TITLE

ETHAN: We tried to think of other titles for it because we weren't completely happy with *Miller's Crossing*. In the end we just stayed with it by default because we never thought of another. Titles are interesting – it is interesting you ask about them. Sometimes you come up with something that feels right – you know you are not going to change it, like *Raising Arizona* – and sometimes it is kind of neutral and stop-gap like *Miller's Crossing*.

THE CASTING

JOEL: First of all, the part that Albert [Finney] played was originally written for Trey Wilson, who was the father in *Raising Arizona*, but Trey died of a brain aneurysm right before we started rehearsing. So Albert came in at the last minute.

ETHAN: He had just walked in his door from Finland where he had been shooting some damn thing for several months. He said, "Yeah, sure, I'm free."

JOEL: We had never imagined Gabriel Byrne's character as being Irish until he came in. It was one of those things where hearing him read the part we thought, that sounds pretty good with an Irish accent. It fitted with the whole idea of the movie, with all the different ethnicities at war with each other.

ETHAN: It wasn't much of a switch, seeing this character as Irish American. Actually the Irishness invaded the movie a little bit by virtue of the score which was adapted to be Irish. So the movie got to feel a little more Celtic.

JOEL: The part was written specifically for [John] Turturro. Again, like with Holly, we had known Turturro for a long time.

THE MOVIE

What is the significance of the hat?

JOEL: It's just an icon of gangsterism. It feels right. Sometimes these things just feel right. Kind of emotionally or intuitively.

Don't you find people come back to your movies and apply symbolism to all these things?

ETHAN: Yeah.

JOEL: But it's not intended that way and I don't think you need to read the movie that way to make sense of it.

ETHAN: Also, it's kind of a reductive way to look at a movie. It assumes you have one reason for putting a hat in where there might be all sorts of reasons that accumulatively make it feel appropriate.

BARTON FINK (1991)

THE PITCH

ETHAN: You know, New York writer goes to Hollywood, hilarity ensues . . . Haha, *decapitations* and hilarity ensue.

THE INSPIRATION

ETHAN: The genesis of that was a couple of things. There was the thing about having Goodman and Turturro's characters together in a claustrophobic setting. And there was this big derelict hotel. Somehow a lot of that, together with those two characters, seemed to point to this premise.

Had you seen this hotel, was there one that inspired you?

ETHAN: No, although we had sort of seen and stolen the slogan for the hotel: "A day or a lifetime", which seemed an incredibly depressing slogan in the place we put up the cast and crew on *Blood Simple* in Austin, Texas.

JOEL: Telegraph Road Apartments: A Day Or A Lifetime.

THE TITLE

JOEL: Just the character.

ETHAN: Just him. I don't personally know any Bartons or Finks.

THE CASTING

JOEL: Again, we wrote the part specifically for John Turturro.

ETHAN: Goodman had obvious appeals.

THE MOVIE

Did the whole idea of writer's block come from personal experience?

JOEL: It is true we kinda got stuck. The plot got so complicated in *Miller's Crossing* and we – it wasn't writer's block – but we decided to think about something else for a while and we wrote *Barton Fink* pretty quickly.

ETHAN: I think the whole concept of writer's block is comical. It's something a self-important character like Barton would dignify himself with having.

Was there any significance to him writing a wrestling movie? Wrestling with his soul, perhaps?

ETHAN: There are all sorts of things that made that appealing. One was pairing him off with John Goodman in size and build. Also, before writing that movie, we read a book called *City of Nuts* by Otto Fredrich. It's about Hollywood in the Forties, and in it he mentions that William Faulkner had worked on wrestling movies.

JOEL: It turns out there were wrestling movies. It was this weird sub-genre.

ETHAN: There were all sorts of reasons in seeing two guys in their underwear grappling with one another: the whole sort of queasy homoerotic thing; the weird connection between the characters; and, like you say, Barton the self-important figure wrestling with his problems.

JOEL: With Barton as this self-important playwright being reduced to writing what is sort of a vulgar genre movie. And you couldn't think of anything more vulgar than a wrestling movie.

THE HUDSUCKER PROXY (1994)

THE PITCH

JOEL: I *wouldn't* pitch that now.

ETHAN: With benefit of hindsight.

JOEL: It's sort of a romantic screwball comedy in the Preston Sturges / Frank Capra mode, set in New York in the Fifties about the man who invents the Hula-Hoop. We never sit in a room and pitch a script, we generally write and then give it to whoever is interested in financing it.

ETHAN: It was already written in this case, with Sam Raimi, although we gave it a fast rewrite before we came back to do it.

THE INSPIRATION

JOEL: Well, you know, the comedies of Preston Sturges and Frank Capra and Howard Hawks. We were thinking in *Hudsucker* of writing a very specific picture.

THE TITLE

ETHAN: Again out of the air, really.

Were you ever asked to change it?

ETHAN: No, because – usually – contractually we have the say.

THE CASTING

How did you get Paul Newman?

ETHAN: That was actually really easy – we sent him the script he said, "Yeah, sure, I'll do it."

Did you consider other possibilities for the role.

ETHAN: The studio suggested all sorts of names, a lot of them comedians who were clearly wrong. He was the bad guy and was comic, but there was something wrong about making him a sort of comic figure. We wanted him to have the sort of weight Paul brings to it.

How about Tim Robbins and Jennifer Jason Leigh?

JOEL: We met the both of them in auditioning.

It's a very Tim Robbins role – nice but dim.

ETHAN: Right, Tim really embraced the dim bit of it. In a good way. And Jennifer, we had met before on other things. We had always liked her work and wanted to work with her, although it wasn't given that Jennifer had to do this because it was in line with stuff she had done previously.

JOEL: It was different.

ETHAN: Once we saw her, it was obvious that she had to do it.

THE MOVIE

Why the Hula-Hoop?

ETHAN: It was really just to fulfil certain plot imperatives. The sort of idea a dimwit could come up with . . .

JOEL: That on the face of it was absurd but everyone would know what it was and it would be a huge success.

ETHAN: It fitted the bill perfectly. It was this embryonic idea that became popular.

The tag line, "You know your kids . . .", did that come from anywhere?

JOEL: No.

How about "The future is now"?

ETHAN: There is something like that . . . Isn't that in *Mirage*? A Sixties Edward Dmytryk movie with Gregory Peck?

JOEL: "The future is here." That's interesting because in *Twelve Monkeys* they use the slogan, "The future is past."

ETHAN: *Mirage* is interesting, the plot hinges around the story of a guy who falls or is pushed out of a window.

How was your first experience with special effects?

JOEL: It was very interesting. Originally we didn't really know how to do those things. In fact, all the computer compositing that we did has only been possible in the last couple of years. Before that we would have had to use blue screen which is not quite as good.

FARGO (1996)

THE PITCH

ETHAN: [*Clearly getting into this now*] Man hires thugs to kidnap his own wife so he can collect the ransom from wife's father . . . hilarity ensues. Dismemberment and hilarity ensues.

JOEL: You've got yourself a picture.

THE INSPIRATION

JOEL: *Fargo* is a true story we heard from a friend. We were attracted to the idea because it took place in Minnesota where we grew up.

Did you notice the similarities to **Blood Simple***?*

ETHAN: I noticed them when we were out on the highway shooting at night. I thought, we've shot this headlights approaching thing before. It was depressingly similar. I guess they are contemporary crime stories and involve . . .

Roads?

ETHAN: Ha! They both involved roads. They both involve plans going horribly wrong.

How close are the characters to their real counterparts?

ETHAN: No idea, except in so far that they did what these characters did. We don't pretend to have made a documentary in terms of characterising people.

THE TITLE

JOEL: Fargo is the name of the town in North Dakota where he went to hire these guys. And we just liked the name of the town. There's no reason beyond that. It's a better name than Brainerd.

THE CASTING

JOEL: Again we wrote the part specifically for Fran. Steve Buscemi and Peter Stormare were people we've worked with before.

THE MOVIE

Was it a relief to make a non-studio film?

ETHAN: We never had that sort of baggage with *The Hudsucker Proxy*. We've been lucky in that we've never had that. The studio, in the case of *Hudsucker*, was co-financed by Warner Bros. and PolyGram. It is a relief in other ways. It was a less arduous shoot.

JOEL: I wouldn't call one harder or easier than the other. On the whole, you might be a bit more comfortable in that it's easier to control all the elements down to the smallest details.

ETHAN: That is one of the great virtues that unlike *Hudsucker* we could control every scene. With *Hudsucker* there were so many different elements, your attention is split more.

Do you find yourself writing more toward the smaller scale?

JOEL: The truth of the matter is you wouldn't want to have to write exclusively small scale, and you wouldn't want to do exclusively large scale. They are different challenges and like anything else you don't want to be tied to one thing. So, if you're lucky you can mix it up.

INTRODUCTION

BY PAUL A. WOODS

THE BIG LEBOWSKI (1998)
THE PITCH
ETHAN: The story is the conceit of setting them [the Dude (Jeff Bridges) and Walter Sobchak (John Goodman)] against each other, and it's the idea of putting the Dude character in the middle of a story that's loosely patterned on a Raymond Chandler novel . . . he wrote these private eye stories in and about L.A. The characters are all emblematic of L.A., and it involves a character journeying among these different characters. In the case of our movie, it's obviously not a private eye movie, the main character's an ageing pot-head. But in the sense of narrative structure, that's what it is.

Fifteen years on from their mood-swathed, homicidal debut, *Blood Simple*, Joel and Ethan Coen had an impressive seven feature-length works of perverse plotting and oddball character study under their belts. ("We're pretty slow, really," confesses elder bro' Joel. "We're lazy. That's why we like the Dude. We tend to make a movie once every two years.") Four of these were derived from the American hardboiled literary style, often called 'pulp' – though only a few of its main exponents ever contributed to the eponymous cheap magazines. *The Big Lebowski*'s shambling old hippie hero, the Dude, though light years away from Chandler's hardbitten white knight of a private eye, Marlowe, is a natural progression.

THE INSPIRATION
JOEL: . . . the Walter character is a composite of several people we know. Bridges is based on an old friend of ours. So we were thinking about those characters in the context of this kind of story . . .

Accusations of coldness and condescension always seem like a misreading of the Coens. "The dudes we know were part of this amateur softball league," says Joel of the friends who inspired Jeff Bridges' stoned amateur tec, "but we changed it to bowling because it was so much more visually compelling, and it's the kind of sport you can do when you're drinking and smoking." Add to the softball players the influence of one Jeff Dowd, an amiably laidback independent film distributor instrumental in their early career, some intense Vietnam vet buddies and gunslinging screenwriter/director John Milius, and you have character composites who are (to them) much too recognisable to dismiss. The Coens *like* their endearingly flawed characters.

THE CASTING
JOEL: We tend to write both for people we know and have worked with, and some parts

without knowing who's going to play the role. In *The Big Lebowski* we did write for John [Goodman] and Steve [Buscemi], but we didn't know who was getting the Jeff Bridges role. **ETHAN:** The only time we ever directed Jeff, was when he would come over at the beginning of each scene and ask, "Do you think the Dude burned one on the way over?" I'd reply "yes" usually, so Jeff would go over in the corner and start rubbing his eyes to get them bloodshot.

While Bridges admits that his personification of the Dude sounds the echo of a younger incarnation of himself, the Coens have stated they wrote *Lebowski* primarily as a means of working with Goodman again. In essence, his Walter – humourless but hysterical, a barrel-chested obsessive for whom everything relates to 'Nam or his conversion to Judaism – is the film's *raison d'etre*.

It's this same leavening of artifice with bar-room (or bowling alley) eccentricity that held the Coens' unique film canon from breaking through into the mainstream. While Ethan observes how it's "the norm, or at least unremarkable in novels" for the central character to be a less than heroic figure stained by life, Joel observes, "People like the main characters in movies to be audience surrogates, or immediately identifiable, someone to root for . . . It helps to promote a kind of narrative uniformity." More at ease conversing with everyday Joes and Janes in bars or taxis than with interviewers, their discerning ear for common speech adapts its nuances for their stylised screen dreams. Reading some of the more deadpan interview responses in this book, the dialogue finds parallels in their own speech: classic American less-is-more laconicism.

THE MOVIE
ETHAN: It only strikes us in retrospect, but it's undeniable, we did it [used a kidnapping scenario] three times [*Raising Arizona, Fargo, Lebowski*]. I guess it's that it's a pregnant plot thing, an ongoing criminal enterprise that seems to suggest all kinds of promising plot opportunities. It's easy for things to spin out of control, to have them go progressively wrong.

While it's as inaccurate to pigeonhole the Coens as comedy makers as it is to credit them as neo-*noir* specialists, there are few of the human condition's absurdities that don't offer up some laughs: deceit, betrayal, even kidnapping and murder. Though inclined only to intellectualise about structure rather than content, the fact that characterisation seems infinitely more important to the Coens than plot minutiae – largely free of unifying themes, grand concepts or personal motifs – suggests to some critics that they might be guilty of offering up nothing more than, gasp, *entertainment*.

O BROTHER, WHERE ART THOU? (2000)
THE PITCH
ETHAN: It's a musical romp about the Depression.

JOEL & ETHAN COEN: BLOOD SIBLINGS

JOEL: The Three Stooges meets Homer's *Odyssey*.

O Brother, Where Art Thou? is, purportedly, a period 1930s version of Homer's *Odyssey*, based around a man trying to find his way home after escaping from a chain gang in the Deep South. As a step up the Hollywood ladder, Ulysses Everett McGill (his name a hybrid of Homer's voyaging warrior and hayseed Irish-American) is played by TV heart-throb-turned-A-lister George Clooney. Ostensibly a period piece, complete with bleached-out, near-sepia colours, 'ol' timey' bluegrass songs and biblical allusions (far more direct than the hokey Homeric conceit), *O Brother* is an old-fashioned 1930s/40s-style piece of 'family entertainment', leavened with enough integrity and ingenious touches to make counting those allusions worthwhile.

THE INSPIRATION
JOEL: We didn't really start with Homer. We started with the idea of these three fugitives escaping from the chain gang and Homer suggested itself later when we realised the movie was essentially about the main character trying to get home and having this series of adventures on the way.
ETHAN: We never actually read it. But we read the comic book version of *The Odyssey* and tarted the movie up with the Cyclops, etc.

From the slightly over-romanticised 'Golden Age of Hollywood' comes one of the Coens' nabobs of movie-making: Preston Sturges, director of 'screwball comedies' like *Sullivan's Travels* (1941), his influence highly visible in *The Hudsucker Proxy*. Sturges, like the Coens, was mocking of the idea of the moviemaker as a moral artist with a serious message to impart, personified by the title character played by Joel McCrea in *Sullivan's Travels*. Throwing himself into a hobo persona and a personal odyssey that takes him from haycart to island prison, self-important Sullivan intends, with echoes of Barton Fink, to use the experience as raw material for his socially-redeeming film project: *Oh Brother, Where Art Thou?*

The Coens' *O Brother* (note how they stress their movie's independence with the missing 'h') is, like Sturges' movies, essentially 'only' entertainment. But it extends beyond homage or pastiche. True, all of its narrative points are grounded in the past: a time when both poor blacks and poor white trash found themselves on chain gangs, principally for the crime of being poor; when the popularity of old-time folk and country songs were segregated on radio from their first cousin, the black country-blues, while outside of radio the music was cross-pollinating; when a pork-barrel populist politician like Pappy O'Daniel (a real character, transplanted here from governorship of Texas to Mississippi, played by Charles Durning) commanded the airwaves with his own radio show and snowjobbed the voters; when the Ku Klux Klan held regular torchlight parades, and to "hang a negra" was a different class of activity to the crime of murder.

The story may belong to a semi-fictional past, but if we don't hear the echoes then we're buying the line that poverty, race and political corruption just aren't the compelling issues they once were.

THE CASTING
ETHAN: In this instance, we wrote for John Goodman: we knew we wanted him to be the sort of Cyclops equivalent, and we wrote the part of Penny for Holly [Hunter]. And we also wrote the Babyface Nelson part for Michael Badalucco.

Everett's partners on the lam make up a charming confederacy of dunces: an antsy hothead named Pete (Coens regular John Turturro) and a big-hearted simpleton called Delmar (film director Tim Blake Nelson) – augmented by Coens veteran John Goodman in a cameo as a Bible-bashing 'Cyclops', Big Dan Teague. Other figures encountered along the way include real-life bank robber George 'Baby Face' Nelson, played by Michael Badalucco as a comic manic-depressive, whose crime career actually took place in the Coens' native mid-West. (Similar artistic licence is taken in *Miller's Crossing*, supposedly set in 1929, when Johnny Caspar refers to a posthumous sighting of Nelson's one-time rival/partner John Dillinger – who wasn't gunned down by the FBI until 1934.)

THE MOVIE
ETHAN: Early on, the issue of music began to inform our thinking about it, and that argued for a Southern setting. One other thing that conspired to make it Southern was the early idea of making the characters chain-gang refugees.
JOEL: In terms of tone, it does sort of resemble *Raising Arizona* more than it does *Fargo* or *Miller's Crossing*. There aren't any bodies in wood-chippers or people throwing up blood.

O Brother, Where Art Thou? is oft described as a collection of set-pieces. Its escapes, fights, near-hangings, damnations and redemptions are held together by the *Odyssey* concept, as well as by an affection for the corny old 'hayseed movies' the brothers cite. It's also in part a musical, albeit one where the songs accompany the narrative rather than being big production numbers. For the brothers' sins, a scene like the Soggy Bottom Boys declaiming their version of 'Man of Constant Sorrow' ties all the threads of cinematic homage and historical accuracy together into one big goofy package marked 'entertainment'.

THE MAN WHO WASN'T THERE (2001)
THE PITCH
JOEL: It's in black and white, set in 1949, and Billy Bob Thornton plays a barber. It's a dark comedy . . .

From such inauspicious beginnings did the Coens make their next step forward into the past. As far from the colourful comic freneticism of their previous two movies as it's possible to be, *The Man Who Wasn't There* is really only as much of a comedy as Samuel Beckett was a master of the one-liner. Cut to a languid, almost static pace, it is, complained *Cahiers du cineaste* and Coens enthusiast Michel Ciment, "A 90-minute film that plays for two hours." Wilfully anachronistic in today's climate of CGI-enhanced blockbusters, Roger Deakins' black-and-white *noir* tones are on decolourised colour stock, resembling an early colour TV on the blink. It fared as badly at the box office as you might expect – pulled by the distributors within an indecently short period after its opening. It's also as potent a film as the Coens have ever made.

THE INSPIRATION

JOEL: I like the sort of skanky *film noirs*, the real low budget Edgar G. Ulmer kind, you know, *Detour* kind of movies.

The way the Coens tell it, *The Man Wasn't There* is only a *film noir* by default. Ed Crane, the barber, isn't really a typical *noir* hero insists Ethan – for all Thornton's superficial resemblance to Bogart, and his heavy chainsmoking, he's far removed from a square-jawed private eye or a man with a past on the run. But then, the Coens' hardboiled inspiration, James M. Cain, never dealt with such solid archetypes. His was an almost poetic pop-literature of little lives and big ideas that combine to fatal effect. (The brothers tip a nod to the debt by naming a secondary character Diedrickson, the name of Barbara Stanwyck's *femme fatale* and her murdered husband in the 1944 screen version of Cain's *Double Indemnity*.)

In this sense, Ed Crane, the barber, is the emblematic *noir* anti-hero: the little man betrayed by forces of chance and deceit, and by his own half-understood actions – thrown onto a course that can only spiral downward, like the ill-fated musician in Joel's favourite B-movie *noir*, *Detour* (1945). While Ethan may have distinguished himself with some post-Chandler crime fiction pastiches in his book *Gates of Eden*, *noir* isn't just a byword for Chandleresque rough stuff so much as an airless cinematic universe, where fatalism and expressionist photography combine. On that basis, *The Man Who Wasn't There* is almost the epitome – whereas the film it most obviously refers to, *The Night of the Hunter* (1955 – an underwater shot of the dead Shelley Winters echoed by Jon Polito as murdered 'pansy' Tolliver in his submerged car) makes the grade for cinematography alone.

THE TITLE

RODERICK JAYNES: *Pansies Don't Float* was an early working title that, thank goodness, they were prevailed upon to discard. They had likewise been coaxed away from more opaque titles aiming to peg the movie generically as a *noir*: *I, the Barber*, *The Man Who Smoked Too Much*, and *The Nirdlinger Doings*.

Originally announced as *The Barbershop Project*, as the mythical Mr Jaynes, the Coens' English editor, acknowledges, the movie was in need of a sharper title. With accidental echoes of Hitchcock's *The Man Who Knew Too Much* (1935/56), this is really the story of 'The Man Who Knew Too Little' – about himself, about his marriage, about the nature of the world he inhabits, and the likely consequences of one rash course of action. The title, befitting its *noir*-ish come-on, also holds an ironic double meaning: as much as the barber is never detected as being 'there' at the scene of the crime he actually commits, he's wrongly fingered as being 'there' at the wrong one; further, he plays such a passive role in his own life ("I never thought of myself as 'the barber'," Ed claims, robbing himself of any worldly significance) that he can hardly be said to be 'there', to exist, at all – until he makes his fatal choices.

THE CASTING

JOEL: We do tend to work with bigger stars now. This movie is sort of an exception to that because Billy Bob and Fran are very well known actors, but aren't the kind of 'movie stars' in the sense that George Clooney and Brad Pitt are.

Billy Bob Thornton, as Ed, is almost a still-life portrait, animated only by a voiceover of his bemused inner monologue. His performance is remarkable: either low-key tragic to those who appreciate it, or the reason the movie moves at such an irritatingly slow pace for those who don't. The supporting cast are no less effective: Frances McDormand, Joel's Oscar-winning wife, as Ed's wife Doris, a sensuous department-store accountant similarly doomed by events; James Gandolfini, TV's Tony Soprano, as Big Dave, the violent braggart who's cuckolding Ed; Michael Badalucco as Frank, Ed's hail-fellow-well-met brother-in-law and fellow barber, driven to hysteria by his sister's destruction, and Jon Polito as the sleazy businessman Creighton Tolliver. Given their subtle impact, they're as effective an ensemble as ever appeared in a Coens movie.

THE MOVIE

JOEL: With this one, we were thinking *noir* to a certain extent, but we were also thinking about science fiction movies from the early 1950s. You know, the flying saucers and the pod people. We were interested in the whole idea of post-war anxiety, you know, atom bomb anxiety and the existential dread you see in Fifties movies, which curiously seems appropriate now.

Some of the audience, perturbed by the appearance of a flying saucer late in the plot, took it too literally. The UFO is symbolic, not only of the unease of the late1940s/early 1950s, and of the film's sense that American suburbia is an unreal façade concealing dark realities, but of the main character's lack of control – Ed is so bewildered by events that conspire to destroy him that flying saucers might just as well be the cause, as Big Dave's widow claims they are.

Even in the film's closing scene, a classic *noir*-ish setpiece, there is a sense of otherworldliness. As Ed faces the chair, the white-hot crackle of electricity seems to offer an escape from his fated life. "I don't know what waits for me, beyond the earth and sky. But I'm not afraid to go," his voiceover calmly states. "Maybe the things I don't understand will be clearer there . . . Maybe Doris will be there," he hopes aloud, and *film noir* melds with existentialism at an emotionally affecting level. "And maybe I can tell her all those things they don't have words for here."

With genre convention and character psychology feeding hungrily off of each other, the atmospherically evocative music of Carter Burwell blending with that of Beethoven, *The Man Who Wasn't There* testifies to the Coens' ability to create their own hermetically-sealed universes.

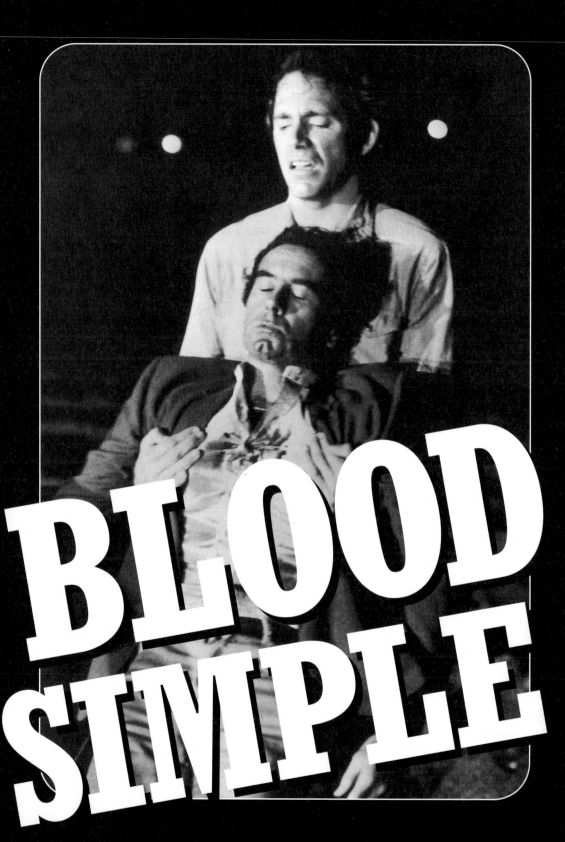

BLOOD SIMPLE

BLOOD SIMPLE

REVIEW FROM VARIETY

An inordinately good low-budget *film noir* thriller, *Blood Simple* first surfaced at the recent USA Film Festival in Dallas where it received positive notices. Written, directed and produced by brothers Joel and Ethan Coen, associated with *Evil Dead* filmmaker Sam Raimi, it is a finely crafted and intriguingly written picture that belies its $1-1,500,000 budget. Indeed, every cent, and then some, is up there on the screen. Picture is a real sleeper and a sure bet to be picked up by one of the U.S. majors' classics divisions, which will need to muster a campaign as terrific as the picture to draw out its full box-office potential.

Aside from the subtle performances, usually lacking in a film of this size, the observant viewer will find a cornucopia of detail. Director's attention to it takes what could have been a flat and lifeless canvas and paints a colourful, moody piece with a texture that's very true-to-life. The involving plot takes a twisty course as it unravels, and one wants to steer the characters straight when they take a wrong turn. Crux of the story-line is that the viewer knows the motivations of all the characters, while they are privy to only their own, thus making for audience around-the-bend anticipation.

Dan Hedaya plays Marty, a brooding owner of a Texas bar whose overbearing and oppressive attitude has taken its toll on his young wife Abby (Frances McDormand). She leaves him for a bartender at the joint. Incensed, Hedaya hires a sleazy, onerous malcreant named Visser (played with appropriate malice by M. Emmet Walsh) to kill his wayward wife and her boyfriend Ray (John Getz).

Walsh takes a snapshot of the lovers asleep in bed, doctors the photo to make it appear he's fulfilled the contract, and meets Hedaya at the bar after hours to collect. Upon payment, Walsh pulls out the wife's gun and shoots Marty dead in the chest. But the victim has swapped the photo and put it in the office safe before his demise, making Walsh's perfect crime not so.

Getz appears on the scene and finds the body and his lover's gun before the police get a chance and, believing she has killed her husband, panics. He cleans up the blood (there's a lot of it) and takes the body in his car to dump it out in the sticks, but on the way, Hedaya proves to be not quite dead yet. Getz, via a device borrowed from Edgar Allan Poe, drags Hedaya into a field and buries him – alive.

He then returns to McDormand, babbling that they must "keep our heads". She hasn't a clue what Getz is talking about, and goes to the bar to find out. Walsh, meanwhile, is trying to hammer his way into the safe to retrieve the doctored photo that links him to the murder that wasn't quite murder. Walsh hides in the closet upon McDormand's arrival, whereupon she sees the battered safe and assumes Getz was breaking into it, got caught by Hedaya, and killed him. Now she suspects Getz, and Walsh suspects both lovers are on to him.

Final confrontation between Walsh and the lovers is paced with mounting suspense, with a chilling face-off between McDormand and Walsh that's outright horrific.

Performances are top-notch all around, Walsh in particular conveying the villainy and scummy aspects of his character with convincing glee. Newcomer McDormand has an aura of animal desire about her that makes Getz's headlong plunge into a doomed situation all the more believable. Hedaya's Marty is a carefully etched study of desperation and tenacity, and Samm-Art Williams as a sceptical bar-hand is credible.

Sound and lighting are a real plus, and add much to the Hitchcock-esque look, as does the eye for detail of the art direction and production design. Catch it if you can.

Abby (Frances McDormand) searches nervously for her husband Marty — unaware of his death, and of who is really manipulating the murderous situation.

BLOOD SIMPLE

BY STEPHANÉ BRAUNSCHWEIG

If one retains the French title (*Sang Pour Sang*), this film by Joel Coen (produced and co-written by his brother Ethan Coen) would appear to be a modern western (a "Texan"), filled with "revenge and blood". Borrowed from Dashiell Hammett, the original American title is much more interesting: it tells us first that it isn't a western but a crime story (hence the Critic's Prize at the Festival International du Film Policier at Cognac, 1985); it places us directly, thanks to two small words, within the atmosphere of the film. "Blood Simple" would perhaps translate more literally as "Hébété par le sang" ("Dazed by blood"). The phrase suggests the demeanour of those who've just killed, who are suddenly no longer really themselves, terrorised by their inconceivable deeds (one of the psychological motors of the plot: the inconceivability of murder), by death (so difficult to attain: as in the murder scene in Hitchcock's *Torn Curtain*, the human body proves extremely resistant), by blood (which marks everything, permeating the film until it becomes a parody of itself – the actors dazed at the sight of so much hemoglobin!). As for the spectators, they can only hesitate before the odious imagination of the Coen brothers, caught between laughter and fright: the film plays subtly on both levels, delivering, at the most atrocious moments, the strongest doses of black humour (the blood on the ground that spreads in the attempt to clean it, transforming the wooden flooring into a fishmonger's display). Add to this the formidable construction of a fool-proof script, built on a traditional frame with three characters (husband-wife-lover) perverted by the intrusion of a fourth, whose existence is only known to those he murders. Superbly crafted from ambiguity and lies, the plot multiplies into as many versions as it has characters, each of whom only discovers a small piece of the truth.

Editing and framing accentuate the dissociation between what (really) happens and what is thought to happen (the imagination and partial knowledge of the characters): Joel Coen steadily alternates close-ups on faces and close-ups on gestures and objects (the film has many cuts), avoiding where possible the long- or close-medium shots which tie gestures and faces to precise actions and intentions, concealing everything except the most significant details, seen only by the camera and the omniscient spectator. Coen also prefers the shot/reverse shot to a medium shot on two characters talking, doubtless (signifying alienation) because in Texas, "everyone pulls for himself." Alas, that systematic editing process produces, in the long run, an impression of monotony and boredom, and the achievements of the camera (rapid tracking close to the ground, low-angle shot under a wash basin or high-angle close-ups of fans, etc.), instead of varying the effect and increasing the tension (which succeeds sometimes: as in the scene of a lorry at night), serve only to make the monotony flashy, turning this exemplary script into an exercise in style.

Translated by Paul Buck and Catherine Petit

GOOSE BUMPS

BY KIM NEWMAN

JOEL COEN: I started working in films as an assistant editor, mostly on independent horror films, including *The Evil Dead*. As I was working as an editor in New York, Ethan and I were writing scripts together. We'd been working for other people and decided to come up with something we could produce ourselves. We wanted to do something that was producable on a relatively low budget, but something that was viscerally engaging to a fairly wide audience, so we decided to make a thriller. That sequence at the end is probably more influenced by horror films.

Blood Simple isn't a horror film, but it has certain horror elements in it. We were generally influenced by a certain kind of hardboiled American fiction of the Dashiell Hammett/James M. Cain school. We like those kind of overheated passion-murder stories, where the characters are all basically doomed from the start.

ETHAN COEN: In a way, there's something old-fashioned about *Blood Simple*. It was fun writing the script, raising audience expectations and figuring out how to subvert those expectations in a way that would keep them guessing, giving them something which they don't expect and which is even better than what they had expected.

JOEL: We both believe that audiences like stories, and that's what engages them, and the fact that, generally, movies suffer from the lack of a story isn't an indication of changing audience tastes, but of laziness on the part of film-makers.

ETHAN: It was fun at the New York festival, which is full of movies you go to because they're good for you. When our movie showed up there, the audience was kind of surprised, and took it as a reward for sitting through the films that were good for them.

Isn't **Blood Simple** *good for you?*
ETHAN: Hopefully.
JOEL: We're not making movies to enlighten the audience. We're making them to make them scream.
ETHAN: I don't know why audiences like being punished by this kind of movie, but they definitely do.
JOEL: Even though, in the bare bones of its plot, *Blood Simple* is a downer, people leave the movie quite chipper. We wanted the audience to leave on an upbeat.

You have a magnificent gag at the end. Would you close your comedy with an axe murder?
JOEL: That's much more challenging.
ETHAN: Funnily enough, our comedy begins with a suicide, but it's a very fun suicide. It won't upset anybody.

A lot of people in Parliament and The Festival of Light were upset by **The Evil Dead.**
JOEL: The movie is really just fun, and it's very sick to take it seriously.
ETHAN: There are certain people you want to offend. There's an expression in the United States, 'if they can't take the joke, then fuck 'em!'

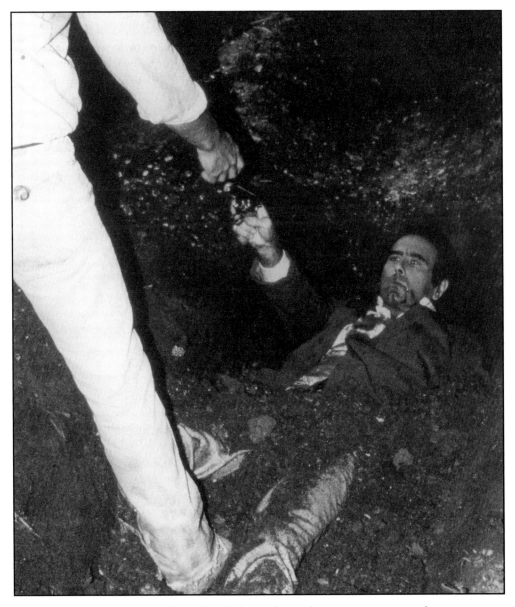

During his burial alive, Marty (Dan Hedaya) makes one last attempt at revenge on the man who cuckolded him, Ray (John Getz — back to camera).

SIMPLY BLOODY

BY ANNE BILLSON

Here be the Rules of Samuel M. Raimi, director of *The Evil Dead*: 1) The Innocent Must Suffer 2) The Guilty Must Be Punished 3) You Must Taste Blood To Be A Man. To these three film-making axioms, the brothers Coen have added one of their own: The Dead Must Walk.

There are no zombies in *Blood Simple,* although Joel Coen reckons all four Rules are applicable to it "in a weird kind of way". Joel, 29, and Ethan, 27, wrote it. Joel (assistant editor on *The Evil Dead*) directed. Ethan produced.

Warned not to go "blood simple", Marty puts his fate into the hands of the sleazy Detective (M. Emmet Walsh).

They set *Blood Simple* in Texas, for reasons that were both practical (weather, unions, cost . . .) and aesthetic. "We wanted a very specific milieu," explains Joel, "and Texas carries a lot of baggage with it, at least for American audiences. It's sort of overblown, mythical Texas." It's a Texas of sleazy motels, neon-lit bars and ramrod highways stretching to the horizon. But it's about as far away from *Paris, Texas* as you're likely to get.

Nor is it anywhere in the neighbourhood of the *Chainsaw Massacre*. Despite its sanguinary handle, *Blood Simple* is not a horror movie. The title was lifted from Dashiell Hammett's *Red Harvest*. "It's an expression he used to describe what happens to somebody psychologically once they've committed murder. They go 'blood simple' in the slang sense of 'simple' meaning crazy." But it's left up to the audience to muse on the title's implications: the film itself never spells them out.

"We always cringe when we hear the title of a movie mentioned in dialogue," explains Joel. "He doesn't love you," Ethan exemplifies with scorn in his voice, "He's just . . . *Romancing the Stone*."

"Makes me grind my teeth," shudders Joel in sympathy.

"*Blood Simple*," says Joel, "was financed completely independently. We set up a limited partnership and then solicited private investment. That was a really time-consuming, frustrating process. It took us about a year. It was probably the hardest part of making the movie. What we *did* do, which proved to be really helpful, was made a two minute trailer *before* we made the movie, and then used that to show to prospective investors, as a sort of foot-in-the-door tactic."

Blood Simple's roots lie in that school of hardboiled crime fiction typified by Hammett, Chandler and, especially, James M. Cain. Although superficially similar to *Body Heat* in its updating of classic *film noir* clichés and characters, it nevertheless forges its own fraught territory, particularly in terms of plot. "*Body Heat*," says Ethan, "was more of a mystery. One didn't know who was doing what to whom. We didn't want to write a whodunnit. We wanted to do a movie where the audience knows what's going on every step of the way."

The audience knows, but the film's characters don't know what the hell's hit them. "The original premise was a sort of central double-cross," explains Ethan, "and beyond that it was a question of figuring out how to make things progressively worse for the survivors." *The Innocent Must Suffer.*

Whodunnit or not, the delicious convolutions of *Blood Simple*'s plot are such that an excessive elaboration of them here would detract from their cumulative effect on screen. Suffice to say, the increasingly sticky webs of murderous intrigue wrap themselves around a wealthy Texan bar-owner; his attractive, young wife; the barman whom she's boffing on the side; and a cheapskate divorce tec, played by M. Emmet Walsh with all the sordid and slimy panache of a walking social disease. There is paranoia to spare, and there's guilt-a-go-go. *The Guilty Must Be Punished.* And there's blood. Lots of it.

"Would you say the ending verges on Grand Guignol?" I ask.

"Yeah" the Coens reply laconically. *You Must Taste Blood To Be A Man.* The precise meaning of taste, as usual, is open to interpretation. There are no vampires in *Blood Simple*.

If the use of the word "blood" in the title trips you into assuming that the film is of the splash 'n' splat variety, then the word "simple" is also apt to send you up the garden path. Simple meaning artless, unsophisticated, not complicated. The film exudes style and stylisation. Tricksy camerawork, arty set-ups, super-real sound effects: they're all there. And the Coens have gone for a soundtrack which counterpoints the action, rather than underlining it. "We didn't want to tell the audience how to feel." Consequently, there's "a very eclectic sonic score" mixed with a lot of Latin-American, a little reggae, and Four Tops and a Balinese Monkey Chant.

Despite its graphic gore, doomed characters and downbeat storyline, *Blood Simple* unravels enjoyably like the long tangles of hair from the coat of a big, black shaggy dog, complete with climactic punch-line. The Coens purposely temper their violence with "a certain amount of humour". They keep a detached, cool, almost cruel distance from their characters, and the most sympathetic of these is also the most despicable. "He probably has the same sort of ironic attitude to the story as we do," admits Joel.

BLOODLINES

BY HAL HINSON

In his novel *Red Harvest*, Dashiell Hammett wrote that after a person kills somebody, he goes soft in the head – "blood simple". You can't help it. Your brains turn to mush. All of a sudden, the blonde angel whose husband you just buried starts getting strange phone calls. You reach into your pocket for your cigarette lighter – the silver-plated one the Elks gave you with your name spelled out in rope on the front – and it's not there. Your lover limps in early one morning with blood on his shirt and a .38, *your* .38, stuffed in his jeans and announces, "I've taken care of it. All we have to do now is keep our heads." Yeah. That's all. Just keep your heads. Might as well go ahead and call the cops.

For the characters in the stylish new thriller *Blood Simple*, passion, guilt and the sight of blood on their hands causes the world to warp and distort just as Hammett said it would, like the nightmare reflection in a fun-house mirror. The movie, which was put together on a shoestring by Joel and Ethan Coen, a couple of movie-mad brothers from Minneapolis, has its own lurid, fun-house atmosphere. The camera swoops and pirouettes as if in a Vincente Minnelli musical; at times it scuttles just inches above the ground, at shoe-top level, crawls under tables, or bounces down hallways. Always some part of the frame is energised by an odd detail or incongruous fillip of colour. Composed in phosphorescent pastels, in neon pinks and greens that stand out against the khaki-coloured Texas landscapes, the movie has a kind of tawdry flamboyance that draws attention to itself, like a barfly adjusting her makeup by the light of the jukebox. *Blood Simple* is only the Coens' first movie – their contributions overlap, with Joel credited as writer-director and Ethan as writer-producer – but already they have an agile sense of visual storytelling and a playfully expressive camera style. They don't make movies like beginners.

If anything, the Coens' technique in *Blood Simple* is too brightly polished, too tightly screwed down. But their excesses come from an over-eagerness to impress, to put their talents on display. *Blood Simple* looks like a movie made by guys who spent most of their lives watching movies, indiscriminately, both in theatres and on TV, and for whom, almost through osmosis, the vocabulary and grammar of film has become a kind of instinctive second language. Made up of equal parts *film noir* and Texas gothic, but with a hyperbolic B-movie veneer, it's a grab-bag of movie styles and references, an eclectic mixture of Hitchcock and Bertolucci, of splatter flicks and Fritz Lang and Orson Welles.

On the face of it, *Blood Simple* may appear to be more about other movies than anything else, and there is an element of movie-movie formalism in their work. But the Coens aren't interested in just recycling old movie formulas. In *Blood Simple*, the filmmakers assume that the audience grew up on the same movies they did, and that we share their sophisticated awareness of conventional movie mechanics. But the Coens don't play their quotations from old movie thrillers straight; they use our shared knowledge of movie conventions for comedy. The movie has a wicked, satirical edge – there's a devilish audacity in the way these young filmmakers use their film smarts to lure us into the movie's system of thinking, and then spring their trap, knocking us off-balance in a way that's both shocking and funny.

The basic geometry of the film is a James M. Cain triangle: husband, wife, lover. The husband, Julian Marty (Dan Hedaya), is a brooding Greek with a militant brow and a puckered chin who owns a gaudy roadside night-spot called the Neon Boot. One look at Marty, who looks like he was born to catch lead, and it's clear why his wife Abby (Frances McDormand) thinks she'd better hightail it before she uses the pearl-handled revolver he gave her as an anniversary present on him. Ray (John Getz), a drawling bartender who works for Marty, becomes involved with Abby innocently enough when she asks him to help her move out. Almost inevitably, Abby and Ray fall into the nearest motel room where a fourth figure, a slob detective named Visser (M. Emmet Walsh), catches them *in flagrante* and delivers his photographic evidence to Marty ("I know where you can get these framed"), along with his own leering account of the evening's bedroom activities, setting the film's tragic spiral of events in motion.

Much of the pleasure in *Blood Simple* comes from watching the filmmakers run their intricately worked-out plot through its paces. The film's narrative is never merely functional in the usual murder-mystery fashion; things don't happen in this movie just to push the plot along. Everything plugs into the film's basic idea: that we are dependent in our judgements upon what our senses tell us, and that our senses lie – that in life we never really know what's going on. The Coens have created a world in which nothing is exactly as it seems. When Marty sees Visser's picture of Abby and Ray nestled together in bloody sheets, we assume, as Marty does, that the hired killer has done his job and the lovers are dead. It's not until the next scene, when Ray saunters into the bar and finds Marty's body, that we discover the photo was doctored. In this movie, a corpse is not always a corpse.

All the characters in *Blood Simple* are able to see only part of the whole picture. Each character has his own point of view in the film, his own version of what has happened and why. And based on the evidence before them, each one behaves appropriately. But each one is limited by his own perspective and it's what they don't know, what they *can't* see from where they stand, that keeps getting them into trouble. Only the audience is given the whole picture. But the Coens never let us relax. Just as we think we're in synch with the film, they shove our assumptions back in our faces. Like their characters, we're making a mistake by believing what we see.

It's this layering of points of view, the interweaving of four versions of the same events, each one complicating and contradicting the other, that distinguishes *Blood Simple* from Lawrence Kasdan's *Body Heat* and other *film noir* re-treads. It's been some time since a low-budget thriller has had this kind of narrative richness. And if at times the Coens are a little too much in love with their own cleverness, occasionally bogging the movie down with self-conscious arty flourishes, they are saved by their drive to provide low-down thrills, to surprise and delight their audience. *Blood Simple* suggests that the Coens are an anomaly on the independent film scene. They don't see a conflict between film art and film entertainment. Nor, in *Blood Simple*, do they break new aesthetic ground. First and foremost, they are entertainers.

Some critics have used this aspect of their work to dismiss *Blood Simple* either as an independent film with a conventional Hollywood heart or as just another schlocky exploitation picture with a glossy, high-art finish. They use the film's accessibility as a club to beat it over the head with, as if to imply that the things that make the movie fun to watch, that satisfy an audience, are precisely the things that compromise its artistic purity. According to this logic, *Blood Simple* is little more than an audition piece, a stepping stone to the world of big-budget studio financing.

But it's the Coens' showmanship, their desire to give the audience a cracking good ride, that gives *Blood Simple* its freshness and originality. The film is most effective when it plays as a comedy. The Coens have a sharp eye for the oddball details of the sleazy Texas milieu they've created. Their humour is droll and understated; their characters spout a kind of terse, prairie vernacular that's dead-on authentic but with a twist, like Horton Foote with a rock in his shoe.

As the scuzzy detective slithering through the movie in a beat-up VW bug, M. Emmet Walsh is a redneck variation on all the bad cops and corrupt gumshoes in the hard-boiled genre. Dressed in a canary-yellow leisure suit, his belly sagging over his western-style belt buckle, Visser is the kind of half-witted vermin who likes to torture puppies in his spare time. Walsh gives his character a mangy amorality; one look at this guy and you know he's for sale at bargain-basement prices. His performance sets a new standard for scumbag character acting.

Dan Hedaya, who plays Marty, does something that even Walsh isn't able to pull off: he shows us what a slime the guy is and still makes us feel almost sorry for what happens to him. Marty is the perpetual outsider, the one who's always put upon and misunderstood. He doesn't even talk like the others. Instead of speaking in a lazy Texas drawl, he spits his words out quickly in a tight North-eastern accent that's clenched like a fist. With his dark, swarthy looks, gold chains, and European-cut shirts, he's on the opposite end of the sleaze scale from Walsh's Visser, but their scenes together are the best in the film.

The Coens aren't as successful with their main characters: John Getz and Frances McDormand are bland and uninteresting as Ray and Abby. In *The Postman Always Rings Twice*, Frank and Cora were so hot for each other that sparks seemed to arc between them; their passion was so volatile that it almost *had* to erupt into violence. There are no comparable sexual fireworks between the lovers in *Blood Simple*; it's a tepid affair, and neither character has enough vitality to engage us. It may be that the Coens have a natural talent for creating lively villains. In any case, in *Blood Simple*, the sympathetic lovers are upstaged by their loathsome adversaries. Their low-watt rapport leaves a dark, empty space at the centre of the film.

The most remarkable thing about *Blood Simple* is that it's satisfying both as a comedy *and* a thriller. What the Coens have learned from Hitchcock, whose spirit hovers over the film as it does in Brian De Palma's movies, is that murder can be simultaneously tragic and comic. The moment in *Blood Simple* when the two lovers confront one another, each one convinced of the other's guilt, and from out of nowhere a rolled-up newspaper arches into the frame, hitting the screen door between them with a sickening smack, is so startlingly unexpected and yet so right, that for a moment you're not sure you actually saw it. Watching *Blood Simple*, you begin to feel uncertain even of the ground beneath your feet. They have that kind of skill.

The Detective squirms as his hand is impaled on the other side of the window frame by Abby, who is convinced that she's under attack by her husband Marty.

JOEL & ETHAN COEN: BLOOD SIBLINGS

This interview took place with Joel and Ethan Coen, and their cinematographer Barry Sonnenfeld, in an apartment on the Upper East Side of Manhattan on the afternoon of **Blood Simple***'s commercial opening in New York. All three were casually dressed and, at the beginning of the session, excitedly talking, not about their opening night, but about their upcoming lunch at the Russian Tea Room, about superagent Sam Cohn ("Does he really eat Kleenex?") and the politics of who sits where. During the interview, the Coens chain-smoked Camels out of the same pack, passing it back and forth across the glass tabletop in front of them.*

Let's start with the basics. You were both born and raised in Minneapolis?

JOEL COEN: Yeah. We both grew up in Minneapolis, but have lived in New York, on and off, for about ten years. I moved here to go to school at NYU and haven't really lived in Minneapolis since then, except for about a year when we were raising money for the movie. We raised a lot of the money there, although some of it came from here and New Jersey and Texas.

ETHAN COEN: I left Minneapolis to go to school at Princeton – I studied philosophy – and after that came to New York.

How did you become interested in film-making?

JOEL: There were two things really. We made a lot of Super 8 movies when we were kids.

ETHAN: They were incredibly cheesy, even by Super 8 standards.

JOEL: We remade a lot of bad Hollywood movies that we'd seen on television. The two that were most successful were remakes of *The Naked Prey* and *Advise and Consent* – movies that never should have been made in the first place. At that time, we didn't really understand the most basic concepts of filmmaking – we didn't know that you could physically edit film – so we'd run around with the camera, editing it all in the camera. We'd actually have parallel editing for chase scenes. We'd shoot in one place, then run over to the other and shoot that, then run back and shoot at the first spot again.

Did these films have titles?

JOEL: Yeah. The remake of *The Naked Prey* was called *Zeimers in Zambia* – the guy who played the Cornel Wilde part was nicknamed Zeimers. We had very weird special effects in that film. We actually had a parachute drop – a shot of an airplane going overhead, then a miniature, then cut to a close-up of the guy against a white sheet hitting the ground.

ETHAN: It was hell waiting for the airplane to fly by. We were nowhere near a flight path.

This sounds amazingly sophisticated.

JOEL: It wasn't, really. They were just hacked together. *Advise and Consent* was interesting, though, because at the time we made it we hadn't seen the original film *or* read the book. We just heard the story from a friend of ours and it sounded good, so we remade it without going back to any of the source material.

When you finally saw the original, which did you like better, your version or theirs?

ETHAN: Well, we're big Don Murray fans, so I like the original.

JOEL: Yeah, guys like Don Murray and the early Disney stars, you know, Dean Jones and Jim Hutton, are big favourites. Kurt Russell, too.

Sounds like you watched a lot of movies on TV.

ETHAN: Yeah, we saw a lot of Tarzan movies and Steve Reeves muscle movies. What was that Tarzan rip-off with Johnny Sheffield?

JOEL: *Bomba the Jungle Boy.* What's-his-name used to introduce those.

ETHAN: Andy Devine.

JOEL: Yeah, he had a thing called "Andy's Gang" . . .

ETHAN: But that wasn't *Bomba*, that was a serial set in India called *Ramar.* Did you ever see *Tarzan's New York Adventure*? That's one of the greatest. And the Sixties Tarzans were kind of weird.

JOEL: A movie like *Boeing Boeing* was big with us. And we were into movies like *That Touch of Mink*, *A Global Affair*, Bob Hope movies, Jerry Lewis movies, anything with Tony Curtis, *Pillow Talk*. We tried to see everything with Doris Day. Those were important movies for us. I saw *Pillow Talk* again recently. It's incredibly surreal.

ETHAN: It's a very weird, wooden aesthetic that nobody's interested in anymore. *The Chapman Report* is great that way too.

JOEL: What's happened is that those movies have now become TV fodder.

*Did the look of those movies have anything to do with your decision to shoot **Blood Simple** in colour? It's kind of **film noir**, which is usually done in black and white.*

JOEL: There was a big practical consideration. Since we were doing the movie independently, and without a distributor, we were a little leery of making a black and white movie. But we never really considered that a sacrifice. We wanted to keep the movie dark, and we didn't want it to be colourful in the . . .

ETHAN: . . . the *That Touch of Mink* sort of way.

JOEL: Right. What we talked about early on was having the elements of colour in frame be sources of light, at least as much as possible, like with the neon and the Bud lights, so that the rest of the frame would be dark. That way it would be colourful, but not garish.

BARRY SONNENFELD: I think we were afraid that to shoot the film in black and white would make it look too "independent", too low-budget.

ETHAN: Yeah. We wanted to trick people into thinking we'd made a real movie.

JOEL & ETHAN COEN: BLOOD SIBLINGS

The film has been criticised for that reason.

JOEL: Yeah, one critic said it had "the heart of a Bloomingdale's window and the soul of a resume". I loved that review.

ETHAN: The movie is a no-bones-about-it entertainment. If you want something other than that, then you probably have a legitimate complaint.

JOEL: But you can't get any more independent than *Blood Simple*. We did it entirely outside of Hollywood. To take it a step further, we did it outside of any established movie company anywhere. It can't be accused of not being an independent film. It was done by people who have had no experience with feature films, Hollywood or otherwise.

BARRY: What this writer means by independent, though, is arty or artistic. It wasn't our intention to make an art film, but to make an entertaining B movie.

As Ray and Abby sleep, the Detective takes the photo he will doctor in order to convince Marty he has murdered them both.

Do you consider yourself linked in any way with other independent filmmakers and what they're doing?

ETHAN: The independent movies that we see aren't really avant-garde. John Sayles is an independent filmmaker who I like. Although I haven't seen his new film, I like what Alan Rudolph does. He'll make a movie for a studio, like *Roadie* or *Endangered Species*, and then go off on his own to make a movie just for himself for $800,000.

JOEL: Also, I like low-budget horror movies that are made independently. They're mass-audience pictures, but they're done independently. I've worked with a lot of people who've done that stuff, like Sam Raimi. Those are the kind of independent filmmakers that we feel closer to than, say, the more avant-garde artists. I liked *Stranger than Paradise*, though, which I suppose is closer to being avant-garde than we are.

ETHAN: I think there's room for all kinds of independent movies. And whenever anyone makes a successful one, no matter what kind it is, it's good for everybody.

I think the distinction that's being made is between art and entertainment.

JOEL: That's a distinction that I've never understood. If somebody goes out to make a movie that isn't designed primarily to entertain people, then I don't know what the fuck they're doing. I can't understand it. It doesn't make sense to me. What's the Raymond Chandler line? "All good art is entertainment and anyone who says differently is a stuffed shirt and juvenile at the art of living."

*Some people see **Blood Simple** as a shrewd manoeuvre to establish yourselves on the scene in order to launch your careers as mainstream filmmakers.*

ETHAN: They're wrong. We made the movie because we wanted to make it, not as a stepping stone to anything else. And we prefer to keep on making this kind of movie, independently.

JOEL: Someone in *Film Comment* said *Blood Simple* was "aggressively New Hollywood". We wanted to make this movie, and the way we did it was the only way we could have done it. The main consideration from the start was that we wanted to be left alone, without anyone telling us what to do. The way we financed the movie gave us that right.

When you were both still in school, you wrote a few feature scripts together. What were they like?

JOEL: The first one was called *Coast to Coast*. We never really did anything with it. It was sort of a screwball comedy.

ETHAN: It had 28 Einsteins in it. The Red Chinese were cloning Albert Einstein.

JOEL: After that we were hired by a producer to write a script from a treatment he had. That was never produced. Then Sam Raimi, whom I worked with on *The Evil Dead*, hired us to write something with him called *The XYZ Murders*. It's just been finished. And we're writing something with him now that Ethan and I are going to do.

*What movies had you worked on before **Blood Simple**?*

JOEL: I was assistant editor on a few low-budget horror films, like *Fear No Evil*. There was another one that I actually got fired from called *Nightmare*, which had a small release here in New York. And *The Evil Dead*. Those are the only three features I've worked on. *Evil Dead* was the most fun. A lot of the stuff in our film, like the camera running up on the front lawn, is attributable to Raimi, who does a lot of shaky-cam stuff.

JOEL & ETHAN COEN: BLOOD SIBLINGS

How do you two collaborate when you're writing?

JOEL: He does all the typing. We just sit down together and work it out from beginning to end. We don't break it up and each do scenes. We talk the whole thing through together.

BARRY: They pace a lot. And there's a lot of cigarette smoking.

How was it determined that Joel would direct and Ethan produce?

ETHAN: We had a thoin coss . . . I mean a coin toss.

JOEL: The standard answer is that I'm bigger than he is – that I can beat him up so I get to direct.

ETHAN: It's those critical three inches in reach that make the difference.

JOEL: To tell you the truth, the credits on the movie don't reflect the extent of the collaboration. I did a lot of things on the production side, and Ethan did a lot of directorial stuff. The line wasn't clearly drawn. In fact, the way we worked was incredibly fluid. I think we're both just about equally responsible for everything in the movie.

ETHAN: Although, on the set, Joel is definitely the director. He's the one in charge.

JOEL: Yeah, I did work with the actors and all that. But as far as the script and the realisation, down to the tiniest details and including all the major aesthetic decisions, that's a mutual thing.

Who sets up the shots?

JOEL: This is where it gets really fuzzy. When we're writing a script, we're already starting to interpret the script directorially. As to how we want the movie to look, even down to specific shots and the kind of coverage we want, that's worked into the writing of the script. Also, before production, Ethan, Barry, and I storyboarded the movie together.

ETHAN: Also, at the beginning of every day, the three of us and the assistant director would have breakfast at Denny's – the Grand Slam special – and go through the day's shots and talk about the lighting.

JOEL: On the set, we'd put it together and look through the viewfinder. Barry might have an idea, or Ethan would come up with something different, and we'd try it. We had the freedom to do that, because we'd done so much advance work.

BARRY: Also, on the set, we'd try to torture each other. For example, I didn't allow smoking . . .

ETHAN: "It degrades the image." [Laughs.]

BARRY: . . . which meant that only one of them would be on the set at any time, because the other one was off having a cigarette.

The atmosphere of the film shows the influence of hard-boiled detective fiction. Have you read a lot of that stuff?

JOEL: We read all of Cain six or seven years ago when they reissued his books in paperback. Chandler and Hammett, too. We've also poured through a lot of Cain arcana.

ETHAN: Cain is more to the point for this story than Chandler or Hammett. They wrote mysteries, whodunits.

JOEL: We've always thought that up at Low Library at Columbia University, where the names are chiselled up there above the columns in stone – Aristotle, Herodotus, Virgil – that the fourth one should be Cain.

ETHAN: Cain usually dealt in his work with three great themes: opera, the Greek diner business, and the insurance business.

JOEL: Which we felt were the three great themes of twentieth century literature.

Marty, the cuckold, seems to be lifted directly out of Cain.

ETHAN: He is, but a little less cheerful and fun-loving.

JOEL: They're usually greasy, guitar-strumming yahoos, which of course Marty isn't. But yeah, that's where he comes from.

Why did you set the film in Texas?

JOEL: The weather's good. And it just seemed like the right setting for a passion murder story. And people have strong feelings about Texas, which we thought we could play off of.

ETHAN: And again, your classic *film noir* has a real urban feel, and we wanted something different.

*Did you set out to create a **film noir** atmosphere?*

JOEL: Not really. We didn't want to make a Venetian-blind movie.

ETHAN: When people call *Blood Simple* a *film noir*, they're correct to the extent that we like the same kind of stories that the people who made those movies liked. We tried to emulate the source that those movies came from rather than the movies themselves.

JOEL: *Blood Simple* utilises movie conventions to tell the story. In that sense it's about other movies – but no more so than any other film that uses the medium in a way that's aware that there's a history of movies behind it.

How were you able to maintain such a delicate balance between the comic and the thriller elements in the story?

JOEL: I think that gets back to Chandler and Hammett and Cain. The subject matter was grim but the tone was upbeat. They move along at a very fast pace. They're funny…

ETHAN: … they're insanely eupeptic …

JOEL: … and that keeps the stories from being grim. We didn't want this to be a grim movie. There's a lot of graphic violence and a lot of blood, but I don't think the movie's grim.

ETHAN: We didn't have an equation for how to balance the blood and the gags. But there is a counterpoint between the story itself and the narrator's attitude toward the story.

JOEL: To us it was amusing to frame the whole movie with this redneck detective's views on life. We thought it was funny, but it also relates directly to the story. It's not a one-liner kind of funny.

ETHAN: It's easy to think that we set out to parody the *film noir* form because, on one hand, it is a thriller, and, on the other, it is funny. But certainly the film is supposed to work as a thriller and I don't think it would work as both at once.

JOEL: Humourless thrillers – *Gorky Park*, or *Against All Odds* – are dull, flat. They take themselves too seriously in a way that undercuts the fun of the movie. We didn't really think about making the situations in the film funny. Our thinking was more like, "Well, this will be scary", and "Wouldn't it be fun if the character were like this?"

In preparing **Blood Simple**, *did you look at other movies and use them as models?*
JOEL: *The Conformist* is one of the movies we went with Barry to see before we started shooting in terms of deciding what we wanted the visual style of the movie to be, the lighting and all that. Also, we went to see *The Third Man*.

BARRY: Which is funny because I read that Richard Kline [the cinematographer] and Larry Kasdan went to see the same two films before they shot *Body Heat*.

JOEL: And came up with a completely different look. We wanted a real non-diffuse image which is the kind of image that Vittorio Storaro got in *The Conformist*. But in *Body Heat* they got this overexposed, halating image with light running through the windows. Maybe they saw a really bad print.

ETHAN: We're also big fans of Robby Muller, particularly *The American Friend*, which we've all seen a number of times. So there are a lot of points of reference. Actually, we just wanted the movie to be in focus.

Do you intend to continue your arrangement as it is at present, with Joel directing and Ethan producing, or do you want to switch it around next time?
ETHAN: We're going to continue the same way. [To Joel] We've got to do *Boeing Boeing* credits next time [in which, to calm top-billing egos, Jerry Lewis' and Tony Curtis' names revolved on an axis].

JOEL: We're thinking that next time we'll have it say, "Ethan and Joel Coen's *Whatever*."
ETHAN: No, I like "Ethan Coen presents a film by his brother Joel."

And you would like to continue working together?
JOEL: Oh yeah. In fact the three of us do. There are certain collaborations which are really fruitful. One of them is with Sam Raimi, which we hope continues on other movies in the future. Another is with Barry.

As a result of the success you've had so far with **Blood Simple**, *are the studios beating a path to your door with offers?*
JOEL: We're getting a lot of talk, but we don't know what it means. You spend one week in Hollywood! [Laughs.] People have been calling. But we'd like to continue to work as

independently as possible. Not independent necessarily of the Hollywood distribution apparatus, which is really the best if you want your movie to reach a mass market. But as far as production is concerned, there's a real trade-off involved. It's true that certain movies require more money to produce right than *Blood Simple* did. But the difference with us is, while we may need more money for the next one than we did for *Blood Simple*, we're still not talking about the kind of budgets that the studios are used to working with. We did this film for a million and a half, and, for me, three - four million dollars is an incredible amount of money to make a movie. And that's attainable without going to the studios.

ETHAN: The bottom line is, even if *Blood Simple* does well, we're comfortable with the idea of making another low budget movie.

JOEL: Right. We're not afraid of making movies for cheap.

Ethan (left) and Joel Coen in the mid-1980s, against a backdrop of the road environment integral to their first two films, Blood Simple *and* Raising Arizona.

JOEL AND ETHAN COEN

BY ERIC BREITBART

The Coen brothers are having a good time. And why not? Their first film, *Blood Simple* – directed by Joel, produced by Ethan, and written by Joel and Ethan – was a hit at the 1984 New York Film Festival, and has opened to good box office and critical acclaim verging on mass hysteria. Being compared to Alfred Hitchcock and Orson Welles hasn't fazed the Coens, but not because the reviews haven't tried – one critic called *Blood Simple* the best first film since *Citizen Kane*. *Blood Simple* may have opened the doors to the magic kingdom, but the brothers Coen aren't ready to rush in just yet.

"I really think our film has been blown up out of proportion," says Joel. "A lot of it has to do with timing. *Beverly Hills Cop* seems to be the movie everyone was going to see. The press was tired of writing about it and was hungry for something else. It looks like we're it. Now they're reviewing each other's reviews. Let's face it: It's only a movie."

*'I ain't afraid of you, Marty.' Abby opens fire on her unseen assailant,
unaware of just who it is that she's killing.*

"Dealing with the publicity is almost as hard as raising money," says Ethan half seriously. "I mean, *People* magazine called to do a story on us – can you believe it?" He gestures around an Upper West Side apartment befitting a couple of graduate students rather than Hollywood minimoguls. "We didn't do it, but it got Joel to clean up the bathroom." He proudly shows off a tile floor clean enough to . . . walk on.

Although the Coens look and act like independent filmmakers – Joel went to NYU undergraduate film school, Ethan studied philosophy at Princeton – their professed allegiance to the action-horror school of filmmaking should be a reminder that the term "independent filmmaking" has always encompassed more than socially committed or avant-garde films. It includes the Corman brothers – Gene and Roger – as well as the Kuchar brothers and the Mekas brothers. "If we see ourselves as part of an independent film movement," says Joel, "it would be the films like *Evil Dead*, *Dawn of the Dead*, or *Halloween* – not avant-garde or experimental films, but films that are commercial and work within a given genre." *Blood Simple* is a movie that sits squarely astride that tradition, but its skillful execution has a shock value all its own.

Even though a film like *Blood Simple* is not foreign to Hollywood, the Coens never really considered selling the script to a studio. "We knew no one would buy it – particularly since we wanted to make it ourselves," says Ethan. From his experience as an assistant editor and sciptwriter on low-budget features, Joel knew that they would need at least a million dollars to do the film the way they wanted to do it – and a million dollars is a lot of money for a producer and director without a proven track record. Or is it?

"We spent about five months spinnning our wheels," says Joel, "but we took it one step at a time. The first thing was to get a lawyer, and we talked to a lot of lawyers. Since the first consultation is usually free, we kept going, getting a lot of advice along the way, until we found one we both liked – and who would defer half of his fee. He set up the limited partnership." The Coens then went back to their hometown of Minneapolis (both their parents are college professors), not because they knew a lot of people with money there, but because they knew a lot of people told them that they would be better off if they started in Minneapolis, that it meant something to be hometown boys.

It meant something to Daniel Bacaner, an investor who became the film's executive producer and helped the Coens to raise most of the money by providing introductions to other potential backers. The Coens hauled around a two-minute trailer they had made, figuring that it would be easy to convince people with a slick, stylised piece of film. "We were wrong about that," says Joel. "We couldn't get people to come to a screening room to see it in 35mm, so we made a 16mm reduction, got a projector, and took it around to people's homes or where they worked. We figured it would be harder for them to get rid of us. We went everywhere – bowling alleys, auto junkyards, banks. I'd say we saw at least twenty people for every one who gave us money."

Sometimes, the home visits had pitfalls. Once, as they were pulling into a hot prospect's driveway, the Coens' car rammed the man's Cadillac. "We had a short discussion on whether to tell him before or after we asked for the money," Joel recalls. Ethan remembers it as a *very* short conversation. "We decided to do it after, so he'd already turned us down when we told him about his car."

One of the advantages of a limited partnership for filmmakers is that the investors don't have creative control over what the film is going to look like. The Coens found that most of their potential investors didn't really care. "A lot of them said they didn't know anything about films or scripts, so why should they read it," says Ethan. "They were just interested in whether it was a good deal or not, and whether they would end up looking foolish." One investor did want to read the script though. "He was a urologist," says Joel. "When we got the script back from him, it was covered with blood." Once they had about half the money, the going became easier, but they couldn't let up: "You've *really* got to want it," Ethan says, "because there are *plenty* of opportunities along the way for you to throw up your hands and say, 'Hey! Why am I doing this?'" When that happened one of the brothers usually had the answer.

The Coens didn't have much of a problem going out on a set for the first time. "I think the technical aspects of filmmaking are vastly overrated," says Joel coolly through a cigarette haze. "There was a kind of conspiracy of imposturing," adds Ethan, "even though we didn't know everything, we knew that no one else did either. We helped each other out." They also had a clear idea of the film they were going to do. Aside from a few subplots that were dropped in the editing room, *Blood Simple* on the screen is very close to the script and the storyboards.

Even when the film was completed, though, the Coens faced the last independent's hurdle – selling the film. Hard as it is to believe, given the film's critical and popular reception, *Blood Simple* was turned down by nearly every major studio as being too bloody, too simple – or both. Finally, it was picked up by a small, independent company, Circle Releasing, with one of the largest cash advances ever paid for an American independent film

The success of *Blood Simple* has brought Hollywood to the Coens' door with a number of scripts and offers of work, but for now, they want to continue on their own. "We're working on a comedy script," Ethan says, "something more dialogue-intensive than *Blood Simple*, a film where everybody steps on everybody else's lines." For now, the guns and knives are back in the drawer.

They may be the toast of Hollywood and New York, but their fame has not yet reached Minneapolis. "We did screen the film for our investors," says Joel, "and I think most of them didn't know what to make of it. A lot of them had their kids there, though, and they told them the film was OK." As for their own parents, "They weren't overjoyed about us being filmmakers at first, but they've come around. They called before to say that they'd missed us on *The Today Show*, but some friends of theirs had taped it and they were going over for brunch to watch it." Our sons the filmmakers. Orson Welles never had such a good time.

CRIMEWAVE

REVIEW FROM VARIETY

Crimewave is a boisterous, goofy, cartoonish comedy in the *Airplane* mould. Pic is not really about anything except people's unrelenting aggressiveness toward one another, and laughs tend to come in bunches rather than being provoked throughout, so final result is more of a mild audience pleaser than a sustained hoot.

Film, previously billed as *The XYZ Murders* (its final U.S. release title will be *Broken Hearts and Noses*, while *Crimewave* is used overseas) is framed by the impending execution of nerdy security man Reed Birney and flashes back to the primary setting, which is a particularly dangerous section of downtown Detroit.

Screenwriters Joel and Ethan Coen (of *Blood Simple*) and Sam Raimi (of *The Evil Dead*), who also directed, quickly assemble the motley cast of characters, which includes weird security systems operators Hamid Dana and (exec producer) Edward R. Pressman, latter's obnoxious wife Louise Lasser, lounge lizard Bruce Campbell, who pursues cutie-pie Sheree J. Wilson and Birney, who ineptly attempts to rescue Wilson from Campbell.

Best of all, however, are hulking Paul L. Smith and ratty Brion James as two exterminators who have expanded their field of victims from rodents to human beings.

A great percentage of pic's humour stems from Smith's maniacal pursuit of his prey. Laughing with menacing relish and betraying a gleefully cruel enthusiasm for his work, Smith stalks everyone in sight and turns in a fabulously enjoyable comic performance that single-handedly keeps the film afloat.

Pic gives the impression of having been storyboarded rather than directed and, despite good execution all around, production looks pretty cheap and its impact evaporates immediately upon final fadeout. However, laughs are abundant enough to make this a passably funny entertainment.

CRIMEWAVE

BY STEVE JENKINS

Detroit. As a car full of nuns speeds through the city, Vic Ajax, about to be executed at the Hudsucker State Penitentiary, proclaims his innocence and recalls the events leading to his present predicament . . . Vic works as an installer of security systems for Odegard-Trend. Learning that Donald Odegard intends to sell their business to the evil Renaldo, Ernest Trend hires a pair of exterminators, Faron Crush and Arthur Coddish, to murder his partner. They carry out the contract, but their lethal machine subsequently also kills Trend. That same night, at the glamorous Rialto Club, Vic comes into conflict with Renaldo over Nancy, whom he has met and fallen for that day. Renaldo leaves with another woman, and Vic and Nancy, unable to pay their bill, are forced to do the washing up after failing to win a dance contest. Trend's prying wife Helene is meanwhile attacked in her apartment by Faron, whom she has seen removing one of the bodies from her husband's office. A man who comes to her aid falls from her window and is then run over and killed by Arthur, driving the exterminators' van. Vic and Nancy arrive back as Arthur is bringing the body into the apartment block, where Nancy also lives. Helene is pursued to the Odegard-Trend showroom by Faron, but manages to elude him; Nancy is captured by Arthur, but gets away in a car, with a corpse as a fellow passenger. A furious chase ensues, with Vic and Arthur slugging it out on the roofs of the speeding vehicles. The exterminators' van is eventually destroyed, leaving Nancy's car perched perilously on a bridge over a river. Faron reappears, but is finally despatched into the river by Vic and Nancy. Vic also ends up in the water, as Nancy climbs to safety . . . Nancy arrives at the prison (she had disappeared and been taken in by nuns) and, breaking her vow of silence, corroborates Vic's story and saves his life. The couple get married. Helene, meanwhile, turns up in a crate in Uruguay.

As a collaboration between Sam Raimi, director of *The Evil Dead*, and Joel and Ethan Coen, responsible for *Blood Simple*, *Crimewave* is unfortunately proof that a whole can be less than the potential sum of its parts. The various contributions are clearly apparent: the frenetic, comic-strip energy of *The Evil Dead*, combined with *Blood Simple*'s rather more knowing and darker brand of humorous excess. But the result is fairly unsatisfactory. The attempt to create a vaguely *film noir* ambience – "The story is set in the present, but the atmosphere is late Forties" as Raimi has put it – sits awkwardly, for example, with the manic "characterisation" of the two exterminators (prefiguring, incidentally, Scorsese's use of Cheech and Chong in *After Hours*), who are simply allowed to run riot, in a manner precisely suggesting the script's anything-goes, catch-all sense of humour. The latter is too often pitched at a banal and obvious level – the romantically inept Vic reading a book entitled *How to Talk to Girls* – and the fault is then compounded by unnecessary and unfunny underlining, as with the gunshots which accompany

The maniacal pest exterminators (Brion James, left, and Paul L. Smith) in Sam Raimi's
Crimewave *who 'kill all sizes' – and all species, including human beings.*

Renaldo's smart remarks to a woman in the Rialto Club. The extended car chase which brings events in the flashback to a climax certainly has the air of an arbitrary wrap-up. Occasionally, *Crimewave* hits the genuinely bizarre note to which it frantically aspires: Faron pursuing Helene through a succession of locked doors of different colours – "The Parade of Protection: The Safest Hallway in the World" – in the Odegard Trend showroom; a policeman's remark to a small boy dragging a body out of a lift: "Where'd you get the Negro, Butch?" But these moments merely suggest the movie which Raimi has ultimately failed to deliver.

H.I. M^{c}DUNNOUGH

NO. 1460

RAISING ARIZONA

RAISING ARIZONA
REVIEW FROM VARIETY

There are not many films in which a man is blown up by a hand grenade for comic effect, but *Raising Arizona* is just such a film. Pic is the Coen brothers' twisted view of family rearing in the American heartlands and although different in style and tone from their debut effort, *Blood Simple*, it is full of the same quirky humour and off-the-wall situations. *Raising Arizona* may not be everyone's cup of tea, but it's fresh enough to find a faithful following with the right handling.

Quite possibly there has never been another film like *Raising Arizona*, with *Repo Man* and *True Stories* perhaps coming closest to its generous look at the denizens of society's underbelly. As written by Joel and Ethan Coen, directed by Joel and produced by Ethan, the film captures the surrealism of everyday life. Characters are so strange here that they seem to have stepped out of late-night television, tabloid newspapers, talk radio and a vivid imagination.

Nicolas Cage and Holly Hunter are the off-centre couple at the centre of the doings. As H. I. McDonnough, Cage is a well-meaning petty crook with a fondness for knocking off convenience stores. Edwina is the cop who checks him into prison so often that a romance develops.

H. I. and Ed soon learn marriage is "no *Ozzie and Harriet Show*" and when she learns she can't have kids or adopt them, they do the next logical thing – steal one. Target is furniture magnate Nathan Arizona (Trey Wilson) and his wife (Lynne Dumin Kitei) who have just been blessed with much-publicised quints.

Once H. I. and Ed have the child things don't get any easier as they are confronted by several models of the "family unit". One neighbouring couple is intent on wife swapping while H. I.'s crazed prison buddies, Gale (John Goodman) and Evelle (William Forsythe) who beat a path to his door after tunnelling out of the joint, are another alternative. And the generically named Arizonas are yet another possible direction for the new family.

Loosely structured around a voice-over narration by Cage, *Raising Arizona* is as leisurely and disconnected as *Blood Simple* was taut and economical. While film is filled with many splendid touches and plenty of yocks, it often doesn't hold together as a coherent story.

Plowing right through the middle of the story is the mad motorcyclist of the apocalypse (Randall [Tex] Cobb), who is the enemy of all families. As the film's central villain, he's a weak and unfocused creation with Cobb's performance lacking the teeth to make the character stick.

While Cage and Hunter are fine as the couple at sea in the desert, *Raising Arizona* sports at least one outstanding performance from John Goodman as the con brother who wants a family too. Here, as in *True Stories*, Goodman is a rarity on the screen, an actor who can communicate friendliness and goodwill in spite of his foolishness. Consequently, scenes with the two brothers are the most animated and entertaining in the picture.

As a director, Coen demonstrates an assured technical touch (though perhaps a bit too much low-angle framing) and camerawork by Barry Sonnenfeld is richly coloured and adds to the texture of Jane Musky's sets.

H. I. and Ed McDunnough (Nicolas Cage and Holly Hunter) become a full nuclear family with the addition of kidnapped baby Nathan Arizona, Jr. (T. J. Kuhn).

RAISING ARIZONA

BY STEVE JENKINS

After serving several sentences for robbing convenience stores, H. I. "Hi" McDonnough marries Edwina, a police booking officer. The couple's happy existence, living in a mobile home with Hi working at a sheet metal plant, is spoiled when they find themselves unable to have children. They succeed, however, in kidnapping Nathan Jnr., one of the quintuplets recently born to unpainted-furniture tycoon Nathan Arizona and his wife Florence. Hi and Ed's family life is then disrupted by the arrival of Gale and Evelle, two escapees from his old prison, and Hi is haunted by a vision of the fearsome Leonard Smalls, the Lone Biker of the Apocalypse, who seems to be on the trail of the two convicts. Hi and Ed are visited by Hi's foreman Glen, his wife Dot and their monstrous children, and Hi loses his job after a dispute with Glen about wife-swapping. Hi then robs a convenience store, involving Ed in the subsequent chaotic gunfight and chase. He tells Gale and Evelle that they must leave, but they want him to join them on a bank raid they are planning. As Hi decides to leave Ed and the baby, because he lacks the character to be a father, the Lone Biker tells Nathan he will find his son for $50,000. Glen tells Hi that he knows the baby's true identity and that he will turn Hi over to the police if he doesn't give Nathan Jnr. to Dot, who is desperate for another child. Gale and Evelle then take the baby, intending to obtain a ransom for him and to rob the bank. Hi and Ed, and the Lone Biker, are soon on their trail. Gale and Evelle carry out the bank raid, but inadvertently leave Nathan Jnr. at the scene of the crime. They are involved in a car crash with Hi and Ed, who then find that the Lone Biker has the baby. After a fight, Hi succeeds in blowing up the biker with his own grenades. Ed and Hi return Nathan Jnr. to his father and announce to the latter, who realises that they are the kidnappers, that they are splitting up. He urges them to postpone a decision for at least one night. Hi dreams of Gale and Evelle returning to prison; of Glen still reporting him to the law; of Nathan Jnr. growing up; and of an old couple, very like himself and Ed being visited by their children and grandchildren . . .

In the production notes for *Raising Arizona*, Ethan Coen describes the film as "totally the opposite of *Blood Simple* . . . (which) was slow and deliberate. We wanted to try something with a faster pace and a lighter tone." Nowhere in the notes, however, is there any mention of Sam Raimi's *Crimewave*, which the Coen brothers wrote with Raimi and which certainly prefigures the new film as regards both pace and tone. *Crimewave* unfortunately sacrificed any kind of telling humour in favour of a catch-all freneticism, and while *Raising Arizona* is much more cleverly judged and infinitely funnier, it too is ultimately flawed by a kind of overkill. Take, for example, the escaped convicts Gale and Evelle, who provide the only direct echo of *Crimewave* (the latter featured a pair of murderous comic exterminators). They literally and brilliantly erupt into the film, yelling as they burst up through the ground outside the prison, with accompanying thunder and rain. The scene is startlingly bizarre, but proves a hard act to follow or, more importantly, to develop.

Thereafter, the pair, and particularly Gale, are given some excellent lines (explaining that they escaped because they felt the institution no longer had anything to offer them; remarking of an impending visit from Hi's foreman that there are "so many social engagements, so little time"), but as characters they finally succumb merely to more screaming hysteria. Typically, the film suggests a possible line of emotional development – Evelle's paternal feelings towards the baby they have kidnapped – but allows itself no opportunity to follow the thought through. This problem recurs throughout, with various figures being made the centre of very funny scenes (Nathan Arizona Snr. attempting to cope with police and journalists and plug his unpainted furniture; the invasion of Hi and Ed's home by Glen and Dot's monstrous children, Glen confiding that "There's something wrong with my semen"), but remaining functions of a dense script which proceeds around them rather than through them.

Blood Simple manipulated its characters in a similar fashion, but there much of the pleasure lay precisely in the exposed mechanism and twists of the plotting; the script here seems aimless and sometimes arbitrary by comparison. This is all the more apparent given a clear attempt to invest Hi and Ed's try for a simple happiness with some degree of emotional depth. The gap between Hi's beautifully clichéd articulation of experience ("Her insides were a rocky place where my seed could find no purchase") and its more banal reality suggests a kind of comic but affecting poignancy. It's a quality Nicolas Cage and Holly Hunter's performances might well have sustained. The film, however, fails to reconcile this element with its overall busyness. In this context, for example, the Lone Biker of the Apocalypse – despite Hi's claim not to know "if he was dream or vision" – remains resolutely unapocalyptic, merely a tedious excuse for tricksy camera movement and numerous explosions.

Given that most current American comedy is blandly designed as audience-reflecting fodder for teenagers or yuppies, it seems almost churlish to take the Coens to task. *Raising Arizona* is undoubtedly witty, sharp and constantly inventive. One only wishes that some of its energy had been dissipated in order to leave more space for its characters to breathe. In a recent article in *Film Comment*, April 1987, the film's cinematographer, Barry Sonnenfeld, remarks that "Every time I put on a lens, Joel and Ethan would ask, 'Does it look wacky enough?'". As regards the finished film, the answer is undoubtedly yes. There are, however, other questions one might have wished them to consider.

ETHAN AND JOEL COEN

BY KEVIN SESSIONS

Film-makers Joel and Ethan Coen possess a choreographer's sense of movement, space. Timing. Each Coen film has been filled with a nervous, yet disciplined, energy. Their camera is Nijinsky as coffee achiever.

Blood Simple, cornball but cruel, was their *film noir*-like first effort. Style – like a well-typed resume – was stapled right onto its content; the Coens had announced their own arrival.

Their latest film, *Raising Arizona*, stars Nicolas Cage and Holly Hunter and concerns a barren couple's attempt to convince themselves that kidnapping is above the law – or, at least, beneath it. The film is brilliant in its farcical depiction of desperation. After *Blood Simple*, there might have been a suspicion that Flannery O'Connor and Alfred Hitchcock had parented this pair of camera buffs. But *Raising Arizona* makes one wonder if Janis Joplin and Charlie Chaplin had a magical tryst outside Tucson. For there is a rough and curious musicality to the Coens' sensibility – rock and roll pummeled from a silent-screen Wurlitzer.

Where did these guys come from?

"We grew up in Minneapolis," Joel confessed. "Both our parents are teachers. Our father is an economics professor and our mother is a professor of art history."

"But it's funny you should mention Flannery O'Connor," Ethan grinned. "We like stealing from her."

"Yeah," Joel's confession continued, the same devilish grin crawling across his face. "That term 'warthog from hell', in *Raising Arizona*, is hers."

Ethan: "From *Resurrection*."

We met the morning after the cast-and-crew screening for *Arizona* and it was the first time I had been confronted with Coen-speak. Joel would just about finish a sentence, then Ethan would run on with it. This characteristic carries over to the screen as well. Although Joel is billed as the director and Ethan as producer (the two share screenwriting credit), their work is not distributed so precisely.

"We both sort of co-direct and co-produce the movie," Joel admitted.

"Well," Ethan, of course, continued, "on the set Joel is more or less the boss. You don't want more than one person talking to the actors. And you just need a clear court of last appeal to get things done efficiently."

Joel lit a cigarette.

Then Ethan.

Same pack.

The two weren't always this close. Even as teenagers, when they were experimenting with a Super-8 camera, they didn't spend that much time together. ("We mostly did remakes back then," Joel joked. "Stuff like *The Naked Prey* and *Lumberjacks of the North*.")

In fact, they went their separate ways in college. Ethan turned to philosophy at Princeton; Joel came to New York and majored in film at NYU. After school, however, they started to write screenplays together, and a bond – one based on business as well as brotherhood – quickly developed.

Would they ever work separately?

Joel: "No. The nature of what we do is so collaborative that I can't imagine working any other way."

Ethan: "Never."

The flavour of both their films has been rather barbecued. How did two guys from an academic Midwestern background hook into the mentality of the Southwest so successfully?

Ethan lit another cigarette. "Well, gee, that's nice as a compliment, but it's all made up, and if it gibes with what people are really like in that area, then fine. If it doesn't . . ."

" . . . that wouldn't really bother us," Joel joined in.

"It's liberating in a way to see something in a foreign culture and to use that culture as a milieu for a movie. Plus, we love Southern writers. Most of what we know of the place, in fact, comes from what we've read."

"Faulkner."

"Faulkner."

"Yeah."

"We started writing, before *Raising Arizona*, something that does take place in New York. But it's also exotic, because . . ."

" . . . we made it period – the late 1950s. It takes place in a skyscraper and is about big business. The characters talk fast . . ."

" . . . and wear sharp clothes . . ."

Weeks later, I spotted the Coens talking fast and wearing sharp clothes themselves at a screening of Barry Levinson's new movie, *Tin Men*, at the Museum of Modern Art. There, among the jostling celebrities and the Jasper Johnses, the two still had the devilish little grins on their faces that I'd first encountered on the morning I met them, sort of smirks smeared into smiles. As I watched them giggling, greeting friends, making new ones, I was struck by the fun they seemed to be having. Still under 30, the two are somewhat bemused by all their success. It is the bemusement of precocious kids who've been invited to their very first adult party.

They've spiked the punch.

INVASION OF THE BABY SNATCHERS

BY DAVID EDELSTEIN

If you've ever left something on the roof of a car and then realized the goof several miles down the road, you'll get a kick out of a bit in *Raising Arizona*, Joel and Ethan Coen's farce about a babynapping and it's afterbath. What's left on the car roof is an infant, and when the awful truth is discovered, the occupants – a pair of escaped convicts – make a squealing 180-degree turn and go barreling back to where the babe has presumably landed. Cut to the infant in his car-seat in the centre of the blacktop, staring off screen with gurgling, Gerber-baby glee, while, behind him, the vehicle rushes in at 90 miles an hour, screeching to a halt about an inch from his little head. And the kid is still smiling.

This is how the guys behind the ghoulish *Blood Simple* invade the American mainstream: The kid is so *cuuute* and the gag so felicitous that you hardly register the perversity. In *Raising Arizona*, a young hayseed couple – excon H. I. "Hi" (Nicolas Cage) and police booking officer Edwina "Ed" (Holly Hunter) – learn they cannot have a child. (As narrator Hi puts it, "Her insides were a rocky place where my seed could find no purchase.") In desperate need of a baby to complete their blissful, suburban existence, they shanghai one of the newborn Arizona quintuplets, sons of Nathan Arizona (Trey Wilson), an unpainted-furniture baron.

In a world where moviemakers often inflate themselves and their motives, Joel and Ethan Coen – 32 and 29, respectively, both childless but presumably fertile – take the opposite approach: They talk coolly about craftsmanship and storytelling, and little else. With *Raising Arizona*, the Coens say, they wanted to make a film as different from *Blood Simple* as possible – galloping instead of languorous, sunny instead of lurid, genial and upbeat instead of murderous and cynical.

"It's not an emotional thing at all," says Barry Sonnenfeld, their cinematographer. "Given any topic, they could write an excellent script. Topics are incredibly unimportant to them – it's structure and style and words. If you ask them for their priorities, they'll tell you script, editing, coverage, and lighting."

When pressed for their attraction to the *subject* – babies, child-rearing, images of the family – the Coens squirm and smoke and do their best in the face of so irrelevant a question. We're in a small Greek coffee shop near Joel's Manhattan apartment, where, in less than half an hour, they have smoked three cigarettes apiece; the air in the room has grown so foggy that we seem to have drifted out to sea.

Finally, out of the cloud, Joel speaks: "You have a scene in a movie when someone gets shot, right? Bang! And the squib goes off and the blood runs down and you get a reaction, right? It's movie fodder, you know what I mean? And in a really different way, a baby's face is movie fodder. You just wanna take elements that are good fodder and do something different with them." He laughs – a reassuring laugh, like old bedsprings – and turns to his brother. "Wouldn't you say that's basically it?"

"Yeah," says Ethan, deadpan, "it's like a real cheap and shameless bid at making a commercial movie. We decided to sell out and that was the first decision."

If the Coens are tightlipped and ironic with interviewers, perhaps it's because they themselves can't account for the warmth and integrity of their movie. "That's your job," suggests Ethan, helpfully.

They don't make it easy. Few journalists are allowed on the *Raising Arizona* set, and when I arrive, there isn't a lot to see. It's the end of a thirteen-week shoot, and all I get to watch is part of a chase scene in a supermarket: There's no dialogue, the shots have been meticulously storyboarded, and the only real challenges are those facing the special effects people. (I spend a lot of time watching them blow popcorn and cereal out of an air cannon.)

But I'm lucky to be there at all, and it's hard to blame the Coens for their wariness of the press. No one paid any attention to them when they made *Blood Simple* on $1.5 million – money they raised themselves from private investors, most in the vicinity of their hometown, Minneapolis. Sometimes their crew consisted of one person, Barry Sonnenfeld. *Raising Arizona,* while no biblical epic, cost four times as much, sports a full roster of production assistants, and is being released by a major studio, Twentieth Century-Fox.

"The attitude on *Blood Simple*," says Sonnenfeld, "was 'Just go for it, 'cause if we screw it up, no one will know about it, it'll be just one more unreleased movie.' I still take chances, but there's no question we're more scared."

By this point in the shoot, however, Joel and Ethan seem anything but antsy. (The Coens co-wrote the script; Joel is nominally the director, Ethan the co-producer with Mark Silverman.) Although I have agreed in advance not to waylay them, they're happy to make small talk – or, in this case, baby talk.

"The babies were great," says Ethan, of the most potentially problem-ridden scene, in which Hi swipes Nathan, Jr. (T. J. Kuhn), from the nursery and accidentally liberates the other infants.

"We kept firing babies when they wouldn't behave," says Joel. "And they didn't even know they were being fired, that's what was so pathetic about it."

What gets a baby fired?

"Some of them took their first steps on the set," says Joel. "Ordinarily, you'd be pretty happy about something like that, but in this case it got them fired."

"They'd make the walk of shame," intones Ethan.

"The parents were horrified. One mother actually put her baby's shoes on backward so he wouldn't walk".

We're in a supermarket in Tempe, Arizona, in the middle of a long, flat stretch of shopping centres outside Phoenix. In keeping with the movie's visual motif of aggressive bad taste, the female extras shop with curlers in their hair and let out sustained shrieks; as Hi dodges their carts, a red-faced manager pulls out a shotgun and starts blasting. No babies are involved, but a pack of dogs have chased Hi into the supermarket. Early on, it's clear that if you're ever pursued by angry dogs, the absolute best move would be ducking into a supermarket – the animals don't have much traction on those shiny floors and get easily traumatized.

"This is worse than when we had babies," says Ethan. "At least with babies, you could smack them around. People are afraid to hit dogs."

Hi, bedraggled and bloody, dragged along by the Motorcyclist of the Apocalypse (Randall "Tex" Cobb).

The Coens remain calm, laid-back. Joel, the taller, has nearly shoulder length hair and dangling arms; ten or fifteen years ago, the look was vintage pot-head. Ethan, unshaven, lighter, and more compact, divides his gaze between the action and the floor, pacing between shots and grinding out cigarettes. Synchronicity is the key: Sonnenfeld has compared them to a two-man ecosystem; and while they do communicate through tiny signals and monosyllables, they seem to be the recipients of what Mr. Spock would term a "Vulcan mind meld".

Jim Jacks, executive producer, narrates their trademark *pas de deux:* "You watch Ethan walk in a circle this way and Joel walk in a circle that way; each knows exactly where the other is and when they'll meet. Then they go to Barry."

This is also how the Coens write; they don't make films so much as pace them out. (Asked where the confidence to make movies comes from, Ethan replies, "Every little step considered one at a time is not terribly daunting.") Ethan, the more silent and cryptic of the two, majored in philosophy at Princeton, and the contrast between his placid demeanour and the nicotine-fuelled churnings of his brain gives pause. The computer in his head seems to try out hundreds of moves before it ever lets him *do* anything.

Between setups, the brothers take turns on a decent game of Ms. Pac-Man. They're going a little stir-crazy by now; Scottsdale, where they've been settled for the last few months, seems (as actress Frances McDormand puts it) like a big golf course; and the nearby desert, though magnificent, is not reliably soul-quenching.

Nicolas Cage sits in silence next to the book rack, idly flipping through magazines. On his canvas chair, a Band Aid separates "Nic" from "olas", the offending "h" obscured. Cage is touchy about misspellings of his first name, and, in a soothing (and poetic) gesture, Ethan ministered to the hurt. That's what producers are for.

Reluctant to discuss his methods, Cage is clear about his goals. He arrives on the set with a ton of ideas; even in the uncomplicated supermarket chase, he proposes a glance at his watch during a tiny lull. Joel politely shakes off the suggestion. Their relationship has been bumpy but respectful. Cage praises the brilliant script and the Coens' professionalism, but he's clearly miffed that he couldn't bring more to the party. "Joel and Ethan have a very strong vision," he says, "and I've learned how difficult it is for them to accept another artist's vision. They have an autocratic nature."

A few minutes after the interview, Cage summons me back. "Ah, what I said about Joel and Ethan . . . with relatively new directors, that's when you find that insecurity. The more movies they make, the more they'll lighten up. The important thing is not to discourage an actor's creative flow."

Not all the actors feel their flow was dammed, however. Holly Hunter, a friend of Joel and Ethan's (inspired by her ramrod Southern tenacity, they wrote the part of Ed for her), insists she always held the reins, but could rely on Joel as a safety net. "Joel and Ethan function without their egos," she says. Then, thinking it over, she amends, "Or maybe their egos are so big they're completely secure with anybody who disagrees with them."

That sounds more like it. "You can convince Joel and Ethan of things," says Sonnenfeld. "I find the best thing to do is bring up your point, drop it, and wait a couple of days."

The Coens radiate confidence, and you can bet their young, nonunion crew picks up on it. The set ("remarkably sex and drug free", I'm told) behaves like a winning clubhouse – kids just up from the minors who know they'll top the standings by season's end. The tone is relaxed but super efficient. In return for artistic control, the Coens are determined to stay on schedule. "They worry more about going over budget than we do," says Ben Barenholtz, who signed both to a four-picture deal with Circle Releasing Company (producers of *Blood Simple*). Fox has left them alone; the day after I arrive, executive vice-president Scott Rudin flies in to see his first set of dailies.

To say the Coens come prepared to shoot is to understate the case. The script has been rubbed and buffed, the shots storyboarded. On the set they rarely improvise. Joel insists that when you make a movie for so little money, you can't afford to mess around. It's strange then, to hear him rhapsodise about Francis Coppola, a director who can't seem to work without a crisis, hammering out scenes and shots on the spot. "I have no idea how you can go into a movie without a finished script," Joel admits.

Sitting with Joel, Ethan and Sonnenfeld in a Scottsdale Denny's before the next evening's shoot, the mood is as comfortable as one of those all-night bull sessions in *Diner*. The Coens aren't limo types, and it takes very little to make them happy – a pack of cigarettes, coffee, a warm Denny's. "When they're in work mode, creature comforts become minimal," says Frances McDormand, who played the heroine of *Blood Simple* and has lived with Joel for the past couple of years. (She was Holly Hunter's roommate before that, and has a brazen cameo in *Raising Arizona*.)

"They love the performance part of their job, like the minute you walk on a stage or the camera starts rolling. For them, the writing is one part of it, the budgeting and preproduction another, but it's all building toward the shoot. And then in postproduction, that's when they get to lead the artistic life: They get to stay up late and get circles under their eyes and smoke too much and not eat enough and be focused entirely on creating something. And then it starts again."

Truly, a design for living.

Joel and Ethan Coen grew up in a Jewish suburb of Minneapolis, the sons of two college professors – a father in economics, a mother in art history. (They have a sister, now a doctor.) Despite their ties to academia, they're almost perversely anti-intellectual about what they do; in fact, they insist that their home was short on high culture. Recalls Joel, "My mother once wrote an article, 'How to Take Children to an Art Museum,' but I don't recall her ever taking us."

Instead, the children were left to their own devices, and weaned on pop culture and television; they set James M. Cain beside Aristotle, and among their most favourite film experiences, cite fifties and sixties sex comedies like *Boeing Boeing* and *Pillow Talk*. (For the record, they also love good movies.)

From the age of eight, Joel made films – remakes of pictures like *Advise and Consent* – and eventually went off to study filmmaking at New York University, where he's remembered for sitting in the back of the class and making snotty remarks. He says he learned almost nothing, but welcomed his parents' subsidy to make movies. (In his 30 - minute thesis film, *Soundings*, a woman makes love to her deaf boyfriend while verbally fantasising about his buddy in the next room.) At Princeton, Ethan was equally out of step. After neglecting to notify the college that he planned to return from a term off, he tried to cut through the red tape with a phony doctor's excuse (from a surgeon at "Our Lady of the Eye, Ear, Nose, and Throat") that claimed he'd lost an arm in a hunting accident in his brother-in law's living room. The school ordered him to see a shrink.

After film school, Joel worked as an editor on Sam Raimi's *The Evil Dead* – the *Don Giovanni* of hack-'em-ups – and quickly struck up a friendship with Raimi, for whom he and Ethan wrote a script called *The XYZ Murders*. It was mangled and discarded by its studio, Embassy (and had a limited Columbia release as *Crimewave*), a disaster that made the Coens more wary of dealing with major studios. "We've always let Sam make those mistakes for us," explains Joel. "'Sam,' we tell him, 'you go do a movie at a studio and tell us what happens.'"

The Coens are pranksters, but colleagues also describe them as affable and generous, not to mention quick studies: They're fond of quoting entire scenes from other movies, along with lines from bad reviews. Their geniality doesn't come through in the rigid, Q & A format of interviews, though, and while promoting *Blood Simple*, their anarchic impulses came out. In their press conference at the 1985 New York Film Festival, for which *Blood Simple* had been selected, Ethan summed up their aesthetic by quoting Raimi: "The innocent must suffer, the guilty must be punished, you must drink blood to be a man."

"That's the great thing about Joel and Ethan," says Sonnenfeld. "They don't wanna be on the *Today* show. They don't wanna be in *People*. They don't give a shit. They wanna have a good time."

My formal interviews with the Coens are, in some respects, exercises in futility – me talking and Joel and Ethan smoking, their faces evoking Redford's response to Newman in *Butch Cassidy and the Sundance Kid*: "You just keep thinkin', Butch. That's what you're good at." Maybe the questions are dumb, or maybe (as they insist) they're just dull guys, movies being their one step out. Perhaps they learned a lesson from their *Blood Simple* interviews. "We wince when we read ourselves in print," says Joel.

Like their movies, the Coens seem suspended between high and low impulses. Ethan studied philosophy, of course, but only "for fun"; there's something absurd, he implies, about being an intellectual in a culture this junky. Like Preston Sturges – one of their models for *Raising Arizona* – the Coens debunk all notions of aesthetic responsibility. Their movies poke fun at ideas, and their characters suffer from tunnel vision, each gripped by an obsession he or she can't be bothered to explain (nor, for that matter, can the Coens).

Perhaps they'd rather just listen. "Their favourite midtown lunch spot is the counter at Woolworth's," says editor Michael Miller. "They go to hear dialogue that will find its way into a script. The opening of *Blood Simple* – many of those lines they'd overheard. Their attention is never more riveted than when they're in the back seat of a taxi. I've seen Joel draw out taxi drivers in a way he doesn't draw out his friends. Once, on the way home from the airport, the driver had a ball game on – the Mets were playing someone and it was in the heat of the pennant drive – and Joel said, 'What's the game?' and the cabdriver said, 'Baseball, I think.' They loved that."

Found objects constitute much of the Coens' work. "It's not meant to be condescending," says Joel. "If the characters talk in cliches, it's because we *like* cliches. You start with things that are incredibly recognisable in one form, and you play with them."

The ingredients might be "movie fodder", but they resonate like crazy when the context is altered. The Coens' principal target is the way Americans conceal their self-interest behind apple-pie slogans and icons, sometimes unconsciously. At the start of *Blood Simple*, homilies about American individualism have a different kind of impact when the narrator is a killer and each character is fatally locked into his or her point of view. In *Raising Arizona*, Hi and Ed return home with the kidnapped Nathan, Jr. and a banner in the living room reads, "WELCOME HOME SON." Ed clutches the infant to her breast and weeps, "I love him *so-ho-ho-ho* much", and Hi hauls out the camera and marks the occasion with a classic family portrait.

The Coens insist that the last part of what they jokingly call their "Hayseed Trilogy" will be a long time in coming but you can see what drew them to this part of the country to make their first films – the absurdity of mass-culture junkiness set against these parched, primal landscapes. Many of their gags spring from an innocent love of this culture (which they share with their characters) combined with wicked insight into its looniness.

A charge implicit in the backlash against *Blood Simple* was that these film-school brats were condescending to the common folk. And, during the shoot of *Raising Arizona*, a Tempe paper got hold of the script and was dismayed to find the place portrayed as a hick town, the film's set and costumes in studiously bad taste. "Of course it's not accurate," says Ethan. "It's not supposed to be. It's all made up. It's an Arizona of the mind."

All their impersonal talk of structure can't conceal the pleasure Joel and Ethan get out of cracking each other up, a pleasure that transcends their devotion to craft, their immaturity as artists. "They laugh hysterically at their own stuff," says Sonnenfeld. "The only person Joel cares about pleasing is Ethan."

"We didn't have that much to do with each other as kids," says Joel. "We kind of rediscovered each other after college, really through making movies." The joy of that rediscovery – of shared assumptions, of a cultural foundation – binds their gags together in ways they're not always conscious of. And that joy pulls us in, too. In a Joel and Ethan Coen movie, we love being in on the joke.

"They're genuinely surprised when people like their films," says Ben Barenholtz. "I remember Joel walked out of a *Blood Simple* screening and started laughing. 'They really liked it' he said!" And Barenholtz imitates Joel shrugging broadly.

I saw the shrug recently, in that same Greek coffee shop. Ethan talks about a test screening of *Raising Arizona* in Fort Worth, Texas, where a woman said, "You depicted very accurately the mentality of Texas prisoners. I ought to know. I spent eight and a half years in a Texas penitentiary. I did some things I shouldn't have."

Joel laughs and shrugs: There isn't a germ of authenticity in the prison scenes. But there's one thing he's forgetting. Mass culture penetrates prisons, too. She'd probably seen all the same movies.

INTERVIEW WITH JOEL AND ETHAN COEN

BY MICHEL CIMENT AND HUBERT NIOGRET

Both your films belong to genres: one crime, the other comedy. Do you prefer to work in a genre framework?

JOEL COEN: We were more conscious of working in a genre with *Blood Simple* than with *Raising Arizona*. *Arizona* seems more absurd, an amalgam of genres. In *Blood Simple* the genre was, in a basic way, guiding the movie we were making.

ETHAN COEN: With *Arizona* we didn't begin by thinking of diving into a genre. We'd wanted to broadly make a comedy with two main characters. We concentrated on them, more than the movie in a general sense.

Tycoon Nathan Arizona Sr. (Trey Wilson) sounds off at the police after the babynapping of his son.

Did you first draw the characters, and then the setting?
JOEL: With *Arizona*, yes. The story was a way of talking about the characters. For *Blood Simple*, we started with a situation, a general plot. The characters went from there. So, the reverse.

Why the South-West with both, Texas, Arizona? You're from Minnesota . . .
ETHAN: Perhaps partly because we're *not* from the South-West, which appears nearly as exotic to us as it is for you. It's like an attraction for us. For the second film, that type of desert landscape seemed the right place.
JOEL: Once again, *Blood Simple* had been conceived in a more planned way, more conscious. By not taking Texas as it really is, but as something preserved in legend, a collection of histories and myths . . . The subject is "deadly passion". If you associate that with a region of the USA, Texas is the most logical place. There are so many identical cases that have occurred in Texas that it's grown in the public imagination. So it was the logical place to construct our story. That situation was important for our dramatic bearings, because the film was supposed to be a slice of life, but still a fiction contrived to fit into an exotic place.
ETHAN: My whole association with Minnesota, where we grew up, was very dull. The movie had to be shot anywhere but in Minnesota.

The "folk tales" have some importance to **Raising Arizona,** *like that of Davy Crockett?*
ETHAN: We decided definitely to have a bond with the imaginary, that the movie wouldn't be a slice of life.
JOEL: When we'd spoken with the cinematographer, Barry Sonnenfeld, regarding the look of the movie, we talked about opening it like a book of stories, with colours that had a certain vibration. That was part of the visual style.

Your influences are more literary than cinematic?
JOEL: For a movie like *Raising Arizona*, I guess you can detect our admiration for Southern writers like William Faulkner and Flannery O'Connor.
ETHAN: Even if we don't share her [O'Connor's] interest in Catholicism! But she has a true knowledge of Southern psychology that you don't find with many other writers. She also has a great sense of eccentric character. For *Blood Simple* the influence was more from crime writers like James Cain.

What you say about Flannery O'Connor is especially striking, because of the director one thinks about after seeing **Raising Arizona:** *John Huston. I'm reminded of sequences from his* **The Life and Times of Judge Roy Bean,** *or from* **Wise Blood,** *adapted from the novel by Flannery O'Connor.*
ETHAN: Yeah, like the fantastic Stacy Keach character in *The Life and Times of Judge Roy Bean*!
JOEL: As far as O'Connor is concerned, our characters haven't the same mystical obsessions as hers. Ours are terrestrial!

JOEL & ETHAN COEN: BLOOD SIBLINGS

One also thinks about Chuck Jones cartoons when viewing **Raising Arizona,** *as in the supermarket scene.*

ETHAN: We thought about these characters who rebound, and collide, and simply their speed of movement. We tried to refine the spirit of animation you find in pinball machines.

JOEL: It's funny that you mention Chuck Jones, because we hadn't thought consciously about him for this film. On the other hand, his *Roadrunner* inspired us for *Blood Simple,* for the long scene where Ray [John Getz] tries to kill Julian Marty [Dan Hedaya], then bury him. There's a Hitchcockian side, but there's also Chuck Jones.

What was the starting point for **Raising Arizona?** *The idea of quintuplets?*

ETHAN: Not really. Essentially, after having finished *Blood Simple,* we wanted to make something completely different. We didn't know what, but we wanted it to be funny, with a quicker rhythm. We also wanted to employ Holly Hunter, a long-standing friend. This isn't really the story of the origin of the project but Holly Hunter, her personality and, by extension, the character we conceived for her. On the other hand, *Blood Simple* started from an idea for a script.

JOEL: The idea of kidnapping the baby was really secondary. We weren't that interested either in the problem of sterility or the desire for having a child, but by the idea of a character who has that desire and at the same time feels outside the law. This conflict allowed us to develop the story, that aspiration to a stable family life, and at the same time a taste for unusual experiences.

ETHAN: Yeah, that tension in the character of Hi was our motive for the movie.

How did the other characters develop? For example, the two halfwit brothers?

JOEL: We like those two guys a lot, they're like Laurel and Hardy. They're there to shake up the story, the other characters, everything. It's like an old idea by Dashiell Hammett: an external character intervenes in a situation and we observe the reactions he provokes.

ETHAN: At some point we said to ourselves: let's make two rough characters enter the story and watch what effect it'll have on the relationship between the heroes.

Was your script very precise or did you leave yourselves some freedom for shooting?

JOEL: We work on the script till we're satisfied, but during shooting we're very faithful on the whole. There's very little improvisation in the dialogue. What changes a lot by contrast is the visual idea of the movie once the actors enter the set. During the retakes, we can think of other ways of "covering" the scene with the camera. That happens mainly in the dialogue scenes. By contrast, for action scenes, they're drawn beforehand and we follow the storyboard exactly. In fact, it's not a matter of referring to the storyboard during shooting, it serves us psychologically. We know what the visual idea of the shot is, we have it on paper and it's reassuring.

ETHAN: Sometimes we look in the camera and discover the shot drawn on the storyboard doesn't work.

JOEL: For various reasons. For instance, the location can pose problems you don't anticipate. And even if we wanted to improvise while shooting we couldn't because our budgets have been very low. *Blood Simple* was made for $800,000 and *Raising Arizona* for a little more than five million, which for Hollywood is very low. To obtain the maximum from that money, the movie has to be meticulously prepared.

Do the actors induce you to change aspects of their characters during shooting?
JOEL: Absolutely. Particularly with Nicolas Cage and Holly Hunter. Nic's a really imaginative actor. He arrives with piles of ideas that we hadn't thought about while writing the script, but his contribution is always in line with the character we'd imagined. He extrapolated from what was written. The same with Holly. Even if she surprised us less because we had her in mind when we wrote her part, and we've known her a long time.

Can you give us examples of the participation by the actors in their roles?
JOEL: We'd spoken at length with Nicolas Cage about his moustache and side burns. We wondered if he had to keep them throughout the movie or lose them at some point.
ETHAN: He was also obsessed by his hair, like Woody Woodpecker. The more depressed the character was, the more flamboyant the tuft became. There was a curious capillary rapport!

And the clothes?
JOEL: That, no, it wasn't in the script, the Hawaiian shirts.
ETHAN: That's clichéd clothing on criminals in the South-West, that style of flashy dressing.

The character of the motorcyclist comes from a dream . . .
JOEL: We tried to imagine a character who didn't correspond specifically to *our* image of an 'Evil One' or a nightmare become reality, but rather to the image that Hi would have. Being from the South-West, he'd see him in the form of a Hell's Angel.
ETHAN: We also tried to connect the characters through the music. Holly sings a lullaby in the movie and we asked the composer to introduce it into the musical theme that accompanies the bounty hunter, that also blends Richard Wayne and country music!

Where did you find the interpreter for Randall "Tex" Cobb?
JOEL: He's not really an actor. He's a former boxing champion. He's been in a few movies. In the beginning he was more someone who brawled in the streets in Texas, then who tried without real success to make a career in boxing. He's less an actor than a force of nature. Not really someone it's easy to work with, and I don't know if I'd rush headlong into employing him for a future film. He played his role well in *Raising Arizona*, but he posed problems.

JOEL & ETHAN COEN: BLOOD SIBLINGS

What kind of language did you want for the characters? It seems like a very stylised argot.

JOEL: It's a mixture of local dialect and a vocabulary we imagined from the likely reading material of the characters: the Bible, magazines. The voice-over was one of the starting points for the story. What we wrote first was the ten minutes preceding the credits.

You established right from the start of the film this mixture of sentimentalism, concerning the baby, and the distancing irony.

JOEL: There are people who find the conclusion too sentimental. Once again, that doesn't reflect our own attitude to life. For us it's written in the context of the character, it fits with his ideas about life, what he dreams of accomplishing in the future.

ETHAN: We hide behind the main character! We hadn't really measured out the quantity of feelings we wanted to inject into that story, the characters guided us.

Both films are visualised very inventively. Did certain images impose themselves on you before writing the script?

JOEL: In some cases, yes. Anyhow, it's different from writing a script for someone else. In that instance, the director generally doesn't want the script telling him the visual elements. Working for ourselves, on the other hand, we allow those elements to be introduced into the script. Sometimes, however, we write the scene and then we ask ourselves what's the best way to express the information, to make the public participate emotionally or to accelerate the rhythm. It's then that we think of the images. But, in fact, it's all very tied together, it's the two faces of the same coin. While writing the script, we knew we'd shoot on a wider plane and with more depth of field than in *Blood Simple*, which was more claustrophobic.

ETHAN: I remember a specific image which pleased us when we wrote the script: to see Holly in uniform hurling orders at the prisoners. It might appear secondary, but that image had great importance in setting the writing in motion.

JOEL: For instance, the first shot with that horizontal line and the character rushing into it was written like that in the script.

How do you share the work?

JOEL: We write together without parting company. We lock ourselves in a room and write the script from A to Z. *Raising Arizona* took three and a half months. On the set it's basically a continuation of the writing. We're always there, both of us, and we consult each other continually. The credits indicate a division of labour more rigid than what really happens. For effectiveness, and to avoid confusion, I speak to the actors and communicate most of the time with the technical crew, but for the directing decisions it's a mutual responsibility. Ethan, for his part, is busier taking care of the production.

ETHAN: The same with the editing and mixing, it's a total collaboration.

Hi McDunnough seeks a radical solution to his wife's infertility problem, in the shape of the baby Arizona.

And the image of the two prisoners who come out of the mud?
JOEL: That sort of primitive birth! We asked ourselves how to introduce those two brutes who'd escaped from prison. That vision came to mind – it appeared to be an appropriate introduction.

It's curious you've mentioned James M. Cain as having influenced **Blood Simple,** *because one thinks more readily of Jim Thompson.*
JOEL: In fact, at that time, we hadn't read him. After *Blood Simple* was released, the novels were republished in paperback in the United States and we started to discover him.

Watching **Raising Arizona** *one sometimes thinks of Preston Sturges.*
ETHAN: We're mad about his films. We adore *The Palm Beach Story.*

How did you get along when you were children?
JOEL: There's three years difference in age and that's important when you're a child. It was only after leaving school that we really got to know each other.
ETHAN: Yeah, above all by writing together. Joel studied cinema at university. Me, I followed a philosophy course, God knows why. Joel then worked as an editor.
JOEL: On horror films. Then we begun to write scripts for others, and finally we wrote *Blood Simple.* When we were kids, we made films on Super 8. They were abstract and surreal. In winter, Minnesota, where we were born, resembles a frozen wasteland. There were fields covered with snow and the scenery was very abstract. We also shot remakes of films we saw on television, like *The Naked Prey* by Cornel Wilde that we made in our garden. And also *Advise and Consent.* That had a more epic dimension, we even had to construct the set inside the living room. We saw many films, those of the Fifties and from the beginning of the Sixties with Doris Day and Rock Hudson, the worst period of Hollywood.

Where did you study cinema?
JOEL: At New York University. Our professors weren't famous directors, they'd made a career essentially in teaching. I studied for four years from 1972.

And philosophy?
ETHAN: I mainly studied the history of philosophy. I wrote a thesis on Wittgenstein. I don't see too many connections with my future work as a film-maker.

You worked as an assistant director?
JOEL: No, I worked as an assistant editor on *The Evil Dead* where I edited between a third and a half of the movie. At that time there was a trend in horror films, low budget, produced independently, like *Fear No Evil.* You always had to put "Evil" on the table . . .

*In **Arizona** there's some superb montage effects, particularly with the motorcyclist on the road . . .*
JOEL: Those cuts were specified in the script.

You like popular culture, and at the same time you're ironical.
JOEL: Yes, we have that relationship with American popular culture.
ETHAN: We have an attitude, a commentary with regard to the material. We make jokes with it . . .

*The characters are very different in **Blood Simple** to **Arizona.***
JOEL: In *Arizona*, the characters were certainly supposed to be sympathetic. We got a lot of pleasure out of writing them. The character of Ed has a restrained sympathy, which is very interesting, something very mature. What's not easy is when a character's very wicked, and at the same time you feel sympathy for him.

There is a dark side with you, and a comic side. You don't seek realism.
JOEL: Some people have been offended by the characters in *Arizona*.
ETHAN: For me, it's a very wild film.

*How was the idea of your first film born – why did you choose a typical **film noir**?*
ETHAN: We've liked that type of story for a long while: James Cain, Dashiell Hammett, Raymond Chandler. It's a genre that really gives us pleasure. And we also chose it for very practical reasons. We knew we weren't going to have much money. Financing wouldn't permit other things. We could depend on that type of genre, on that kind of basic force.
JOEL: The story called for special effects, exotic locations. And we knew we could realise a certain number of things for very little money. You can limit the number of characters, distribute them around a confined space. There's no need to spread out on an enormous scale, shoot things that create expenses. It was a pragmatic decision to choose that style of film.

Barry Sonnenfeld, the cameraman, has shot both films.
JOEL: Yes, he's an old friend, from way before the movie. The collaboration is very close. Well before we began to shoot he saw the sets. We spoke about the movie, the way we were going to shoot certain places. He was involved very early, which once again, from a practical point of view, helps you work more efficiently. At the moment you begin to shoot, you can't suddenly start spending loosely. Everything has to be discussed beforehand.

JOEL & ETHAN COEN: BLOOD SIBLINGS

In **Blood Simple,** *there are shots with astonishing effects, like the revolver firing through the wall, when one sees the hits via the light which comes through . . .*
JOEL: When you speak about scenes constructed from images, that's a good example, because the image determined the situation there, which was then elaborated to integrate into the context of the story.

How was your first film financed? With many partners? Independently?
ETHAN: We'd never made a movie before. We had no references. It was difficult to find a production company who trusted us, who would give us money to make a movie. So we spoke to private investors, large numbers of them. For the second film, that was incredibly easy. We went to see the American distributor of *Blood Simple*, Circle Films, who were interested in us producing another film. They liked our script. They said "yes".

What's your ideal mode of production: to be independent or work with a "studio"?
ETHAN: We produced independently because of circumstances, particularly on the first one.
JOEL: For the second, there was a path of least resistance. We could've sought the money elsewhere, perhaps from a studio. Because of *Blood Simple* we knew Circle Films. We trusted them, it was natural to work with them. There was no ideology behind those choices. As long as we could maintain the type of control we want, we could accept the financing of a studio.
ETHAN: The problem is to get the money.
JOEL: The problem is all the ties attached. The whole idea with regard to independent production is that it helps you to make the movie you want to make, and in the way you want to make it. If the studio permits the same thing, then that's all well and good. Some do it and manage very well, even with movies that don't correspond to the "Hollywood formula". Some directors are very successful in that system, making movies they want to make.

What's been the shooting time for each of your films?
JOEL: Eight weeks for *Blood Simple*, ten for *Arizona*.

Your film appears at the same time as **True Stories,** *which is very different. But there's a common irony, pop-cultural roots, and a very modern visual approach.* **True Stories** *is more static while your film is more dynamic.*
JOEL: It's coincidence. As is the fact that John Goodman [the larger of the two escapees in *Arizona*] acts in both movies. We chose him before *True Stories* was shot, and he came to film with us directly from shooting David Byrne's movie.

How do you make the distinction between Arizona and Texas? The people? The feelings?
JOEL: Arizona doesn't carry all the baggage of Texas for an American audience. Texas is associated with many things, which isn't the case with Arizona.
ETHAN: Arizona is now like so many towns in the Mid- and South-West spread. The stores are the same as everywhere.
JOEL: Once again, Arizona for us was one of the rare states where you can find that type of landscape. That type of desert only really exists in Arizona, closer to Mexico too . . .

What American film-makers of the last twenty years do you feel closest to? Not those you prefer!
JOEL: That question's much more difficult than those you admire! It's much easier to say the ones you like.

Who do you like?
JOEL: Scorsese, Coppola, David Lynch.

Kubrick?
JOEL: Yes.

Kubrick's black humour?
JOEL: Yes, *Dr Strangelove.*
ETHAN: I like Walter Hill a lot, he's done some very interesting things.

And Bob Altman?
JOEL: I like some of his movies. He did a great job of adapting Chandler with *The Long Goodbye.*
ETHAN: Yeah, it's a very good movie. But I read somewhere it's the one he likes least. I can't understand why . . .

No, he likes it a lot.
ETHAN: Ah! That's okay then.

Translated by Paul Buck and Catherine Petit. Interview conducted in Cannes on 8 May 1987.

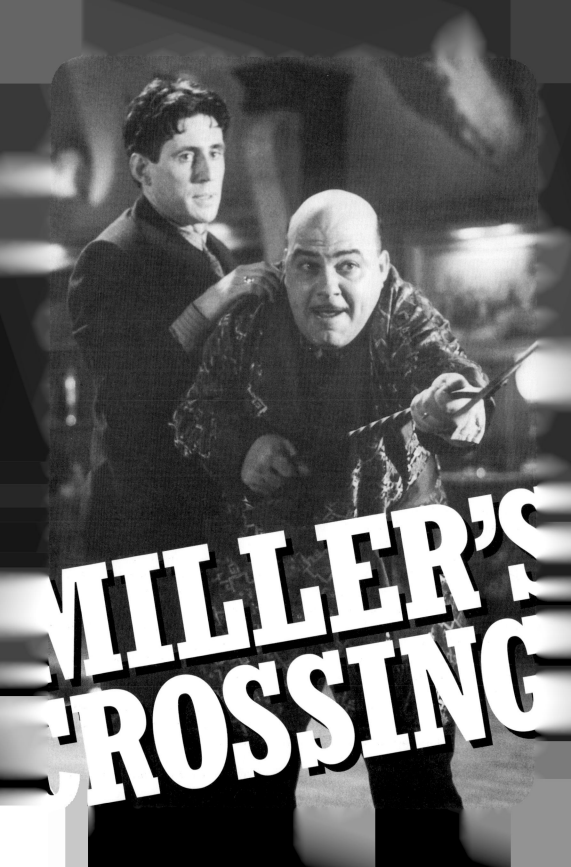

MILLER'S CROSSING

REVIEW FROM VARIETY

I t'll be *Miller's Crossing* not *Dick Tracy*, that's remembered as the standout 1930s gangster film of the year. For substance – the missing ingredient in so many of the year's flashy filmic exercises – is here in spades, along with the twisted, brilliantly controlled style on which filmmakers Joel and Ethan Coen made a name.

Classic-quality outing surely will put Fox square at the box-office if the studio's marketers can mount a campaign as good as this film.

Formal constraints of a richly composed genre piece are apparent in *Miller's Crossing*, but bumping around beneath them are the same wild-at-heart impulses that made the Coens' Texas *film noir* thriller *Blood Simple* so nervily compelling. Result: One never knows what's going to pop.

Story unspools in an unnamed Eastern city where dim but ambitious Italian gangster Johnny Caspar (Jon Polito) has a problem named Bernie Bernbaum (John Turturro). Seems Bernie is angling in on his angle so he can't fix a fight anymore without somebody riding his hip for a chunk of the profit.

"If you can't trust a fix what can you trust?" complains Caspar.

He wants approval from the city's Irish political boss, Leo (Albert Finney), to rub out the cause of his complaint, but Leo's not giving in. He's fallen in love with Bernie's sister, Verna (Marcia Gay Harden), who wants Bernie protected.

Leo's cool, brainy aide-de-camp Tom (Gabriel Byrne) sees that Leo is making a big mistake, and it's up to Tom to save him as his empire begins to crumble.

The complication is that Tom also is in love with Verna, though he's loath to admit it, making it tough for him to get a clear fix even on his own motives.

The pic is about character, friendship and ethics in the gravest of contexts – Caspar as much as says so in the marvellously twisted opening scene. But it's mainly about heart. According to Verna, Leo has one but Tom doesn't. Irony is that Tom's heart is bigger than anyone's, and that, along with gambling, is both his downfall and his redemption.

Rarely does a screen hero of Tom's gritty dimensions come along, and Irishman Byrne (*Julia and Julia*, *A Soldier's Tale*), who's destined to earn widespread recognition with this performance, brings him gracefully and profoundly to life.

Like Verna, he's a tough loner who trusts nobody and nothing, least of all sentiment. Everything he does, he does for Leo – not that anyone would know it. Like Verna says, he always takes the long way around.

Tom figures Verna's taking Leo for a ride, and he despises her but he still can't stay away from her. As portrayed by screen newcomer Harden, Verna has the verve and flintiness of a glory-days Bette Davis or Barbara Stanwyck.

Tom and Verna have some great scenes together. "Intimidating helpless women is part of my job," he tells her after hunting her down in a women's room. "Then why don't you find one and intimidate her," she snaps.

Tom Reagan (Gabriel Byrne), the figure at the centre of internecine gang/political warfare in an unnamed city during the late 1920s, early 1930s.

Also outstanding is Finney as the big-hearted political fixer who usually has the mayor and the police chief seated happily across his desk. He's as cool in a spray of bullets as he is vulnerable in affairs of the heart.

But it's not as if the urge to create full-fleshed characters has taken the fun out of the Coens' game. There's still Polito as the apoplectic Caspar, twisting the tough ethical questions around his thick tongue and thick brain, and the hysterically rude portrayals of his wife and kid.

There's still his human watchdog, the Dane (as in Great Dane, it seems), played by J. E. Freeman, plus a gallery of leeringly satirical fringe characters.

Not at all least, there's Turturro as the weasly Bernie, marvellously despicable with his wheezing laugh and fidgety shrug ("Someone gives me an angle, I play it. Does that mean I should die?").

Animating these characters is a script chock-full of lovingly resurrected period dialogue, phrases like "What's the rumpus?" and lines like "We're a coupla heels, Tom, you 'n' me."

Graphic violence and vivid spectacle abound here, but in this case, as in few other recent pics, they add up to something.

The Coens have brought along a number of their *Blood Simple* and *Raising Arizona* mates, including Carter Burwell, whose subtle, lilting Irish score offers a wry contrast to the action.

Cinematographer Barry Sonnenfeld, who went wild in *Raising Arizona*, bows artfully to convention in this dark-hued, richly composed film, though at least once he jerks his leash.

Buffs will note cameos by director Sam Raimi, with whom the Coens collaborated on his *Evil Dead*, and Frances McDormand, who made her indelible debut in *Blood Simple*.

Pic's rather bland title refers to a lonely spot in the woods where a certain corpse is destined to fall. The thickly twisted script – likely to be deemed one of the best blueprints of the year – was written by the Coen brothers.

MILLER'S CROSSING

BY STEVE JENKINS

Leo, the political boss of an American city during Prohibition, is approached by Johnny Caspar, a rival gangster anxious to kill Bernie Bernbaum, who has been profiting from fights fixed by Caspar but who pays protection to Leo. Because of his romantic involvement with Verna, Bernie's sister, and against the advice of Tom Reagan, his right-hand man, Leo refuses to sanction the killing. Unaware that Tom is also involved with Verna, Leo has her tailed by Rug Daniels. When Rug is killed, Leo blames Caspar and decides to use his power over the mayor and the chief of police to smash Caspar's rackets. Tom tries unsuccessfully to persuade Verna to leave Leo alone and is visited by Bernie, who knows about Caspar's next fixed fight from Mink, the boyfriend of Caspar's lieutenant Eddie Dane. Tom rejects Caspar's offer to pay off his gambling debts if he will give him Bernie, and tells Verna he thinks she or Bernie killed Rug; she claims Tom is jealous of her relationship with Leo. Leo survives a violent attack on his home by Caspar's men, but is enraged when Tom reveals his relationship with Verna, whom Leo now intends to marry. With Verna urging him to leave town with her and Bernie, Tom goes to Caspar, who wants him to prove his new allegiance by shooting Bernie. Unbeknownst to Caspar's men, however, Tom spares Bernie's life, sends him into hiding, and tells Caspar it was Eddie Dane and Mink who sold out the fix on the fights. Dane tells Verna that Tom killed Bernie; Bernie threatens to resurface if Tom does not kill Caspar. Tom is about to be killed by the suspicious Dane, but is saved when Bernie's body is found (the corpse is actually that of Mink, shot in the face by Bernie). Tom now calls Bernie's bluff and threatens to tell Caspar that he is still alive. Caspar kills Dane after Tom tells him that Dane has double-crossed him on the next fight. Tom tells Verna that Bernie is still alive and sends Caspar to a rendezvous, supposedly with Mink. Caspar is killed by the waiting Bernie who, after revealing that Mink killed Rug, is shot by Tom. The latter uses Caspar's money to place a bet on the fixed fight and thus clear his debts. At Bernie's funeral, Tom is snubbed by Verna but Leo, believing that Tom has been acting in his interests all along, offers to forgive him. Tom rejects the offer and Leo walks away.

The belated U.K. release of *Miller's Crossing* means that it now appears as part of a gangster film revival (after *Dick Tracy* and *GoodFellas* and just before *The Godfather Part III*) and also in the middle of a wave of *noir*-ish adaptations from American hardboiled fiction (see *The Hot Spot* and a flood of Jim Thompson). In fact, by choosing to make a Dashiell Hammett movie, albeit without officially adapting one of his books (much as they dealt with James M. Cain in *Blood Simple*), the Coens are returning to the roots of both areas, a move which gives their film a strange air of both self-consciousness and purity, a kind of knowing classicism. For the record, *Miller's Crossing* does borrow strongly from *Red Harvest* (the corrupt interlinking of crime and politics in the running of the unnamed city) and more particularly *The Glass Key* (the ambiguous triangular relationship between Leo, Tom and Verna, and the strong hint of sadistic homo-eroticism that weaves through the complex plot). But the film's particular strength derives from a sense that the film-makers have tapped a kind of essence of Hammett, outside any specific theme or plot, and worked outwards from this, basing their own highly expressive visual and rhythmic style on solid generic foundations.

What is most Hammett-like here is anchored in the characterisation of Tom, and in Gabriel Byrne's quietly judged performance. When Bernie pleads for his life a second time, and again asks Tom to look into his heart, Tom merely asks "What heart?" before shooting him. This has less to do with any clichéd idea of a cynical, hardboiled ethos than it does with Tom's inscrutable motivation. In the film's final scene, when Leo explains away Tom's defection to Caspar to suit his own purposes, Tom's only response is to query whether anyone ever knows why they do things. This is not so much rhetorical as a precise encapsulation of Hammett's style and method, whereby his protagonists and the world they inhabit effectively function independently of each other. His pared-down prose never turns places or events into an expressionist projection of his central character's state of mind, since the latter is always inexpressible. Which is why Hammett's relationship to *film noir* is crucial but also rather indirect.

By making Tom a kind of tragic cipher, furthering a pattern of events in relation to which he is always the outsider, the Coens give *Miller's Crossing* an almost abstract centre, emphasised paradoxically by the dark solidity of Byrne's look and persona. This cleverly highlights the tortuous complexity of the plotting in which Tom is caught up, in terms of relationships, allegiances, double-crosses, etc., all too appropriate in a genre so concerned, particularly in its Mafia strand, with what Caspar describes as "ethics". As he succinctly and exasperatedly puts it, "If you can't trust a fix, what can you trust?" One double-cross leads to another until, Caspar asks, "Where does it all end? Interesting ethical question." It ends, in fact, in a series of repetitions and variations through which the narrative is carefully structured: the repeated line "What's the rumpus?"; the chief of police and the mayor dealing first with Leo and then with Caspar; two occasions on which Tom finds Bernie sitting in his room; two visits by Tom to the place of execution in the woods at *Miller's Crossing*; the two occasions on which Bernie pleads for his life, etc. The shadowy ties between Leo, Tom and Verna (a triangle itself doubled by Eddie Dane, Mink and Bernie, with Bernie the link, having been educated in sex by his "sick twist" of a sister) are both the catalyst for this pattern and its unknowable opposite, queering the pitch for ethics.

In this context, the fact that the Coens' visual stimulus for the film, according to the production notes, was an image of generic incongruity ("big guys in overcoats in the woods") makes perfect sense. *Miller's Crossing* consistently plays off visual solidity (perfectly iconographic hats, coats and faces; dark autumnal shades and colours; large wood-panelled rooms) against sudden eruptions of violence, hysteria and humour, with the latter elements often blended. Thus Caspar viciously slaps his grossly fat young son, believing that with "Kids you gotta be firm"; Leo's machine-gunning of an assailant turns the latter's demise into an ecstatically prolonged dance of death, to the strains of "Danny Boy"; and a boxer screams repeatedly and hysterically as Caspar beats Eddie Dane to death. The sense of pacing in certain scenes is quite uncanny, with extended moments of calm preceding and accentuating the physical grotesquerie and violence.

The duplicitous Tom with Verna (Marcia Gay Harden), his boss's girl, with whom he's having an affair.

The film's credit sequence illustrates a dream of Tom's, which he later recounts to Verna, in which his hat is blown off by the wind while he is walking in some woods. Her keenness to interpret the imagery (did he chase the hat? did it turn into something else?) is countered by his simple insistence that it stayed a hat. In fact, the image is so strong and strange that it needs no interpretation, and much of the strength of *Miller's Crossing* springs from a Hammett-like sense of things as they are, combined with an unerring feel for the genuinely surreal twist. Caspar believes that ethics are important because without them there is only chaos and anarchy. Here the Coens convincingly demonstrate that he is right, and in so doing turn an exercise in genre reworking into something much more rich and strange.

SHOT BY SHOT

BY STEVEN LEVY

O nce Joel and Ethan Coen decided to do a gangster movie, it was inevitable that something like the Thompson jitterbug would find its way onscreen. The New York-based brothers, creators of *Blood Simple* and *Raising Arizona*, are known for infusing their intricately plotted screenplays with uniquely macabre twists. Their new film, *Miller's Crossing*, does not abandon this tradition.

Quite simply, the Thompson jitterbug – thus named by its wisecracking creators – refers to a gruesome dance performed involuntarily by a hood who's being riddled with bullets while his dead fingers continue to squeeze the trigger of a Thompson submachine gun. Though the antics are improbable, presumably the combination of shells pumped into him from below and the recoil of the still-firing tommy gun holds the dead man aloft, jerking him up and down as the bullets tear apart the room. In one scene of 22 quick cuts in this Thompson jitterbug, we see him shoot his toes off.

And another thing: all the while, the soundtrack blares an Irish tenor singing "Danny Boy".

Presumably a throwaway moment in the midst of the movie's key sequence, it is prime Coen: a borderline-tasteless, bloodstained piece of slapstick that results from blending the sensibilities of Stephen King and Samuel Beckett. "It isn't intended to be riotously funny, but there's something . . . *fun* about it," says producer Ethan Coen, an amiable fellow in his early thirties who looks mildly preppy with his short brown hair and polo shirt. "It's a Big Death, you know?"

Director Joel Coen, who in contrast to his younger brother has long dark hair and work clothes (a vaguely Neil Young-ish look), is mildly surprised that the jitterbug has been raised as an issue: "We didn't set out to make *Scenes From a Marriage*," he explains.

They did set out to make something different. The Coen brothers – self-described as "poky" – work on one project at a time and try not to repeat themselves. "We didn't want to do another out-and-out comedy, like *Raising Arizona*," says Joel. "We wanted to do something that was a little bit morbid. Less of a comedy, more of a drama. We've always liked gangster movies, so it was what we started to think about when we did another script."

They initially intended to explore the conflict between Irish and Italian gangs, a power struggle between second-generation immigrant groups. Eventually, a plot emerged, centring on the local mob boss, an Irishman named Leo, and his cagey lieutenant, Tom. The delicate ecosystem of their Prohibition-era town is upset when Leo falls for Verna, the sister of a Jewish bookie, and foolishly protects her brother from the Italian mobsters who hold a grudge against him. The crooked cops and politicians formerly in Leo's employ wait to see who prevails. Meanwhile, Tom is also having an affair with Verna and has some demons of his own to fight. Trying to play all the angles, he winds up in a nightmarish situation in the wooded area that lends its name to the film.

The Coens changed the concept somewhat as the cast filled out. The darkly Celtic Gabriel Byrne was cast as Tom. The part of Leo was written specifically for Trey Wilson, the irascible Nathan Arizona in the Coens' previous film. But two days before *Miller's Crossing* was to begin shooting, Wilson died of a cerebral hemorrhage. Stuck with the task of finding an immediate replacement, the Coens got lucky: Albert Finney, whom they greatly admire, was available. With Byrne and Finney in hand – and with Byrne reading his lines in a heavy brogue – the ruling gang members now represented a less-assimilated stripe of Irishman, and the Coens beefed up the ethnic character of the movie.

"We got mugged by the Irish," explains Ethan.

Then there was the task of recreating a dirty industrial town, circa 1929. Normally, they would have considered such beefy towns as Chicago or Albany. But they didn't want to deal with cold or snow, and this was a winter shoot. "We looked around San Francisco, but you know what that looks like: period but upscale – *faux* period," says Ethan. Then someone suggested New Orleans, parts of which surprisingly fit the bill. Outside of the distinctive French Quarter, there were plenty of places that could pass for a generic Anytown in the late 1920s. "New Orleans is sort of a depressed city; it hasn't been gentrified," says Ethan. "There's a lot of architecture that hasn't been touched, storefront windows that haven't been replaced in the past 60 years."

The centrepiece of *Miller's Crossing* is the explosive assassination attempt that occurs when the Italian family sends its gunsels to rub out Leo. On one level, the Coens see the sequence as a tonic to what they consider a perilous amount of dialogue in the film thus far: "It's about time at that point to shed a little blood," says Ethan. "The movie's in danger of becoming tasteful, you know?"

On another level, the failed rubout is central to the audience's understanding of Leo's character: by fending off four would-be assassins with spectacular nonchalance, Leo shows us that his vulnerability as a boss might be overestimated. "This is Leo as the boss, Leo as the guy in control of the situation, as opposed to situations in the movie where he seems a bit naive," says Joel. "This is Leo in his element."

The scene also represents the Coens in *their* element: tour de force filmmaking. The rubout scene is an elaborate, explosive montage. But it also drips with irony, primarily because behind the gangster-movie images – blazing machine guns, body parts jerking from direct hits, a house burning down, and a car crash – we hear a soppy rendition of "Danny Boy", ostensibly the song playing on Leo's Victrola.

The scene begins with a long tracking shot in which we see Leo's just-killed bodyguard slumped over, his cigarette igniting a newspaper. The killer lets an accomplice into the parlour, and the pair climb the stairs to Leo's bedroom. Leo, meanwhile, has noticed smoke coming from beneath the floorboards – he's already stubbed out his cigar and grabbed his revolver. As the gunmen burst in, he's ready for them, rolling under the bed and shooting one in the ankles, then in the head. Then, appropriating the victim's machine gun, he dives out a window, dropping to street level outside the burning house. He dispatches the second gunman (Monte Starr), who is still in the bedroom – the jitterbug; ducks bullets from a speeding car full of more assailants; and then, patiently walking up the tree-lined street, keeps firing the tommy gun until his bullets reach the auto, which spins into a tree and explodes.

Needless to say, the logistics were considerable. Because the sequence was shot in various locations, ranging from studio interiors and a residential street in suburban Metairie to a house near the French Quarter to a vacant house (now occupied by novelist Anne Rice) in the Garden District, the tightly edited montage was filmed over a period of several weeks. Exactly which part was filmed when is hard to remember – with one exception. "We burned down the house the night of the Academy Awards," says Joel.

Perhaps the hardest shot to get right was the one in which Leo rolls under the bed to shoot. The Coens used an elevated set, about three feet off the ground, so the cameras would be level with the bed. The challenge was to coordinate the action with the technology – Finney had to shoot while the muzzle of the gunman's Thompson blazed, squibs in the mattress above him exploded, and an air gun shot feathers downward from the mattress. Eventually, the Coens were satisfied, but when the footage reached the editing room, they found that the first gunman's death was insufficiently vivid – the squib didn't "read" (it didn't explode properly and jerk the hood's head) when Finney shot him. So they reshot that part.

More edifying was the fate of the second gunman, the unwitting performer of the Thompson jitterbug. Not one but two men played the poor victim, whose extended dance of death still evokes silent mirth as the Coens review it in the editing room months afterward. Starr stood in for the head-on shots, but the reverse shots required the hardy stunt coordinator Jerry Hewitt.

"Thompsons are not light guns," explains Joel Coen. "It's difficult to hold one while it's firing and bucking, and also with squibs going up your back."

"It's hard," agrees Ethan. "You have to sell all that body language, taking the bullet hits. What sells the hit is the dance."

Ah, the dance. "We always knew we wanted to do that," says Ethan.

"You keep thinking of things you want to add to the scene," says Joel. "He shoots up the chandelier, the paintings, his toes. All kinds of fun things. It was a lot of fun blowing the toes off. The only regret is that it goes by so fast, you almost kind of miss it. They're a highlight."

Bernie Bernbaum (John Turturro), Verna's smug brother, during his first onscreen meeting with Tom.

In the course of planning this scene, the Coen brothers became expert in the lore of Thompson guns, several of which they procured for the film. While they are enamoured of the gun's output – given sufficient ammunition, the monster can choke out 800 rounds a minute – they had to accept its predisposition to jam, a drawback that forced innumerable retakes.

Overall, though, they considered the Thompson guns a big plus. "The gun is incredibly loud, and it does vibrate," says Joel fondly. "You can see it sort of jingle. The whole thing was a very satisfying experience."

Even Finney got into the Thompson mania. Toward the end of the segment, as Leo walks down the street firing the gun at the speeding getaway car, Finney had to maintain a cool demeanour while controlling the powerful weapon. As an added challenge, the Coens set up a bucket behind him to see how many expelled cartridges he could land in it. "He got a very high percentage," says Ethan, as Joel collapses in laughter. "Technically, he's a very good actor."

Finney's machine-gun virtuosity helps end the sequence with a flourish. But what really makes the scene is "Danny Boy". The Coens recruited Irish tenor Frank Patterson – he played the vocalist in John Huston's *The Dead* – to perform the song. After the scene was edited, Patterson went into the studio with an orchestra and watched the monitor so he could tailor the cadences of the song to the mounting body count. At the end, when Finney, cigar stub in his mouth, sighs in satisfaction as he watches his last assailants die in flames, the music swells in old-world mawkishness: " . . . and I will sleep in peace . . . until you come to . . . meeeeee!" – a deliciously droll commentary on the Thompson jitterbug that came before.

CHASING THE HAT

BY RICHARD T. JAMESON

Ice dropping into a heavy-bottomed glass: cold, hard, sensuous. The first image in *Miller's Crossing* hits our ears before it hits the screen, but it's nonetheless an image for that. Tom Reagan (Gabriel Byrne) has travelled the length of a room to build a drink. Not that we saw him in transit, not that we yet know he is Tom Reagan, and not that we see him clearly now as he turns and stalks back up the room, a silent, out-of-focus enigma at the edge of someone else's closeup. Yet he is a story walking, as his deliberate, tangential progress, from background to middle distance and then out the side of the frame, is also a story – draining authority from the close-up Johnny Caspar (Jon Polito) who's come to insist, ironically enough, on the recognition of his territorial rights.

The place is a story, too, which we read as the scene unfolds. A private office; not Caspar's, but not Reagan's either – it's city boss Liam "Leo" O'Bannion (Albert Finney) who sits behind the camera and his big desk, listening. An upstairs office, we know from the muted street traffic (without stopping to think about why we know). Night outside, but sunlight would never be welcome, or relevant, here. A masculine space, green lampshades amid the dark lustre of wood, leather, whiskey. A remote train whistle sounds, functional and intrinsically forlorn; the distance from which it reaches us locates the office in space and in history. This room exists in a city big enough to support a multiplicity of criminal fiefdoms and a political machine that rules by maintaining the balance among them, yet it is still a town whose municipal core lies within faint earshot of its outskirts. Urban dreams of empire have not entirely crowded out the memory of wilderness, of implacable places roads and railroads can't reach, even if one of them has been wishfully designated *Miller's Crossing*. Hence we are not entirely surprised (though the aesthetic shock is deeply satisfying) when the opening master-scene, with its magisterial interior setting and dialogue fragrant with cross purpose, gives way to a silent (save for mournful Irish melody) credit sequence in an empty forest. And then to a title card announcing, almost superfluously, "An Eastern city in the United States, toward the end of the 1920s."

It has always been one of the special pleasures of movies that they dream worlds and map them at the same time. *Miller's Crossing* dreams a beaut, no less so for the fact that Joel and Ethan Coen's film is a reverent, rigorous reimagining of the world of Dashiell Hammett, especially as limned in *The Glass Key* and *Red Harvest*. (A phrase from *Red Harvest* supplied the title of the Coens' filmmaking debut *Blood Simple*.) The look is right, from first frame to last – even the aural "look" of that ice: this is a movie that knows what drinking is about in Hammett, what it has to do with rumination and gravity, coolheadedness and rash error, and every coloration of brown study. The mood is instinct with the private pain that separates reticence from caring and conceals itself, with desperation and anger, in seeming not to care. Even the narrative spaces are true to Hammett. There is a man named "Rug" Daniels who enters the film dead, whose murder is the least insistent and finally least significant of the film's mysteries, offhandedly explained amid the backwash from gaudier mayhem ("I don't know, just a mixup"); the cast has to wonder – though the audience need not – why Daniels' corpse should be missing his eponymous toupee. Floyd Thursby might envy a death surrounded by such perplexity and pixilation.

The terrain is worthy of mapping. But more importantly, the mapping itself becomes cinematic terrain in *Miller's Crossing*, each adjustment of distance and perspective invested with exquisite sensibility. Sometimes the effect is startling, like the delayed revelation that the precariously politic dialogue between Leo and Caspar, with Tom kibbitzing, also involves a fourth man: the Dane (J. E. Freeman), Caspar's partner in crime, who, though standing directly behind Caspar the entire time, is never seen by the audience till his fierce visage towers in sudden closeup several minutes into the scene. That silent detonation is the most effective shock cut since Dennis Hopper in *Blue Velvet* offered to "fuck anything that moves". But one takes no less satisfaction when, a moment later, after Caspar and the Dane's angry departure, Tom Reagan leaves off lounging at the window ledge behind his friend and boss, moves to a couch along the wall, settles in, takes a deep drink, and says, "Bad play, Leo." 99 directors out of a hundred would have played that line in closeup. Joel Coen frames Tom within enough space that we feel both director and character have a judicious respect for patterns, for the ways in which moves and designs can go wrong, and for the crisis whose resolution is going to drive Tom and Leo forever apart.

When John Wayne noticed that Dean Martin, as the drunk in need of redemption, seemed to have the ripest part in *Rio Bravo*, he asked Howard Hawks what he ought to do to hold up his own end of the screen. Hawks replied, "You look at him like he's your friend." Tom Reagan is Leo O'Bannion's friend in *Miller's Crossing*, but he has the devil's own time looking out for the interests of both of them. Johnny Caspar starts out wanting only to send a red letter to "the Schmatte", Bernie Bernbaum (John Turturro), a bookmaker who's been screwing the play everytime Caspar fixes a prizefight. Leo refuses to lift protection on Bernie, partly to insist on his own authority, but also because Bernie is the cherished brother of Verna (Marcia Gay Harden), whose dark beauty has stirred banked fires in his heart. Tom wishes his friend could keep his mind on business. He also wishes he knew what to do about the fact that he himself is secretly Verna's lover.

Reportedly, Albert Finney came late to the role of Leo, after Trey Wilson, the 43-year-old actor who played the father of the quintuplets in the Coens' *Raising Arizona*, died of a stroke. Finney's extra decade introduces an imbalance into the friendship between Tom and Leo and adjusts the nature of their rivalry for Verna; besides being a hefty powerbroker ill-made for romantic conquest, his Leo takes on the pathos of age and last options. But if Finney's Leo is less than equal on the field of love, he's more than equal as a figure of estimable regard. The screenplay obliges Leo to disappear for most of the last two-thirds of the movie; excellent player that he was, it's doubtful whether the late Wilson could have loomed so large in absentia as Finney's Leo does. The sense of rueful aspiration that drives Tom Reagan during his often mystifying maneuvers to set the cockeyed world of *Miller's Crossing* right finds expression mainly through the Irish music that marks his passage, and our memories of Leo – apart from his beefy authority and boyish candour – reverberate as a kind of music. Not only the playing of "Danny Boy" over the most audacious of the film's tour-de-force sequences (an exhilarating first-act high that would render the remainder of any other movie anticlimactic), but also the mortally wounded sighs Leo emits after learning of Tom and Verna's affair. And the way Finney gets the history of a long day and Leo's life and his friendship with Tom into responding to the offer of a late-night drink – "I wouldn't *mind*."

That line reading is one of a thousand things to love about *Miller's Crossing*, along with a zephyr of smoke through waxed floorboards, the rubbing together of stark trees above a killing ground, the arrival of a small man to conduct the beating a giant couldn't manage, the way men and guns fill up a nocturnal street like autumn leaves drifting. And one loves a screenplay with the fortitude to lay all its cards on the table in the first sequence and then demonstrate, with each succeeding scene, that there is still story to happen, there is still life and mystery in character, there is reason to sit patient and fascinated before a movie that loves and honours the rules of a game scarcely anyone else in Hollywood remembers anymore, let alone tries to play. Johnny Caspar is a brute posing as a philosopher, but he knows the word that fits the Coen brothers' moviemaking: "et'ics".

One of the Coens told a *New York Times* writer that *Miller's Crossing* had its genesis in the image of a black hat coming to rest in a forest clearing, then lifting to soar away down an avenue of trees. That image accompanies the main title, a talisman of the movie's respect for enigma and dedication to the irreducible integrity of style. It also crops up verbally as a dream Tom describes to Verna – the closest he gets to sharing a confidence. Yeah, says Verna, and then you chased the hat and it changed into something else. "No," Tom says immediately, "it stayed a hat. And I didn't chase it." But one way or another, this man in grim flight from his heart, who cannot, must not "look at him like he's your friend" till the last world-closing shot of the film, chases his hat all through *Miller's Crossing*. So do the Coens. And that it doesn't change into something else is the best news for the American cinema at the dawn of the Nineties.

THE JOEL AND ETHAN STORY

BY JOHN H. RICHARDSON

Joel and Ethan Coen's new movie, *Millers Crossing*, opens with an oddly poignant shot of a hat blowing through an autumn forest. A little later, Tom, the hero, tells Verna, his mistress, that he dreamed he was walking in the woods when the wind blew off his hat.

She responds cynically: "And you chased it, right? You ran and ran and finally you caught up to it and picked it up, but it wasn't a hat anymore. It had changed into something else – something wonderful."

Tom turns away and takes a drag off his cigarette. He's a hard drinker, it's dawn, and he's worn out from the effort of keeping his balance in a slippery world of criminal intrigue – a world of crosses, double crosses, and double double crosses. "No," he replies wearily. "It stayed a hat. And no, I didn't chase it. I watched it blow away – nothing more foolish than a man chasing his hat."

Later still, we learn that this stretch of woods is called Miller's Crossing, and it is a place where gangsters take people to kill them. In fact, Tom himself takes someone there to kill. Which makes the hat and the forest the pivotal images in the single most impressive movie of the year so far. Chosen to open the 1990 New York Film Festival, *Miller's Crossing* is a brilliant mixture of satire and seriousness, style and substance, a bitter love story embedded in a gangster gothic, a film that is at once an homage to *films noirs* past and an extraordinarily assured leap into the future.

Although their previous film, *Raising Arizona* dipped its toes into the warm bath of sentiment, the Coens have always been ironists – cold and distant, puppet masters in the grand tradition of Hitchcock. Not that they've given that up for a happy ending and a trip to Disneyland; if anything, *Miller's Crossing* is darker than their other films. What they have done is drop their ironic distance. If *The Godfather* found greatness by taking the then-dismissed gangster genre seriously, *Miller's Crossing* is a post-postmodern *Godfather* that rollicks in the silliness of the genre but still somehow plumbs the depths of emotion. This is a movie teeming with caricatures that keep on revealing real characters underneath. We see a buffoonish gangster, then meet his child, we see a tough guy, then meet his male lover. Even a dead man still has a toupee between him and the bald truth. It's an unsettling combination of the grotesque and the touching, a tongue-in-cheek tongue kiss.

But ask the Coen brothers why the movie is called *Miller's Crossing* and you get deadpan responses, Beckett by way of Hammett by way of Rocky and Bullwinkle.

ETHAN: We couldn't think of a better title.

JOEL: It's okay. A friend of ours came up with it. Or we wouldn't have had any title.

ETHAN: Yeah, it's an okay title. We'd give it like a B, B-minus. It's … yeah. Sometimes they come, and sometimes they don't.

So what is it with this hat thing, anyway?

JOEL (laughing): That's a really good question – "So what is it with this hat thing, anyway?"

I'm a highly trained professional.

JOEL: No, it just sounds really good. Yeah, what is it with the hat thing, anyway? I don't know. You know, those gangsters, they wore fedoras. You're no gangster without the hat.

*But you could've called it **Five O'Clock Shadow**. You don't have gangsters without that, either.*

ETHAN: Actually, well, yeah, right. But we didn't call it *The Hat* or *The Fedora*.

JOEL: Yeah, it's called *Miller's Crossing*.

There is a striking similarity between the dialogue of the movie and the Coens' own speech – the terse suggestiveness, the irony, the existential flatness of tone. It's the sound of cheap detectives making wisecracks into the void. This is the Coen style, onscreen and off, which is why most of the articles written about them have titles like "The Brothers From Another Planet" or "Warped in America". In person, as onscreen, the Coens never apologise and never explain.

It's true that they're a bit different. They seem normal – just look at them and you know they hung out in the English or film or philosophy department of some damn college, and they went to lots of movies, and they read lots of novels. Joel slouches in a corner with his scraggly long hair half covering his face, and Ethan looks attentive but slightly abstracted in his wire rims. They wear blue jeans and T-shirts.

But they have these eccentric habits. They tend to finish each other's sentences and talk in a private argot of jokes and code words. Although Joel is credited as the director and Ethan as producer, they are so joined at the hip professionally that crew members treat them as interchangeable beings. By Hollywood standards, they are virtually freaks. They live in new York. They rarely go to parties, and when they do, Ethan usually takes a book to read. And they have this weird quirk of making aggressively self-conscious movies but playing dumb when it comes time to talk about them. "They'll never talk to you conceptually," says cinematographer Barry Sonnenfeld, who has shot all three Coen films – *Blood Simple, Raising Arizona* and their latest. "They'll never say 'The hat in *Miller's Crossing* represents this.' In fact, if you ask them about it, they'll say, 'We wanted to make a movie about men in long coats wearing hats.' "

The Coens are hot commodities in Hollywood, and *Miller's Crossing* is apt to make them hotter still. Twentieth Century Fox had to fight off bids from other studios for distribution rights to their next film, *Barton Fink*. Fox ended up providing almost the entire budget, reportedly nine million dollars, in exchange for domestic rights alone – and this for a period piece about writer's block.

From the beginning, the Coens have had final cut, a power many far more experienced directors would kill to get. And they have used their power to make not artsy black-and-white "films" but their own twisted versions of classic Hollywood genres, risky movies without viewer-friendly characters and happy endings.

Hollywood looks at the Coens the way it looks at Woody Allen: their films don't make much money, but everyone wants to be associated with them. (*Raising Arizona* made $22 million.) Fox may be concerned because *Miller's Crossing* appears dark and uncommercial, but it would be "a black eye for the company to let these guys get away", says Universal Pictures executive Jim Jacks. Jacks should know, since he's been trying to lure the Coens to Universal for years. "You want to be in business with the Joel and Ethans, the Spike Lees, and the Phil Kaufmans. These are the people who are going to make the great movies of our time."

Bernie begs for mercy in the forest area called Miller's Crossing. Despite Tom sparing his life, both he and the whining hoodlum will betray each other.

And possibly even the hit movies. One day, Jacks says, "the Coens will write a script that they think is off-centre, and between the time when they write it and when it comes out, the centre will have moved just enough that they will hit it right in the middle, and they will be appalled."

The Coens may be kings of their medium-budget mountain, but it took some scrambling to get there. They grew up in the suburbs of Minneapolis, bright but otherwise unremarkable kids. They shared a room, skied a little, and were bored in school. "What they really remind me of is two guys who grew up in bunk beds," says a longtime friend. "There wasn't much back then to suggest that anything would happen," says their father, Edward, an economics professor at the University of Minnesota. It's true they made three Super-8 films, but the movies were "so primitive, it never occurred to me that this would become something serious".

The only hint of an artistic future was an elementary-school play that Ethan co-wrote. "In one scene, King Arthur was about to leave the castle, and his nurse says to him, 'Don't forget to put on your sweater,' " says Edward, who, like his sons, chuckles constantly. "There were laughs like that pretty much all through it."

The Coen brothers did have one unusual characteristic: they were tenacious. Especially Ethan. "He always knew what he wanted and insisted on it," his father says. "He would never eat any green vegetables, so we made a deal with him. 'We'll start eating vegetables next year.' He'd say, 'Okay', and when next year rolled around we didn't get any compliance."

The boys left high school early and went to a private Massachusetts school called Simon's Rock of Bard College. From there, Joel transferred to the New York University film department, and Ethan went to Princeton and studied philosophy. After college, Joel edited horror films and took odd film jobs until Ethan graduated and joined him in New York.

They began writing scripts. One was a murder mystery called *Suburbicon*. Another was *The XYZ Murders*, co-written and directed by Sam Raimi and released under the title *Crimewave* in 1985. Then there was *Blood Simple*.

"They were very, very worried when they were making *Blood Simple*," their father says. "Everything would turn on that, and they realised it. But when they were raising money, they would walk in and seem very calm."

When the film was finished, all the studios passed. But it happened that a cash-rich Washington, D.C.-based distributor called Circle Releasing was interested in producing its first film. Circle snapped up *Blood Simple*, and when it earned a respectable if not spectacular three million dollars on the art-house circuit, the studios came running. "There was nothing on paper," says Jacks, then an executive with Circle. "I half expected them to say, 'Look, we can make movies for studios now.'"

But the Coens were loyal. In return Circle gave them final cut and put up three million dollars in cash to shoot *Raising Arizona*. Three weeks into production, Twentieth Century Fox put up another three million dollars. The unusual relationship continues to this day. "The primary thing is, we really love the kind of movies they make," says Circle co-owner Ted Pedas. "We really do."

The Coens aren't tight lipped just with journalists. They don't like explaining themselves on the set either. "It was really weird that nobody mentioned the hat all the way through the movie," says Gabriel Byrne, who plays Tom Reagan, the lead role in *Miller's Crossing*. "I said to Joel at one point, 'What is the significance of the hat? Is the hat significant?'

And he said, 'Mmm hmm.' And that was it."

Jon Polito plays a gangster wackily obsessed with ethics. The film begins with his monologue: "If you can't trust a fix, what can you trust? For a good return, you gotta go bettin' on chance, and then you're back with anarchy. Right back inna jungle. On account of the breakdown of ethics."

"I remember going through it at first, and I got one word wrong," says Polito. "After it was over, they go, in stereo, 'You missed that word.'" But the Coens never discussed the meaning of the speech with him. "They really don't talk about things like that," Polito says. "They sort of giggled, then they would say, 'Go further.'"

The Coens tend to approach things physically. Marcia Gay Harden, who plays Verna, mistress to both Tom and his boss, Leo (Albert Finney), reports that they flew her to the film's location in New Orleans for an unscheduled costume fitting that went on until "the wee hours of the morning", redesigned her dresses to make them more clingy, had her spend a week on makeup tests, had her eyebrows plucked and her hair cut. "That was important to them," she says. But they left her on her own conceptually. "We would just use words like 'smoky, sensuous, sexy', and Joel would go, 'Yeah, yeah, those words.'"

Byrne had a similar experience. "I would say, 'I'm going to put this glass down and walk out of the room,' and Joel would say, 'No, no, Tom would never leave a drink in the bottom of the glass.' We would get into a discussion of Tom's maybe being an alcoholic, but nothing too deep. Usually it was 'Close the door after you', that sort of thing."

They are famous for their meticulous planning. They put virtually all the visual and cutting cues in the script and storyboard every shot. They don't let actors change a single word. "It would be completely inappropriate to say, 'I got a great idea: Verna's really English,'" says Harden.

The Coens also control their budgets which inspires audible gratitude from their backers. For example, they almost gave up on the memorable shot from above the ceiling fan in *Blood Simple* because it was taking too long to set up. "They say they'll do something, they do it, and often for less," says Pedas.

Between them, the Coens are a self-contained filmmaking unit. "They're the real creators of the movie," says John Turturro, who plays Bernie, Verna's brother, in *Miller's Crossing*. "They do everything. They write it, they cast it, they work on the editing, they're involved with the music. They don't hire people to go out and do those things," says Sonnenfeld. "They are so insularly self-confident, it doesn't matter what anyone else thinks." They don't try to create a feel-good atmosphere. "It wasn't a fun set to be on at all," recalls Byrne. "People were there to work really hard."

But within rigid boundaries, they are flexible. It's significant that these "control freaks" usually write their scripts without an outline or even a glimmer of an ending. "They literally make it up as they go along," says Jacks. "When they come to a crossroads in the story, they always figure what's the weirdest way of going."

The Coens also manage to make their actors feel free – mostly, it seems, by using laughter. They have a remarkable ability to turn strangers into co-conspirators in their private joke. It's a "deceptive" way of directing, says Polito. "They sort of giggle and make you laugh along with them, until finally you realise you're going in a way they planned years before. They have a wonderful way of catching you off guard."

The Coens' combination of flexibility and control seems to inspire everyone. All their actors use the same word to describe their feelings for the brothers: trust. Turturro says he tried wildly different approaches on every take of the almost embarrassing scene in which his character pleads for his life. The result is a tour de force of acting. "I knew I was taking a risk, but for them I would basically do anything," he says. "I felt very free."

Until *Miller's Crossing*, none of the Coens' characters were capable of much thought. If they weren't actually blood simple, they were hayseed dumb. But the hero of *Miller's Crossing* is a guy with a million angles. Tom always seems to be one step ahead of everyone else. That's his job, in fact; he's the brains to Leo's crime boss. The Coens up the ante by pushing him into a situation in which his survival depends on how fast he thinks.

"He's a character who sort of throws everything up in the air and intentionally creates confusion", says Joel. "This is an old [Dashiell] Hammett idea – 'If I stir things up, I'll be able to deal with the consequences, whatever they are. Something will emerge that I can exploit.'"

But the Coens put a twist on the power of positive thinking by making their hero win the world and lose the girl. Is the only thing more foolish than a man chasing his hat a man trying to use the head under the hat?

"You don't know any smart guys who've ever lost girls?" asks Ethan, turning helpful. He points out that Leo listens to his heart. The name is no accident: he's lionhearted. And Leo also gets the girl – "so maybe," Joel reluctantly concedes, "there's a moral there".

Ethan makes a brief for simple instinct. "I mean, the whole hat thing, the fact that it's all hats, is good, because even if it doesn't mean anything, it adds a little thread running through the whole thing that's the same thread. It feels good."

"It's the same with decisions you make while you're making the movie," Joel continues, "because you're always confronted with things like, 'Should the wallpaper be this colour?' 'Should the actor be sort of taking it to this level or keeping it at that level?' And you really have to be fairly intuitive about it. You just have to say, 'This seems to fit the idea, this seems to be of a piece with what we're doing, and this doesn't.' But you're not always thinking about it."

But then complications arise. After all, the one time Tom listens to his heart, when he decides not to kill his ladylove's brother, it ends up being the biggest mistake he ever made. "It was an irony we kind of liked," says Ethan, pronouncing the word "EErony" to turn it into a joke. And Leo's heart upsets the balance of criminal power and brings death and destruction on the city – another "Erony." And the simplicity of Leo's man of action is also tied to his love of blood; he's "an artist with a tommy gun".

When things get this complicated, you get the itchy feeling you may be watching "art". It has the ring of truth, even if you can't figure out what the truth is – or maybe *because* you can't. The Coens have taken the leap from the stylish confectionery of *Blood Simple* and *Raising Arizona* to what novelist John Gardner called "moral fiction". *Miller's Crossing* ultimately isn't about film, it's about humanity.

It's only appropriate that the Coens resist this compliment emphatically. "It's not about humanity, it's about the characters, you know?" says Ethan. "If you wanna say, inasmuch as we resemble the characters, it's about all of us, then it's true, but emptily true."

So what's profoundly true is the way the specific story works out? What the specific characters do? And nothing more than that?

The Coens answer firmly, in harmony: "Right."

Maybe the Coens are just the most unself-conscious self-conscious artists in history. Their evasive and jokey approach to interviews – much like that enigmatic hat – reveals as much as it conceals. For the Coens' disdain of abstract thinking goes far beyond the traditional artist's distrust of ideas. It goes, finally, as deep as style itself – which in many ways is what the Coens are all about. Theirs is a style that's exuberantly attentive to surfaces, to the look of things, to style itself.

Barry Sonnenfeld tells a story about the memorable shot in *Blood Simple* in which the camera, tracking along a bar and coming to a drunk who has fallen asleep across it, simply bumps up and over the drunk. It is a signature Coen shot, echoed in *Raising Arizona* when the camera tracks over a car, up a ladder, and in through a window, and in *Miller's Crossing* when a camera dollies in on a screaming man's face.

But that shot was cut from the first edit of *Blood Simple*. "I asked Joel why, and he said, 'I don't know. It just seemed too self-conscious to me,'" Sonnenfeld recalls. "I looked at him in total disbelief and said, 'Joel, this *whole movie* is self-conscious.'"

No wonder, then, that one of the Coen trademarks is the extended wordless sequence, like the fifteen-minute burial scene in *Blood Simple*, a moment of pure film, at once a bravura bouquet to the art of moviemaking and a chest-beating announcement of the Coen brothers' considerable powers: Look, Ma, no words! We don't need 'em; we can make pictures talk! Hell, we can make them *sing*!

With *Miller's Crossing*, the Coens have taken the truths of style a step further and found depths in the surface itself.

JOEL: I mean, the hat thing, what can you say about the hat, it's like, you know –

ETHAN: Yeah, it is hard to talk about it, it's sorta not – it doesn't sort of –

JOEL: But that's the weird thing. It's not because there's any, like, hidden mysteries or anything, it's just because, you know, it's all there, you know – it's all there –

A HAT BLOWN BY THE WIND

BY JEAN-PIERRE COURSODON

One of your actors, questioned about your collaboration on the set, explained that: "In reality, Joel is the director — and Ethan too!"

JOEL COEN: That's true, we co-direct. The division of labour suggested by the credits is pretty arbitrary.

Are there sometimes conflicts between you two during shooting about the best method of directing?

ETHAN COEN: No, we write the scene together, we imagine it the same way. Everything happens in the most straightforward way.

Do you make any changes during shooting to the script, and do you let the actors themselves improvise or provide changes?

JOEL: In *Miller's Crossing* the actors didn't change one single word of the dialogue. We follow the script very faithfully, and a large number of the production elements are already included. That said, in the middle of shooting we rewrote the whole second part of the script.

Do you think that situation of two directors can sometimes unsettle the actors?

JOEL: I don't think so. Like Ethan said, we're generally agreed on the type of interpretation we want. We didn't have any surprises on the set because we had a lot of rehearsals beforehand. When we auditioned the main actors, they read not just one scene or two but the whole script.

Albert Finney is a last-minute choice . . .

JOEL: The part had been written for Trey Wilson, who died just before the beginning of shooting. We had to delay it for ten days. It just happened that Finney was available and could commit himself for a few months. We didn't rewrite the dialogue for him, but the result would undoubtedly have been very different with Trey.

ETHAN: What's strange is that the part would never have been written without Trey in mind, whereas now it's impossible for us to imagine any other actor than Finney in the Leo role.

Who had the idea of making Finney and Gabriel Byrne speak with a strong Irish accent?

JOEL: The characters are of Irish extraction, but their parts weren't planned to be spoken with an accent. When Gabriel read the script he thought it had a style, a rhythm

Tom's final meeting with his friend and gang boss Leo (Albert Finney), at Miller's Crossing. Tom finds (but does not desire) forgiveness for his double-dealing.

that was authentically Irish, and he suggested trying the lines with his accent. We were sceptical at the start, but his reading convinced us. So Finney took on the accent too.

The film is out at the same time as other gangster movies.

JOEL: It's a coincidence. It's very different from the others, in any case from Scorsese's *Goodfellas*, the only one I've seen. I love it but the story and the style are completely different, like day and night.

ETHAN: When they describe all those movies as gangster movies, it suggests a wider community that doesn't really exist. It's the type of situation journalists like to exploit, because they always try to identify fashions, trends. It makes good copy but doesn't mean a lot. Anyway, *Miller's Crossing* is really closer to *film noir* than to the gangster movie.

The film unfolds in New Orleans, a city one doesn't usually associate with the genre. What dictated your choice?

JOEL: We had to shoot in winter, and we didn't want snow for the exterior shots, so we had to choose a Southern city. New Orleans happens not to be very industrially developed and many districts have only slightly changed since the Twenties.

ETHAN: We took care not to show the picturesque or tourist aspects of the city. We didn't want the audience to recognise New Orleans. In the story the city's an anonymous one, the typical "corrupted town" of Hammett novels.

In your interviews you always give the impression that you avoid the issue when asked about the symbolism of the images, the motivation of the characters, the social implications of the film, etc.

ETHAN: Apparently, nobody wants to be satisfied with the movie, as if they absolutely need explanations beyond the images, the story itself. That always surprises me. But if you don't comply, journalists get the impression that you're hiding something from them.

JOEL & ETHAN COEN: BLOOD SIBLINGS

In his New York Times review Vincent Canby complains that Gabriel Byrne is often hard to understand, and also complains about the obscurities of the film: some characters are only names in the dialogue and what happens to them is not clear. Are you sensitive to that kind of criticism?

JOEL: Not really. It doesn't really concern me if the audience sometimes loses the thread of the plot. It's not that important to understand who killed the Rug Daniels character, for instance. It's far more important to feel the relationships between the characters. The question of intelligibility concerns me more, but, until now, I haven't received any bad reactions concerning that.

The relationships between characters are rather obscure: Leo and Tom, for instance. It's a friendship that degenerates into rivalry.

JOEL: Because of Verna's character. It's the heterosexual triangle of the movie.

You spoke in your press conference about a homosexual triangle – Bernie, Mink, Dane – balancing the other one. The homosexuality of those three characters is scarcely evident (except perhaps for Bernie) and their relationships even less. How important is that triangle?

JOEL: It's difficult to say what made us think of it. It's not very important, it's a pretty minor point but it's somehow satisfying to us, a kind of symmetry or counterpoint maybe. It introduces a certain variety, and the process seems legitimate to us insofar as we don't do violence to the story or the characters.

Tom, the hero, cheats, lies and manipulates throughout the entire film. Does he nevertheless have ethics?

JOEL: Yes, I think there's a certain purity in his intentions, but it manifests itself in a very twisted way. He has principles that are in conflict with themselves.

ETHAN: It's everybody's problem, in fact. The movie is a gangster story because it's a genre we're attracted to – a literary rather than a cinematic genre, by the way – but the conflicts of the characters, the morality, have a more universal application.

What got you started, a theme, the idea of a character, or an element of the plot?

JOEL: Certainly not a theme. In reality the starting point of the script was an image, or a series of images, the desire to make a movie whose characters would be dressed in a certain way – the hats, the long coats – and would be placed in certain settings that were unusual for the genre: the countryside, the forest . . .

The hat is more than an accessory in the film, it's a recurrent theme as soon as the credits start, with that hat blown by the wind in the forest. What is the significance?

JOEL: Everybody asks us questions about that hat, and there isn't any answer really. It's not a symbol, it doesn't have any particular meaning . . .

ETHAN: The hat doesn't "represent" anything, it's just a hat blown by the wind.

JOEL: It's an image that came to us, that we liked, and it just implanted itself. It's a kind of practical guiding thread, but there's no need to look for deep meanings.

In a sense, Tom himself puts us on our guard against interpretation when he recounts his dream: he specifies that the hat doesn't change into something else, it stays a hat.

ETHAN: Sure, you can take it like that. Verna wants to give a meaning to Tom's dream, and it's gratuitous. Tom remains objective.

How long did you take to write the script?

JOEL: Much longer than for the two previous movies. All in all, eight months more or less, but we stopped to write the script of the next one, which took two months.

Would you contemplate shooting somebody else's script?

ETHAN: No, I don't think so, we've grown so used to working like this since the beginning. For us, creation really starts with the script in all its stages; the shooting is only the conclusion. It'd be very difficult for us to direct a script written by a third person.

You've changed designers for **Miller's Crossing.**

JOEL: We like to work with the same collaborators, but Jane Musky, the designer of our first two movies, wasn't available. David Gassner, who worked with Coppola, helped us a great deal in the choice of colours. The colours are more controlled than in the previous movies.

ETHAN: David had the idea for the building columns, to have the architecture reflecting the trees in the forest . . . He was our designer again for the movie we just shot, *Barton Fink*.

What is Gabriel Byrne's musical contribution?

JOEL: He suggested a certain number of traditional Irish songs. We'd already decided to use "Danny Boy", but the other song, on which Carter Burwell based the main theme, is an old ballad suggested by Gabriel.

What relationship do you have with Circle Films?

ETHAN: As you know, it's the independent distribution company which distributed *Blood Simple* and which later produced *Raising Arizona*. Fox contributed to *Raising Arizona*'s budget and were the distributors, as they are for *Miller's Crossing* and the next one, *Barton Fink*, but our relationship with Circle remains the same. Ben Barenholtz as a distributor has always been interested in independent cinema, American and foreign, he's always taken risks. We're on the same wavelength.

Translated by Paul Buck and Catherine Petit. Interview conducted on 22 September 1990, in New York City.

BARTON FINK

REVIEW FROM VARIETY

Barton Fink is one of the most eccentric films to come out of, or take place in, Hollywood in many a moon. Accomplished on every artistic level, Joel and Ethan Coen's hermetic tale of a "genius" playwright's brief stint as a studio contract writer is a painstakingly miniaturist work that can be read any number of ways.

As with the Coens' previous pics, critical reaction should be strong, but the 1991 Golden Palm winner's circumscribed world and private meanings will limit commercial interest to the cognoscenti.

This new film will appeal to buffs at least as much as did the brothers' last, *Miller's Crossing*, and for the same reasons: extraordinarily colourful period language spoken by superlative actors, leading of scenes into odd, unexpected places, and impeccable craftsmanship.

With the partial exception of *Raising Arizona*, however, the Coens' films have proven elusive to a wide public, and that's likely to remain the case this time. Much of the action unfolds in a single dreary hotel room as a writer struggles to write.

Under this heavily constricted condition, the brothers generate some marvellous scenes in their engagingly surreal rumination on "the life of the mind", but don't provide a reliable key to entering their confidential world.

Title character, played with a creepily growing sense of dread by John Turturro, is a gravely serious New York dramatist who scores a soaring triumph on Broadway in 1941 with a deep-dish think piece about the working class. Fink gets to deliver a boilerplate anti-Hollywood speech before capitulating to a lucrative studio offer, but assures himself he will remain true to his ideals.

Before he can say proletarianism, however, he is assigned a Wallace Beery wrestling programmer and told to come up with something by the end of the week. He is coddled by studio chief Jack Lipnick (Michael Lerner) and, checking into a huge, slightly frayed and weirdly under-populated hotel, becomes friendly with the hulking fellow bachelor next door, Charlie Meadows (John Goodman), an insurance salesman with a gift for gab.

Working at home, Fink suffers from intense writer's block, and shades of Kafka surface as scenes of the scribe staring at his blank page turn to such odd distractions as wallpaper peeling off walls and a mosquito buzzing about the room.

After a little more than an hour into the pic, one of those startling screen occurrences (like Janet Leigh's murder in *Psycho*) takes place and throws the film in a wholly unexpected direction. There is a shocking murder, the presence of a mysterious box in Fink's room, the revelation of another's character's sinister true identity, three more killings, a truly weird hotel fire and the humiliation of the writer after he believes he's finally turned out a fine script. Ending is as lovely as it is enigmatic.

Scene after scene is filled with a ferocious strength and humour. Fink's encounters with the studio boss represent astounding displays of character domination and debasement. Lerner's performance as a Mayer-like overlord is sensational.

But much more of the action involves Fink and his friendly neighbour as Charlie expounds upon life, gives him a wrestling demonstration and invariably interrupts the writer just when he's about to get cracking.

It could plausibly be argued that the Meadows character actually doesn't exist, that he is simply a physical manifestation of extreme writer's block. He also stands in for the real working man that Fink idealises and tries to write about, but in fact doesn't know at all.

Barton (John Turturro) with sympathetic everyman-figure Charlie Meadows (John Goodman) – who will become his satanic nemesis.

The fat man has a thousand real-life stories he's willing to tell, but the writer is scarcely interested. Fink comes off as remote and difficult, with inflated notions of his work's importance, but hopeless as a social creature. Turturro invests this creative worm with convincing anxiety, sweat, desperation and inwardness.

Goodman is marvellous as the folksy neighbour, rolling his tongue around pages of wonderful dialogue. Judy Davis nicely etches a woman who has a way with difficult writers, and John Mahoney turns up as a near dead ringer for William Faulkner in his Hollywood period.

Replacing Barry Sonnenfeld behind the camera for the Coens, Roger Deakins has created many brilliant images. Production designer Dennis Gassner's earth-toned sets, Roderick Jaynes' editing, Richard Hornung's costumes and Carter Burwell's score all contribute strongly in creating a Hollywood as it might have been sketched in a surrealist short story rather than a fleshed-out novel.

BARTON FINK

BY STEVE JENKINS

1941. Following the successful Broadway opening of *Bare Ruined Choirs*, his play about fishmongers, young Barton Fink moves to Hollywood to work for Capitol Pictures. After checking into the rundown and rather eerie Hotel Earle, Barton meets studio boss Jack Lipnick and is told to script a wrestling B-picture to star Wallace Beery. Attempting to work in his hotel room, Barton is disturbed by strange noises, but is then befriended by the culprit, his neighbour Charlie Meadows, an insurance salesman. To help him over his writer's block, Barton is advised by his producer, Ben Geisler, to talk to Bill Mayhew, a famous novelist who is also under contract to the studio but who has a bad drinking problem.

Barton is attracted to Audrey, Mayhew's secretary, but she tells him that she and Mayhew are in love. Complaining of an ear infection, Charlie again visits Barton and demonstrates his prowess at wrestling. He later tells Barton that he has argued with a doctor about his ear and is going to New York for a few days. Barton argues with Mayhew when the latter drunkenly hits Audrey, and subsequently appeals to her for help with his script. She visits him at the hotel and reveals that she writes Mayhew's work.

They make love, but Barton then wakes to find Audrey's murdered corpse beside him. Charlie offers to help the hysterical Barton and removes Audrey's body. He later tells Barton that he is going away again and leaves a box with Barton which he says contains everything from his life. Barton is then visited by two detectives and learns that Charlie is actually a psychopathic murderer, Karl "Madman" Mundt, whose victims include the ear doctor.

Barton finally manages to complete his script and goes dancing to celebrate. Returning to his room, he is questioned by the two detectives about Charlie, but the latter returns, sets fire to the hotel and kills the detectives. Charlie is furious at Barton for never listening to him, but spares his life. Barton leaves the hotel and goes to see Lipnick, who tells him that he didn't like the script but will keep him on contract. Still carrying Charlie's box, Barton goes to the beach and watches a girl looking out to sea . . .

The fact that *Barton Fink* proved such a resounding success at last year's Cannes Film Festival but a failure at the US box office ought, one feels, *somehow* to connect with the situation of its protagonist: a writer whose triumph on the "respectable" New York stage is matched by a nightmarish failure to connect with the formulaic demands of a Hollywood studio. But as a neat way into the film's concerns and methods, the link is actually as unhelpful as it is obvious. Despite its setting, *Barton Fink* actually shows little concern with notions of classic Hollywood or what kind of culture it represents.

Characters like Lipnick, the studio chief, and Mayhew, the Faulkneresque drunken writer, are simple (and in the case of Lipnick, very funny) stereotypes, who serve as obvious distorted projections of Barton's prejudices about art and its social function ("I try to make a difference", as he pompously puts it). Barton's problem could be reduced to the fact that he doesn't listen: a final accusation made by the psychopathic Charlie, whose attempts to tell Barton the truth about the "common man" have been drowned out by the writer's ravings about the importance of theatre. But the film itself works out from rather than towards this conclusion. And its key location, and focal point, is not Hollywood but the Hotel Earle.

Thus Barton's inability to write his wrestling script is displaced and abstracted on the film's soundtrack, where every noise is amplified, echoed and distorted, becoming an ironic expression of writer's block, the point at which language fails and words are replaced by sounds. The link between the hotel setting and a writer's problems recalls *The Shining,* an impression heightened by repeated tracks down corridors. But the general atmosphere is more akin to the enclosed world of *Eraserhead,* particularly in images like that of wallpaper peeling as the paste melts. And the Coens share with Lynch an ability to find brilliant aural and tactile devices to suggest a world gone awry. But while *Wild at Heart* showed the dangers of simply allowing this facility free rein (a sense of excess for its own, wearying sake), *Barton Fink* gains a tragic edge by forcing its protagonist to embrace murder and madness with a real sense of desperation.

Blood Simple and *Miller's Crossing* were essentially adaptations, although based on no named work, of the writings of, respectively, James M. Cain and Dashiell Hammett. And in this sense, *Barton Fink* completes a kind of trilogy. For with its alienated hero trapped in a shabby hotel room and ensnared in an inexplicable murder, it captures the essence of that other great Thirties crime writer, Cornell Woolrich. But while Woolrich was obliged to "justify" his nightmarish scenarios with improbable explanations, the Coens choose instead to take their central character through apocalypse (the astonishing image of Charlie in the burning hotel corridor) to a kind of double limbo.

Barton Fink finally resolves itself, if not the details of its plot, with the scene of Barton sitting on the beach with Charlie's mysterious box, gazing at a girl gazing out to sea, an image previously seen hanging on his hotel wall. Prior to this, he has been told by Lipnick that he will be kept under contract, but that nothing he writes will be produced until he grows up. Barton thus remains caught in a space where word and image will never quite come together. By invoking Woolrich, however, and recalling that the film is set in 1941, one might predict that Barton's experiences will eventually resurface via the shadows of *film noir.*

A ROCK ON THE BEACH

BY MICHEL CIMENT AND HUBERT NIOGRET

Barton Fink *is about the artistic block of a scriptwriter. What brought you to write the screenplay?*

JOEL COEN: It happened when we were midway through writing *Miller's Crossing*. It's not really that we were ourselves "blocked", but our rhythm was slowed up and we wanted to put ourselves at a certain distance. In order to get out of the problems we had with that story, we began to think about another one. This was *Barton Fink*, which has two points of origin. First we wanted to work again with John Turturro – who we know well – and to create a character he could play. Then, the idea of a huge neglected old hotel, which preceded even our decision to set the story in Hollywood.

ETHAN COEN: We wrote the script very quickly, in three weeks, before returning to *Miller's Crossing* to finish that. It's one of the reasons why both movies are released so close together. When we finished shooting *Miller's Crossing*, we had the script ready to film.

Why have you situated the action in 1941, a key era for writers in Hollywood? Fitzgerald and Nathaniel West died, Preston Sturges and John Huston, two popular scriptwriters, moved on to become directors . . .

JOEL: We hadn't thought of that. On the other hand, we liked the idea that the world outside the hotel was on the verge of the Apocalypse since, for America, 1941 was the dawn of the Second World War. That appeared to fit the story. The other reason – which hasn't really materialised in the movie – is that we thought of a hotel where only old people, eccentrics, and the physically handicapped resided, because all the others would've left for the war. The more the script developed, the more that theme withdrew, but it prompted us, at the start, to choose that period.

ETHAN: Another reason was the main character: a serious playwright, honest, politically engaged and rather naïve. It seemed natural he came from Group Theatre and the Thirties.

JOEL: The character had a little of the same background as a writer like Clifford Odets, though the resemblance stops there. Both wrote the same type of plays on proletarian heroes, but their personalities are very different. Odets was much more open to the external world, a very sociable guy even for Hollywood, which isn't the case with Barton Fink! The man Odets was also very different from the writer Odets; he was more sophisticated than what he wrote. There was a lot of passion in him.

Have you read the Odets diary that he kept during 1940?

ETHAN: John Turturro read it. But there's still a distance that separates Odets from Barton Fink.

JOEL: Turturro was also interested in the acting style of Group Theatre. At the start of the movie, the voice you hear off-screen is Turturro, and at the end, when he's typing a section of his script at the machine, it resembles Odets.

The character of W. P. Mayhew is directly inspired by Faulkner.
ETHAN: Yeah, the Southern alcoholic writer. It's obvious that we chose John Mahoney for that part because of his resemblance to Faulkner, but it was also because we were very keen to work with him. There again, it's a starting point and the parallel is superficial. In the details Mayhew is very different from Faulkner, he hasn't had the same experience in Hollywood at all.
JOEL: It's obvious Faulkner had the same disdain as Mayhew for Hollywood, but his alcoholism didn't paralyse him and he continued to be productive.

Was the character of Jack Lipnick, the producer, inspired by Louis B. Mayer?
JOEL: Michael Lerner resembles him a little, but Lipnick is more of a composite. The incident with the uniform, for instance, came from the life of Jack Warner, who enrolled in the army and asked his wardrobe department to make up a uniform. Lipnick also has the vulgar side of Harry Cohn.
ETHAN: What's ironical is that that colonel uniform, which is one of the most surreal elements in the movie, is at the same time one of the few to have been drawn directly from Hollywood lore!

One of the great qualities of your films, and of **Barton Fink** *in particular, is the totally unforeseeable nature of their unfolding. How do you construct your screenplays?*
JOEL: In this case we had the course of the movie in mind from the start. The structure was even looser than usual and we were conscious that, towards the middle, the narrative would take a turn. We wanted the start of the movie to have a certain rhythm and to take the audience on a kind of journey. When Barton awoke and discovered the corpse near him, we wanted it to be a surprise without clashing with what had gone before.
ETHAN: We were conscious that the demarcation line was very tight. We needed to astonish the audience without alienating them from the movie. Because of the way the hotel is presented, his arrival in Hollywood is not seen as totally "normal". But it's obvious that this movie is less bound to the conventions of a cinematic genre than, say, *Miller's Crossing*, which belongs to the tradition of the gangster movie.

At what stage did you think of the image of the woman on the beach that heralds the last sequence?
JOEL: That came as soon as we began to ask ourselves what would be in that room. We wanted it to be very sparsely decorated, the walls to be bare, and just that view from the window. In fact, we wanted the only opening onto the external world to be that image. It seemed important to create a feeling of isolation. We needed to establish from the start a state of dislocation in the main character.

ETHAN: The image of the beach had to inspire a feeling of comfort. I don't know exactly why we stuck to that detail, but it served to create even more oppression within the room itself.

With the sequence where Barton flattens the mosquito, the film passes from social comedy into the fantastic.

JOEL: Some people have suggested the whole second part of the movie is only a nightmare. It certainly wasn't our intention to make it a literal bad dream, but it's true that we wanted an irrational logic. We wanted the climate of the movie to reflect the psychological state of its hero.

ETHAN: We wanted the audience to share the interior life of Barton Fink, and his point of view. But there's no need to go further. It would've been silly if he woke at the end into a larger reality than that of the movie. In the sense that it's always artificial to speak of the "reality" of a fictional character, we didn't want people to think he was more "real" than the story.

JOEL: There's another element that enters into play with that scene. You don't know who killed Audrey Taylor. We didn't want to exclude the possibility that it was him, though he proclaims his innocence repeatedly. It's one of the classic conventions of crime movies to create false trails for the audience for as long as possible. With that said, we wanted to remain ambiguous until the end. But what's suggested is that the crime has been committed by Charlie, the neighbour in the room next door.

From that point of view, the choice of John Goodman to play Charlie Meadows is fundamental — given that he usually plays the "pleasant type". For that reason, the audience is with him in the first scenes.

ETHAN: That role was written for the actor, and we were obviously conscious of that warm, affable image the audience feels comfortable with. We exploited that expectation in order to finally turn it round. Yet, as soon as he presents himself, there's something menacing, disquieting about him.

The fact that Barton Fink takes the proletariat as the subject of his plays also obliges him to appear friendly towards Meadows, otherwise he would feel full of bourgeois prejudice.

JOEL: That's partly true, but Charlie also gains sympathy simply through his friendly behaviour at the start.

ETHAN: Charlie is equally conscious of the role Barton Fink intends to make him play, in a perverse way.

While shooting this film you didn't know you'd be in competition at Cannes, and were even less aware that Roman Polanski would be president of the jury. It's ironic he's had to judge a film where **The Tenant** *out of* **Cul-de-Sac** *meets* **Repulsion.**

JOEL: It's clear we've been influenced by his films, but, at this moment, we have too many scruples to speak about it because it'd give the impression we kissed his ass. ★

The three films you mentioned influenced us, of course. *Barton Fink* doesn't belong to any genre, but, if it has a lineage, it's obviously one that begins with Polanski.

One thinks also of The Shining *as well as the world of Kafka, and the black humour of the Jewish culture of Central Europe.*
JOEL: That's true, except *The Shining* belongs more to the international horror movie genre. Several critics have also mentioned Kafka and that surprises me, because, to tell the truth, I haven't read him since my university days when I devoured *The Metamorphosis*. Some of them have alluded to *The Castle* and *In the Penal Colony*, but I've never read them.
ETHAN: With so many journalists wanting us to be inspired by *The Castle*, I've got a newfound desire to discover it for myself.

How do you share the writing of the script?
ETHAN: It's very simple and very informal. We discuss each scene together in detail without ever allotting the writing of such or such scene to either of us. But finally it's me who types. As we've said, *Barton Fink* was particularly quick to write, while *Miller's Crossing* was longer, almost nine months.
JOEL: Usually we spend four months on the first draft that we then show to our friends, before dedicating two more months to polishing.

How did you write Barton Fink *so rapidly?*
ETHAN: Perhaps we owe it to the feeling of relief after the difficulties of *Miller's Crossing*. Anyway, it was very easy.
JOEL: It's strange but some movies present themselves almost entirely formed in your head. You know how they'll be visually and without perhaps knowing the end exactly, you have an intuition of the kind of emotion that'll manifest itself. Other scripts, on the other hand, are a little like slowly progressing journeys where you don't really know where you're going. For this movie, we practically knew what state Barton Fink would be in at the end. Likewise, at the very start we wrote the ultimate tirade of Charlie, where he explains himself and says that Barton was only a tourist in town. It makes things much easier knowing in advance where you're leading your characters.
ETHAN: We had the impression of knowing them really well, perhaps because we're very close to the two actors, and that made writing their roles very easy.

Miller's Crossing *is also a film where many characters and places and different plots intersect.*
JOEL: It's true that *Barton Fink* is much more contained. The story of *Miller's Crossing* is so complex that we had a tendency to get lost while we were writing it!

ETHAN: *Barton Fink* is more the development of an idea, rather than all the narrative intricacies that made up *Miller's Crossing*.

How did that name come to mind?
JOEL: We found it at the start of working on the script, but we don't know where it came from. It seemed to arrive just like that, by pure chance.

There's much humour in the film, from the wallpaper that falls from the walls to the two police detectives. More of a duality of drama/comedy than in your previous films.
JOEL: That's right. The movie's neither really a comedy nor a drama. *Miller's Crossing* tended more towards drama and *Raising Arizona* towards comedy.
ETHAN: It seems we're incapable of writing a movie which, in one way or another, doesn't get contaminated by comic elements.
JOEL: It's funny, because at the beginning I saw *Miller's Crossing* more as a comedy, while *Barton Fink* appeared to me as humour of the blackest kind.
ETHAN: But unlike in *Miller's Crossing*, here we torment the main character for comic effect.

Jon Polito has a role similar to the one in* Miller's Crossing. *In both cases he's humiliated.
ETHAN: Except that in *Barton Fink* he's oppressed for twenty years. He finally got used to it.

The first image one sees of Hollywood is unexpected in this type of film: a rock on a beach.
ETHAN: It's funny you mention that because we filmed other shots to create a more conventional transition, but we decided not to use them. All we needed was a rock on the beach, which also ushers in the end.

It's the second time you've worked with the designer Dennis Gassner.
JOEL: We shot at least three weeks in that hotel where half the movie takes place. We wanted an art-deco style and a place that was falling to pieces, having known better days. The hotel had to be organically linked to the movie – it had to be the externalisation of the character played by John Goodman. Sweat falls from his brow like wallpaper falls from the walls. At the end, when Goodman says he's a prisoner of his own mental state, that it's like a hell, the hotel has already taken on that infernal appearance.
ETHAN: We used a lot of green and yellow to suggest a feeling of putrefaction.
JOEL: Ethan always described the hotel as a ghost ship set adrift, where you get indications of the presence of other passengers without ever seeing them. The only clue would be the shoes in the corridors. You can imagine it peopled with travelling salesmen who've had no success, with their sad sex lives, crying alone in their rooms.

JOEL & ETHAN COEN: BLOOD SIBLINGS

You look at the Hollywood of 50 years ago, but in another way you're confronted by the same problems. Do artists still meet philistines like Jack Lipnick?

JOEL: Very probably. But *Barton Fink* is really very far from our own experience. Our professional life in Hollywood has been particularly easy, which I'm sure is very unusual and very unfair. It isn't a personal comment in any way. We financed our first movie *Blood Simple* ourselves, and the three that followed have been produced by Circle Films in Washington. Each time we've presented them with a script, which they've liked, then agreed on the budget. We have no rejected scripts in our drawers. There are, of course, projects on which we've begun work but haven't finished writing for one reason or another, because there were artistic problems we couldn't resolve, or because their cost became prohibitive.

Is there an unfinished project that was particularly dear to you?

JOEL: No, because finally you're taken by another movie which seduces you, and which becomes your main preoccupation. We'd still like to realise one or two shorts we've written, but it's very difficult to produce them in America because there's no market.

Why have you called in Roger Deakins this time?

JOEL: Our usual cameraman Barry Sonnenfeld wasn't free, and as we'd liked Deakins' work we asked him to work for us. He seemed suitable for the project.

ETHAN: We very much liked his night shots and interiors in *Stormy Monday*. We'd also seen *Sid and Nancy* and *Pascali's Island*.

Have you made a storyboard as with your previous films?

ETHAN: Yes, in some detail. But, of course, many changes happen when we're on the set, though we still arrived with each shot prepared. This was a simpler movie to make than *Miller's Crossing*, and the budget was a third less, as was the shooting time: eight weeks instead of twelve.

Did you shoot sequences that were removed in the editing?

JOEL: For *Miller's Crossing* entire sequences were shot which didn't find their way into the movie. That wasn't the case with *Barton Fink*, nearly everything was used. I remember some shots of studio life in Hollywood we decided not to keep: they were pretty banal.

Compared to your previous films, which had scenes like the night shooting in **Miller's Crossing,** *Barton Fink has a much more rigorous style.*

JOEL: That wasn't intentional. It's probably because *Miller's Crossing* had so much dialogue that, at a certain stage, we wanted to give the viewers some visual punches. The gangster genre also permits those grand action scenes. But for *Barton Fink* that style of thing didn't seem appropriate. Big spectacle would've upset the balance.

The "writer victim" of Hollywood is part of the legend of cinema.

ETHAN: Yeah, it's almost a cliché. On top of that, we give them the dignity of victim status that they probably don't deserve, because Barton Fink is probably not a great artist and Mayhew is no longer capable of writing.

Do you feel close to some of your contemporaries in American cinema?

JOEL: There are quite a lot of things we like, but we don't see affinities with our work. The American film industry is in pretty good health today; a good number of directors are getting their ideas successfully onto the screen, either in the factory products from the big companies – which are mostly formulaic, though there are exceptions – or the independent cinema.

Your style of cinema contrasts strongly with most of the Hollywood films of today. For example, you begin all your films right in the middle of a scene without setting up the context, as in **Miller's Crossing.**

JOEL: At the beginning of *Miller's Crossing*, we have two shots: the first is of a glass with ice, then a close-up of [Jon] Polito. We didn't want to show straightaway who was holding the glass. You saw someone with the glass, heard the tinkle of ice, but the person is blurred in the shot; then, you see Polito, hear his monologue. The ice is a crucial element in the shot. Then you see Albert Finney, but you still don't know who's holding the glass, and finally, you arrive at Gabriel Byrne in the background. All of that was prepared in the storyboard.

ETHAN: We wanted to create a mystery around the character who was going to become the movie's hero.

JOEL: Polito's important in that scene because he gives the information, he begins to recount the story.

ETHAN: We held back Gabriel's entrance in the conversation. He's the last to speak, five minutes after the movie has begun.

How do you explain the relative commercial failure of **Miller's Crossing,** *despite positive worldwide critical reception?*

ETHAN: It's always difficult to speculate. Maybe the story is too complicated to follow.

JOEL: After all, the plot of *The Big Sleep* was pretty hard to understand, too! It's difficult to analyse why it failed, but it was still a disappointment to us.

★ *On the evening of this interview,* Barton Fink *received the Palme D'Or.*

Translated by Paul Buck and Catherine Petit. Interview conducted in Cannes, 20 May 1991.

BARTON FINK AND WILLIAM FAULKNER

BY MARIE-JOSÉ LAVIE

One of the strongest scenes in the *Barton Fink* script, a sceenplay not lacking in vital moments, is a face-to-face given a sense of realism via its setting in a toilet. This is where two scriptwriters are brought together by the two scriptwriters of this film. The first, who's a novice, is none other than Barton Fink himself, while the other, the experienced one, is the spitting image of Faulkner . . . and truer than life itself. A grand burlesque is presented by the Coen brothers, with their crude, cruel accentuation of the character's features and a spirit both caustic and respectful.

Although legally assured that "any resemblance to . . . is purely coincidental", the audience is presented with a carbon copy of Faulkner's face. The dialogue also plays more fascinatingly if the audience has noticed that Barton Fink resembles this same William Faulkner. Thus the scene baroquely sets "Faulkner against Faulkner", and tragically contrasts one scriptwriter, the enthusiastic beginner, against the seasoned, blasé counterpart Barton himself will become a few years later.

The inexperienced screenwriter, Barton Fink, is stuck after the three first lines of the script he's been asked to write on the life of a wrestler, a part planned for Wallace Beery. It just so happens that the very first job given to Faulkner by Sam Marx at MGM, on 7 May 1932, was drafting a remake of *Champion*, the story of a boxer earlier played by Wallace Beery. The remake was to be entitled *Flesh*, with Beery in the role of a wrestler. As one can see, "any resemblance . . . ". For various reasons Faulkner didn't write the script, which was entrusted to Moss Hart, just as the one in *Barton Fink* is similarly transferred to another writer.

The man with the Faulkner face appears before us from the start as an incurable alcoholic with a very distinguished appearance (any resemblance…). A cynic, who's lost all illusions, he is soon to prove his incapability of writing scripts, reduced to having them written by his studio secretary – being also his mistress – whose resemblance to Meta Carpenter is also coincidental! This will irritate those who know Faulkner's Hollywood reputation of an exceptional capacity for work. Here the Coen brothers maintain a greater distance from the reality that supports their screenplay, as far as Faulkner is concerned anyway, as their referential nods and winks evoke many other characters beside the writer. Nevertheless, they present Barton Fink as lured to Hollywood courtesy of the New York success of one of his theatre plays, like Faulkner in his time following the New York craze for his novel *Sanctuary*. Though Meta Carpenter never wrote a single line for Faulkner she was still his scapegoat, like the woman in *Barton Fink* who only coincidentally looks like her.

William Faulkner was as unknown when he arrived in Hollywood as Barton Fink, though he was quickly sought out by a voguish director named Howard Hawks. He was taken with one of the writer's stories, *Turn About*, via the passion for aviation that had already encouraged him to shoot *Air Circus* (1928) and *The Dawn Patrol* (1930). Having bought the rights to *Turn About* for a sum well over $5,000, Hawks was planning a co-production with MGM and wanted Faulkner secured to adapt his own story.

W. P. Mayhew (John Mahoney) with the long-suffering Audrey Taylor (Judy Davis) – the alcoholic screenwriter inspired in part by William Faulkner.

The story of that adaptation is interesting. As we'll see, it bears testimony to Faulkner's great ability to adapt to studio imperatives. And yet, at the same time, it shows the reasons for his mediocre cinematic reputation. Finally, it offers a wonderful example of the oft-amazing conditions the Hollywood screenwriter had to face.

The story *Turn About* related the exploits of an English sailor and an American pilot during the Great War, emphasising the perpetual risks of battle from a classically tragic perspective. Its plot and progression were bare, with no other goal than to present the two men's lack of concern in the face of danger, both animated by the same patriotic instinct. The audacity of the pilot impresses the sailor who, in his turn (hence the title), surprises his comrade with the risks he takes. As for the reader, he couldn't fail to be gripped by the two simultaneous adventures unfolding aimlessly. The story was constructed according to a rigorously simple symmetric plan: one hazardous aerial expedition followed another more dangerous naval action. The adaptation posed no problems: imagery, structure and chronology were all particularly suited to cinema, depicting conflict and action in an exclusively masculine world.

To Hawks' request, Faulkner simply replied that he would get back to him in five days. At that meeting Faulkner arrived not merely with an answer, but with the finished adaptation. Hawks liked the script immediately, shooting would start as soon as an agreement was reached with MGM, whose vice-president at the time was Irving Thalberg. His opinion was entirely favourable, though with the simple condition that a leading female character had to be added before anything else to create a part for Joan Crawford, then under contract at MGM. Leaving contract stars inactive was against studio procedure and good financial management, as well as MGM's concern to maintain the fame of its contracted players. That the transformation was fundamental, requiring a complete reconstruction of the story and a shift of theme, was not taken into consideration. Screenplays, in Hollywood practice, are created purely to service the studio.

If Faulkner was disconcerted by having to modify his basic outline, he still managed to conceive additional scenes without distracting from the action. He wrote a second version at a pace, adding, for instance, childhood scenes which foretold the bonds woven between the different characters. The whole story acquired the dimension of a powerfully moving work. If Hemingway had considered it to be one of the greatest war stories, Bruce Kawin – who was aware of the altered script – found it bore all the strength and unity of a stage play.

It's well known that in Hollywood, to prevent anything depending on one single person, the smallest task was always given to a team – if not to several teams. In that spirit, Sam Marx designated Dwight Taylor to collaborate with Faulkner, resulting in a few scenes altered to the detriment of the dramatic purity of the whole. Then a woman of renowned talent, Edith Fitzgerald, joined the two men to take into account the feminine point of view. What had been a coherent ensemble conceived by Faulkner became dislocated by this diffusion. The altered script was never entirely finished, as the childhood scenes which rooted the drama had to be dropped due to the impossibility of finding young American actors with an English accent! Not a lot remained of the film conceived by Faulkner after the title itself was changed to *Today We Live*. From that second adaptation of Faulkner's script – which, still preserved in archives today, reads remarkably well – came a mediocre film. The adaptation had slipped from the author's hands to such an extent that the last two collaborators were credited as screenwriters, while Faulkner was credited only as author of the dialogue and the original story.

Such vicissitudes were demanded by the Hollywood machine, which ruled everything from a project's seminal stages to its final exploitation. One can understand how the Faulkner of *Barton Fink* had reason for abandoning his illusions about the opportunities cinema could offer him, and how he no longer wanted to write what he knew in advance was doomed anyway to rejection or modification. However, the real William Faulkner, despite the image of him as dominant and uncompromising, never slid towards rancorous disappointment but maintained, throughout those years spent in Hollywood, a great capacity for work that was appreciated at the time, and a great quality of inspiration which was rarely valued. Faulkner appears never to have lacked enthusiasm for his work: for the script of *The DeGaulle Story*, for instance, he wrote more than a thousand pages! Faulkner maintained his profound originality and his quest for excellence whilst working on more than 40 scripts for MGM, Fox and Warner Brothers, without once succeeding in imposing the strength of inspiration which, today, is entirely apparent when reading his work. He worked for a dozen years as a scriptwriter, tied by a succession of deceitful contracts to such a degree that Jack Warner could boast about "employing America's best writer for peanuts".

Faulkner's creative genius, caught up in the studio's organisation, had no effect on such an anonymous, all-powerful bureaucracy. The writer was submitted to an omnipotent, elusive hierarchy which, sometimes from as far away as New York, decided everything without regard to the projects-in-progress, without giving reasons or the smallest opportunity to anyone to explain themselves. The scriptwriters, as with all the studio's employees, had to silently obey administrative orders which, on the spur of the moment, could pass them from one job to another without consulting them or worrying about the creative consequences. Projects aborted, transformed, resumed, suspended or abandoned often provoked frustration in anyone at all interested in their work. Faulkner often found himself dispossessed of the results of labour sustained for weeks or months. Few films resulted from all that he imagined or wrote, with few justifications given. Unfortunately, too few of his writings archived by the studios are publicly accessible for the reputation of Faulkner the scriptwriter to equal that of Faulkner the novelist.

Faulkner is present from beginning to end in *Barton Fink*, reminders of his erudition and disappointment abounding in details like the expression on Barton Fink's face when asked to write a script about a wrestler. That small, almost imperceptible line reminds us of how wounded Faulkner's face must have looked on the day *he* was asked to write a story about a wrestler. Or, taking things further, that office in the scriptwriter's sad pavilion bearing the legend of *Slave Ship*, a project which Faulkner worked on for Twentieth Century Fox.

It's difficult to measure the influence of an author on his art when the necessary documents are lacking. It's therefore difficult to appreciate the part Faulkner could have played in the evolution of the cinema, except for the fascination he exerted on the directors of the French New Wave via his literary work that bore such a remarkably cinematic "editing" style. Whoever innovates is usually less recognised in their chosen field. With time, however, Faulkner would have contributed to the evolution of cinema by making commonplace that which was not acceptable before. Reading Faulkner screenplays 50 years later, their formerly risk-taking style is entirely familiar to our way of thinking. However, at the time they remained unappreciated by the men who defined the art (!), anxious about profitability and thus opposed to all innovation.

Barton Fink offers a perfect entertainment, dedicated to all those unknowns who have worked, in the shadows, toward the development and richness of cinematic language. The Coen brothers have paid tribute with love and humour to many of them, and particularly to one of the most prestigious: William Faulkner.

Translated by Paul Buck and Catherine Petit.

FINKING IT

BY JOHN POWERS

Let me begin, as you secretly want me to, by boasting about the weather. The day is bright, the temperature a placid 27 degrees, and the smog's been carried up-country by the Santa Ana winds that Raymond Chandler made part of the local mythology. In short, it's one of those natty Los Angeles mornings that once prompted that Julian Temple (remember him?) to remark over brunch, "If we had days like this in London, we wouldn't have Mrs Thatcher." Yes, there's something about the sunshine that makes it possible to believe almost anything. For the last five years Twentieth Century Fox has believed that the Coen brothers, writer-director Joel and writer-producer Ethan, were destined to become Hollywood superstars.

When *Blood Simple* came out in 1984, the Coens received the kind of reviews that most young film-makers would kill for, unaware that such over-praise usually winds up killing them. But despite the critical fanfare – Joel was called the next Welles, the next Leone, the next Scorsese – the public found it slow and cold and filled with hateful characters.

Still, the industry was high on the Coens' talent and expected that their next film would prove them mainstream crowd-pleasers like *Back to the Future*'s Bob Zemeckis and Bob Gale. But for all its raves and saturation advertising, *Raising Arizona* enjoyed only a brief, lacklustre run. And *Miller's Crossing* did even worse. After opening the New York Film Festival to the familiar gaga reviews, it was last seen limping trembling through the grass like that hare in Keats.

This pattern will continue with their new comedy, *Barton Fink*, which snatched the top prizes at Cannes (including the Palm d'Or) and has been hailed by even those critics who, like me, had savaged their earlier work for its adolescent smirkiness. *Barton Fink* has no chance of finding a large audience and for once I think it's a pity, because it's both an amusing send-up of Forties Hollywood and a sly commentary on the role of the artist. The eponymous hero is a self-absorbed, pseudo-radical Forties playwright who's hired by Hollywood to impart "that Barton Fink feeling" to a wrestling picture for Wallace Beery. Stricken by writer's block, he spends all his time looking for help; yet he's so busy blathering self-absorbedly on about the "life of the mind" and "telling the stories of the common man" that he never listens to anybody, least of all the common man.

Fink, in fact, looks like the Coens' parody of the kind of self-important message-mongering artist they absolutely refuse to be. For all their winking at the audience and taste for classic genres, they are essentially *formalists*, constructing hermetic worlds whose meanings are self-referential and profoundly abstract. (I've been told that Ethan's a great reader of Wittgenstein, but that might have been a joke.) The Coens' work exults in self-conscious plot twists and narrative echoes, recurrent imagery and running jokes, camera moves that pull you away from the action to make you admire instead the director's proficiency and cheek. Whatever ideas these brothers do have about love and loyalty, art and life, are invariably approached at the obliquest of angles – the surest road to box office failure. *Barton Fink* makes it obvious that the Coens don't care about making popular hits.

"The life of the mind" takes a malevolent turn for Barton Fink, when he discovers Audrey's body - murdered in his bed at the Hotel Earle.

And, for the moment anyway, Hollywood doesn't seem to mind; the Coens are still seen as hot young film-makers. Fox executives are proud to have backed a Palm d'Or winner, if only as penance for their unholy success with *Home Alone*. Besides, they feel sure that two young guys as talented and hip as Joel and Ethan Coen will eventually succumb to the inevitable – and produce a box office smash.

COEN BROTHERS A-Z: THE BIG TWO-HEADED PICTURE

BY MARK HOROWITZ

During the last six years, and with only four films, the Coen brothers, Joel and Ethan, have dazzled and baffled audiences to distraction. In order to aid viewers and reviewers who want to develop their own theories for organising the data in the growing Coen file, *Film Comment* provides this easy-to-use, interactive guide for the perplexed. Properly employed, this hypertextual tool will render even the most mysterious and poetic Coen sequence as straightforward and accessible as a Saturday morning cartoon.

[*Note to reader:* This is Interactive Film Criticism. **Boldface** denotes a separate linked entry. Readers are encouraged to devise interpretations by starting anywhere and following their own critical paths.]

ANAL Of or pertaining to an excessive devotion to cleanliness, order, and control. A character in *Blood Simple* says of another, "He's real careful. Fact is, he's anal. He told me once himself." She taps her head. "In here." (see **Freud**)

BARTON FINK Coen film about **head**s. Not to be confused with *Miller's Crossing*, their film about **hat**s. Barton (John Turturro), a pompous New York playwright who bears a superficial resemblance to Clifford Odets, checks into a seedy Hollywood hotel to write a wrestling movie for Wallace Beery. Barton comes down with a world–class case of writer's block. Complications ensue. Near the end of the film Barton, mad as a **hat**ter, screams at a bunch of soldiers on leave, though really at no one in particular: "I'm a writer, you monsters! I create!" He points at his **head**. "This is my uniform! This is how I serve the common man!"

CREDITS Joel and Ethan Coen, writers-producers-directors of *Blood Simple* (1985), *Raising Arizona* (1987), *Miller's Crossing* (1990), and *Barton Fink* (1991), were raised in suburban Minneapolis; both parents are college professors. Ethan attended Princeton and majored in philosophy. (see **Mind-Body Problem**) Joel went to film school and has long hair. On the question of who does what, Joel is cagey: "In our partnership I'm credited as the director and Ethan is credited as the producer and we share the writing credit, but actually what we do is a lot more fluid than the credits suggest. We could share the credits, but our standard answer is that I'm bigger than he is. In actuality it's very equal in terms of what we do." Sam **Raimi**, who knows both Coens well, claims that

Ethan has the literary mind and has more of a say on scriptoral matters, leaving Joel more time to worry about visual issues. Question for further research: If Ethan is the **head** and Joel is the **heart**, then where is the pineal gland? (see **doppelganger**)

DESCARTES, RENE (1596-1650) French philosopher and Coen precursor who observed, "I think, therefore I am." Laboured hard over the location of the soul. His solution, uniquely French, was that the soul was rooted in neither the mind nor the body, but operated instead through the pineal gland. (see **Mind-Body Problem**)

DOPPELGANGER Ten-dollar German word meaning "double-goer"; refers to a person's ghostly counterpart whose destiny is tied to his. In fiction, the doppelganger often acts out the main character's deepest and darkest desires, thus he must be destroyed if the main character is to survive in the world. In *Raising Arizona*, the half-**heart**ed outlaw impulses of Hi (Nicolas Cage) emerge from his nightmares – from his **head** – full-blown in the form of a leather-clad outlaw biker named Lenny (Randall "Tex" Cobb). In *Miller's Crossing*, Tom Reagan (Gabriel Byrne) finds his doppelganger in Bernie Birnbaum (John Turturro). They are both gamblers and crooks, either of whom might say (though it's Bernie who does), "Somebody hands me an angle and I play it." Twice Tom discovers Bernie sitting in Tom's apartment like a ghost, uninvited and unannounced (Tom's apartment was designed, according to production designer Dennis Gassner, a longtime Coen collaborator, to feel like the inside of Tom's **head**); indeed, after Tom fakes Bernie's death, Bernie literally comes back to haunt him. In the midst of writing *Miller's Crossing* the Coens experienced a severe case of writer's block, and turned instead to the composition of *Barton Fink*, the story of a writer experiencing writer's block, as a form of therapy. *Barton Fink* is the filmic doppelganger of *Miller's Crossing*. One is the dreadful parallel dream running alongside, beneath, and behind the other. Like Shaw's *Don Juan in Hell*, written to be performed midway through another play, *Man and Superman*, *Barton Fink* might be projected between the fifth and sixth reels of *Miller's Crossing* without diminishing either film. And for those who care about such things, the building where Tom Reagan lives in *Miller's Crossing* is the Barton Arms.

EVIL DEAD, THE Before teaming up with his brother, Joel Coen was assistant editor on this first feature directed by Sam **Raimi**, a pal whose four produced films are as wild-assed, uninhibited, and vulgar as a Coen film is careful, preplanned, and precise. Coen films are featured at prestigious film festivals; Raimi films open on Times Square. Raimi is unsurpassed at coming up with new and stunning uses for a camera, and many aspects of the Coen visual style that stick in the mind – the groundlevel high-velocity tracking shots, the odd angles, the relentless Hitchcock-on-speed POV shots – derive from Raimi. It is unlikely that the Coens, try as they may, will ever produce anything as startlingly magnificent as the flying eyeball shot in *The Evil Dead II: Dead by Dawn*, Raimi's awesome high-budget remake of his own film that even surpasses the original. In interviews, the Coen brothers, cerebral and literary as they are, pretend to be old-fashioned, inarticulate craftsmen, interested in nothing but entertaining their audience. They are really self-conscious and thoughtful artists but they wish they were Raimi, an intuitive creator of pointless, hellbent, in-your-face entertainment. Like Barton Fink, Bernie Birnbaum, and Hi, the Coens are too smart for their own good. Raimi is not. Where the Coens are control freaks, Raimi lets it all hang out. Where Coen films are virtually finished by the time their detailed screenplays are typed, Raimi's scripts are unfinished sketches, worthless from a literary point of view, mere pretexts to allow his crazy visual imagination to run amok. Raimi is the Coens' **doppelganger**. He is the filmmaker the Coens would be if there were only one of them, not two, and if they were unburdened by self-consciousness, not trapped in the hall of mirrors that is the life of the mind.

FLYING EYEBALL SHOT An eyeball pops out of a head, hurtles through the air, and lands in the mouth of a young woman, who swallows it and chokes. For one moment we are flying alongside the flying eyeball, its ganglia trailing behind like tail feathers. The effect is hilarious and breathtaking all at once. This influential shot occurs in **The Evil Dead II: Dead by Dawn** by Sam **Raimi**, who consistently pushes his moving POV shots as far as they can go, racing his camera through the air, along the ground, up and down holes and pipes, even (in *Darkman*) tracking alongside a speeding bullet. Raimi's influence extends far beyond Coen films. Whenever audiences ooed at a camera mounted on a flying plate in *War of the Roses* or aahed at the flying arrow POV shot in *Robin Hood: Prince of Thieves*, somewhere Sam Raimi smiled.

FREUD, SIGMUND (1856-1939) Austrian neurologist, founder of psychoanalysis. Proposed that human destiny is in the grip of powerful mental forces of which individuals are often totally unaware. Also seemed to think all problems are in the **head**. Freud's most vivid childhood memory took place in the streets of his native Vienna when he watched helplessly as an anti-Semitic ruffian knocked his father's hat off.

GEOMETRY Inspired by the three-part disharmony of James M. Cain, a recurring form in the Coen world is the murderous triangle. It appears at its purest in *Blood Simple*, then reappears in *Miller's Crossing* double-barreled. First there is the foreground triangle: Tom is sleeping with Verna (Marcia Gay Harden), the fiancee of his best friend Leo (Albert Finney). And then there is the shadowy homosexual triangle in the background: Bernie is seeing Mink (Steve Buscemi), who "belongs" to Johnny Caspar's enforcer the Dane (J. E. Freeman). Linking the two triangles is Bernie, Verna's brother. The gay subtext points to the story's deepest secret: Tom loves Leo, and loses him to Verna, and to his own coldheartedness. To the insular pair of Coens, two's company, three's always a crowd. (see **sex**)

HAT The hat motif, like so much else in *Miller's Crossing*, comes from somewhere else. (see **pulp**) Ned Beaumont, the hero of Dashiell Hammett's novel *The Glass Key* – the source of much plot and character in *Miller's Crossing* – discovers a recently murdered body and observes, "His hat wasn't there." Ned's boss, Paul Madvig, the model for *Miller's Crossing*'s Leo, replies, "He won't need it now." The missing hat, which plays a crucial part in Hammett's novel, reappears in *Miller's Crossing* metamorphosed into a hat-surrogate, the wig belonging to and supplying identity to deceased gangster "Rug" Daniels. There is, of course, a much more crucial, true hat, the one worn and borne and chased by Tom Reagan. It operates not so much as a clearly defined symbol but as a palimpsest of Tom's feelings about longing and loss, about losing his **head** (literally or figuratively), about control, and about death. Finally, the hat is less important than Tom's odd obsession about holding on to it at all costs. When *Miller's Crossing*'s star Gabriel Byrne asked Joel Coen what the significance of the hat was, Joel answered, "The hat is very significant."

HEAD (antonym: **heart**). The word "head" or its synonym (skull, brain, mind, etc.) occurs 64 times in the screenplay for *Miller's Crossing* and 77 times in *Barton Fink*. By way of comparison, the term appears a mere 24 times in *It's a Wonderful Life*, which should come as no surprise since Capra has been a lifelong materialist. However, the word appears only seventeen times in *Chinatown*, which is surprising since **Polanski** is a primary influence on the Coens' work. However, if "nose" is allowed as a synonym for 'head' (since it is an appendage thereof), the total figure jumps to 38.

HEART (antonym: **head**). Conventionally identified with warmth, generosity, passion, love; source of extreme distraction among observers of, if not necessarily characters in, Coen films. The Coens have been accused of being too coldhearted and calculating as artists. A similar charge has been levered at **Kubrick**. In *Miller's Crossing* Tom Reagan, we are told, has "no heart", yet he borrows a lot of trouble for himself by listening when Bernie Birnbaum says, "Look into your heart!" (But only the first time. The second time he shoots Bernie in the **head**.) Tom does not give his feelings away, except to the camera, and then only in the last shot of the film. This makes for exquisite tension or self-righteous dismissal, depending on who is watching or not watching, and whether they believe cold passion is less valid than hot passion. (see **geometry**)

IMPROVISATION "We storyboard our films like Hitchcock. There's very little improvisation because we're chicken basically." (see **anal**)

IN THE DARK The two household gods of screenwriting, Aristotle and Syd Field, say pretty much the same thing about how to write a movie: there's a beginning, a middle, and an end, in that order. The Coens have a better idea: paint yourself into a corner and then try to get out of it. "Circumvent the audience's expectations," says Joel. "Dream up horrible situations to put the characters through." Then, as Ethan told one interviewer, "Make it worse." The characters rarely understand what's going on, and when they do manage to extricate themselves it's usually by mistake, or plain dumb luck. When it's over, the audience remains "the only privileged party to know what actually happened". And at the end, "the characters are still in the dark"

J. J. HUNSECKER The best Coen film not made by a Coen is *The Sweet Smell of Success*, written in battery acid by Ernest Lehman and directed with consummate perversity by Alexander Mackendrick, a portrait of the wonderful life of press agents and sycophants who circle like moths around the megalomaniacal flame of New York gossip columnist J. J. Hunsecker. Lehman's script was rewritten by Clifford Odets, a real–life model for *Barton Fink*. There exists an unproduced Coen screenplay, *The Hudsucker Proxy*, co-authored with Sam **Raimi**, described as a screwball version of *Executive Suite*, screenplay by Ernest Lehman.

KUBRICK, STANLEY (b. 1928). Noted control freak and filmmaker. Directed film full of ominous tracking shots down long corridors of a hotel where a writer moves in, gets writer's block, and loses his mind, not called *Barton Fink*.

MIND-BODY PROBLEM Perennially popular philosophical tongue-twister. What is mind? Where is the soul? Is there life after death? In *The Tenant*, **Roman Polanski** sums it up nicely: "If I cut off my leg, there's me and my leg. If I cut off my arms, there's me and my arms. But if I cut off my **head**, is there me and my body or me and my head?" The issue has intrigued the Coens from the start. They share with Sam **Raimi** a bizarre fascination with severed heads, and once told an interviewer that the film they would take to a desert island would be *Bring Me the* **head** *of Alfredo Garcia*, even though they had never seen it; they heard it was good, though, and "liked the title". Raimi, who didn't major in philosophy at Princeton, takes the easy way out. He finishes the question by regularly showing animated and fully functioning heads without bodies and bodies without heads. The Coens are dissatisfied with this approach, dismissing it as "totally fakey, it couldn't happen". In their first film, *Blood Simple*, the Coens seem to side with the body half of the mind-body question; Visser (M. Emmet Walsh) says, "Well, give me a call whenever you want to cut off my **head**. I can crawl around without it." *Raising Arizona* marked a change in attitude. Its plot features a figment of Hi's fevered mind that comes to life and hunts him down. The corporeal world is now merely an extension of the mental, a position best expressed by Sherwood Anderson: "Men do not live in facts; they live in dreams." In *Miller's Crossing* and *Barton Fink* the Coens continue to believe that the self resides entirely in the mind, but they do not seem happy about it. Both lead characters are prisoners in their own fevered **head**s, unable to connect with those closest to them.

MIRRORS Self-consciousness, a pitfall of the life of the mind, was once considered the bane of true art; now it is the *sine qua non*. The Coens cannot avoid self-consciousness, since there are two of them. One is always watching the other. As one associate pointed out, "In the end the only person Joel has to please is Ethan, and vice versa." In their films self-absorbed thinker heroes are always contrasted with their un-self-conscious, natural counterparts: Leo in *Miller's Crossing* and Charlie Meadows (John Goodman) in *Barton Fink*, both natural men, warm, gregarious, and easygoing, both killers. ("I'll show you the life of the mind!" Charlie bellows. "Heil Hitler!")

POLANSKI, ROMAN (b. 1933) Diminutive Polishborn genius. (see **quid pro quo**)

PULP The Coens are usually regarded as movie babies whose primary influences are other movies, in the manner of Spielberg and Lucas. In fact, their source material is primarily literary, in particular the plot-laden, language-besotted novels of Dashiell Hammett, James M. Cain, Raymond Chandler, and their lesser contemporaries. Cain inspired *Blood Simple* but the title came from Hammett, as did most of *Miller's Crossing*, whose plot and characters are largely lifted from *The Glass Key* with a few smidgeons of *Red Harvest* thrown in for good measure.

QUID PRO QUO Several years ago, Joel Coen was quoted thus: "Roman **Polanski** is a favourite, he's terrific. *Knife in the Water, Repulsion, The Tenant, Chinatown, Rosemary's Baby* − I love them all." *Barton Fink* is, on one level, a love letter to Polanski, drawing heavily on the imagery and angst of *Repulsion* and *The Tenant*. In 1991 *Barton Fink* was awarded an unprecedented three awards at the Cannes Film Festival. The president of the jury was Roman Polanski.

RAIMI, SAM Born in 1959 in Royal Oak, Michigan; raised in Detroit. Director of **Evil Dead** ('83), *Crimewave* ('85), **Evil Dead** II: *Dead by Dawn* ('87), *Darkman* ('90), and the forthcoming **Evil Dead** III: *Army of Darkness*. (see **doppelganger**).

REPRESSED, RETURN OF THE Chaos and violence are unhealthy and terrifying. Order and control are good. (see **anal**) Sweep that bad stuff under the rug, flush it down the toilet, wash it down the drain. Sometimes though, it doesn't work. In *Blood Simple*, Ray (John Getz) tries to kill Marty (Dan Hedaya) − he buries him alive − but Marty keeps trying to dig himself back out of the grave as Ray is trying to cover him up. Barton Fink fancies himself as a liberated radical, a man of the people, the creator of a New Theatre for the masses, but inside he's a repressed, pompous, pointy-**head**ed snob who couldn't smell the coffee if he were soaking in it. Charlie is Barton's secret nightmare come true; he's unrepressed reality, meaningless and chaotic, living right next door. Every artist, to some extent, has the Barton Fink nightmare, that he can't make meaningful order out of the insane chaos of life, and naturally, since Barton is Barton, he gets it in spades. (see **doppelganger**)

SEX Closely associated with the body, generally more trouble than it's worth. (see **geometry**)

UNREALISED PROJECTS *Crimewave*, directed by Sam **Raimi** and written by Raimi and the Coens, was disavowed by all three, saying their original conception was butchered by the distributor before release. Another Raimi-Coen project, *The Hudsucker Proxy*, remains unproduced. (see **J. J. Hunsecker**)

WORDSWORTH, WILLIAM (1770-1850). Romantic poet. The only Coen film that qualifies for the epithet "Wordsworthian" is *Raising Arizona*, the duo's sweet ode to reconciliation, a film about the two conflicting dreams beating within the male breast: domestic bliss versus the outlaw road. We all know the feeling. Whereas the other three films end on notes of loneliness and alienation, *Raising Arizona* concludes with a blissful coming-to-the-table, a dream of family harmony. "The Child is father of the Man; and I could wish my days to be bound each to each by natural piety."

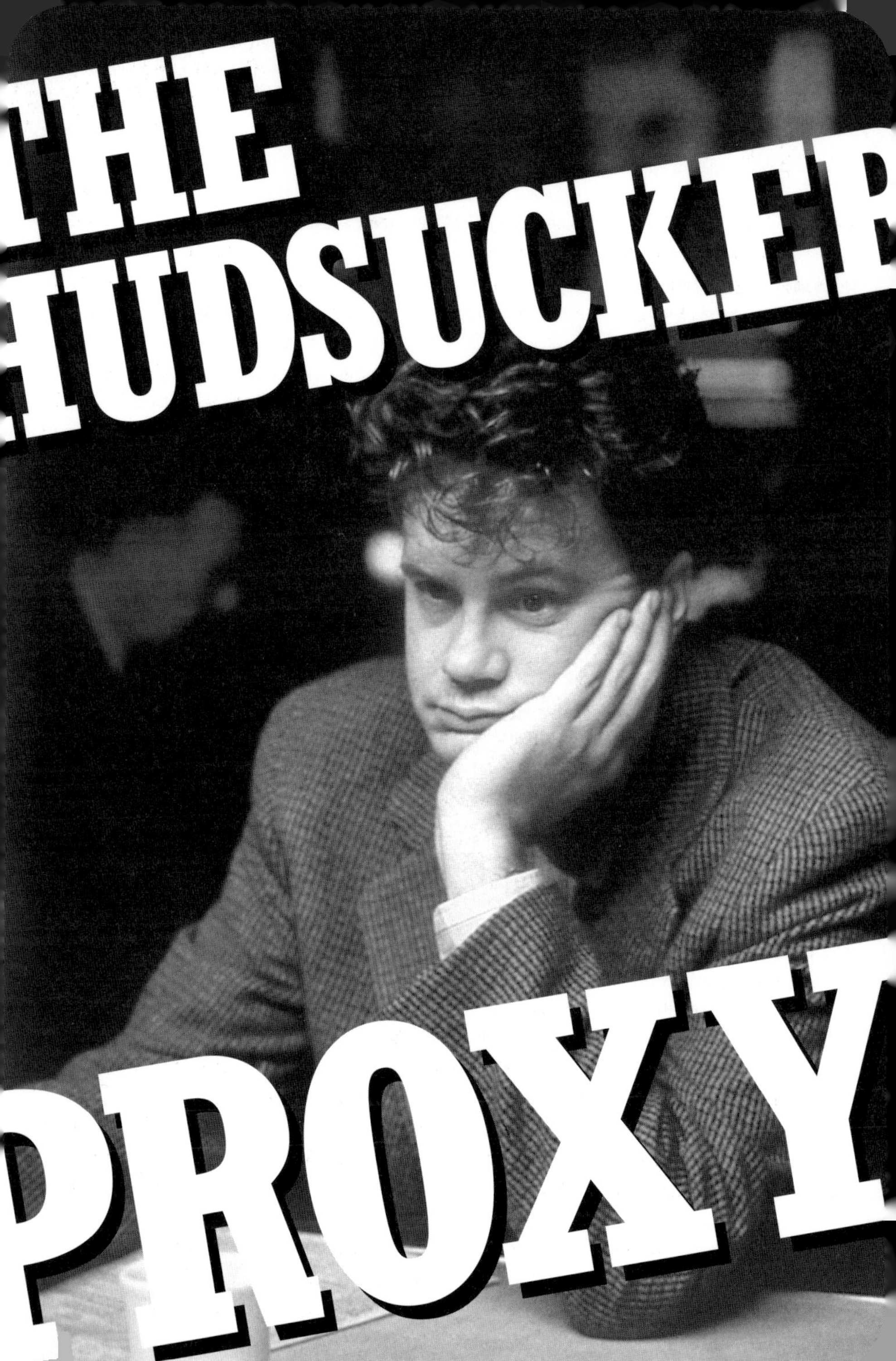
THE
HUDSUCKER
PROXY

THE HUDSUCKER PROXY

BY TODD MCCARTHY

T**he** *Hudsucker Proxy* is no doubt one of the most inspired and technically stunning pastiches of old Hollywood pictures ever to come out of the New Hollywood. But a pastiche it remains, as nearly everything in the Coen brothers' latest and biggest film seems like a wizardly but artificial synthesis of aspects of vintage fare, leaving a hole in the middle where some emotion and humanity should be.

In an unlikely pairing of two of America's most idiosyncratic artists with Joel Silver's production company, and costing somewhere in the vicinity of $40 million, this reps by far the Coens' biggest commercial roll of the dice. Some top reviews and strong support from Warner Bros. should lead to decent mid-level box-office upon pic's release but its pleasures are a tad esoteric for widespread mainstream acceptance.

The Coens' one distinct commercial success, *Raising Arizona*, was their one film most recognisably set in a real world inhabited by working-class characters. The rest have taken place in a relatively stylised and remote gangster milieu (*Blood Simple, Miller's Crossing*) or a brilliantly designed capital of industry (Hollywood in *Barton Fink*, New York here) in which little people are manipulated and buffeted about by the string pullers.

Hudsucker plays like a Frank Capra film with a Preston Sturges hero and dialogue direction by Howard Hawks. Startling opening sequence recalls *Meet John Doe* and *It's a Wonderful Life*, as a desperate young man prepares to jump from a Manhattan skyscraper at midnight on a snowy New Year's Eve, 1958-59.

Flash back a few months and the same young man, Norville Barnes (Tim Robbins), literally bright-eyed, bushy-haired and straight off the bus from Muncie, Ind., is hitting the pavement looking for work. He lands a mailroom job at the enormous Hudsucker Industries just as the successful company's founder (Charles Durning) less decorously hits the pavement after pirouetting out of the boardroom's 44th-floor window.

In a pristine example of one of Sturges' dufus heroes having "greatness thrust upon him", Norville is installed as the firm's president by the cigar-chomping Machiavellian executive Sidney J. Mussberger (Paul Newman), who intends to forestall a public take-over by lowering investor confidence, thereby driving down the price of shares and allowing the board to purchase a controlling interest.

Initially, this strategy works well, especially when hot-shot, tough-talking, Pulitzer Prize-winning reporter Amy Archer (Jennifer Jason Leigh), after worming her way into Norville's confidence and employ, exposes him in an article headlined "Imbecile Heads Hudsucker".

Twisting him around her little finger a hundred times, this dizzyingly clever impostor is Barbara Stanwyck's *Lady Eve* to Norville's Henry Fonda in Sturges' romantic comedy classic, right down to the very verbal seduction. But Norville surprises one and all when, after having baffled everyone with the design of his brainstorm – a simple circle on a piece of paper – he pushes through on his invention "for kids", the hula hoop.

The huge success of "the dingus" deals an unexpected setback to Mussberger's scheme, but for him, "business is war", and it isn't long before he hatches another plot to bring Norville down for good.

Plotwise, it's all been done before: The little man goes up against the evil titans of big business (or government) and gets ground up, only to prevail through his own native ingenuity and decency, and the hard-bitten career woman rediscovers her vulnerability through the love of a simple, good-hearted man. The Coens, and their co-screenwriter this time out, Sam Raimi, aren't saying anything new here.

So it's the way they say it that commands attention, and for connoisseurs of filmmaking style and technique, *Hudsucker* is a source of constant delight and occasional thrills. The Coens' approach, in large measure, consists of the fabulous and ornate elaboration of small details and moments; they make entire jaw-dropping sequences out of incidents that other directors would slide right by.

Three such scenes are an outrageous memory flashback in which Mussberger, literally hanging by a thread over the street far below, becomes sure he won't fall by recalling how his tailor double-stitched his pants; the movement of pneumatic mail capsules through tubes lacing Hudsucker h.q. and, best of all, an incredible episode detailing how the hula hoop became a national sensation.

Throughout, the rhythms of Thom Noble's editing are extraordinary, the montage on a par with just about any classic examples one could cite. This, on top of the orchestration of the other superior elements – Dennis Gassner's formidable architectural production design, Richard Hornung's impeccable costume designs that draw upon diverse periods, Roger Deakins' moody yet vivid cinematography and, perhaps best of all, Carter Burwell's sumptuously supportive score – must certainly establish the Coens among the most imaginative and supple craftsmen of the cinema.

But rehashes of old movies, no matter how inspired, are almost by definition synthetic, and the fact is that nearly all the characters are constructs rather than human beings with whom the viewer can connect. With his gangly frame and appealing pie face, Robbins calls to mind Gary Cooper and Jimmy Stewart, but there's no authentic sweetness or strength underneath all his doltishness to make him seem like a good guy the audience can get behind.

Partly for this reason, no rooting interest develops in the curious romance between Norville and Amy. Leigh skillfully plays the latter with a Katharine Hepburn accent, Rosalind Russell's rat-a-tat-tat speed in *His Girl Friday* and Stanwyck attitude in a lot of things, but the character never seems quite right, although her habit of slugging guys whenever they make the slightest suggestive remark is good for a number of laughs.

Beautifully decked out and speaking with a pronounced rasp in his voice, Newman is elegant and mean but never seems entirely, deeply evil in the old Edward Arnold fat-cat role. Durning has delicious fun with his few moments as the departing tycoon and does his share to make the climactic sequence – when the film returns to see what happens to Norville on the ledge – a doozy.

William Cobbs has some wonderful moments as the man who runs Hudsucker's giant clock and knows all, and Peter Gallagher, all too briefly, is uproarious as a Dean Martin-like singer.

Ethan and Joel in a publicity shot during production of The Hudsucker Proxy – *their most intentionally commercial production, and a huge commercial failure.*

STRANGE BEDFELLOWS

BY JOHN CLARK

The Filmmakers are having trouble with the balls. The balls are a sort of early New Age artifact, a perpetual-motion toy that demonstrates the laws of inertia. The filmmakers are phlegmatic director-writer Joel Coen and slightly less phlegmatic producer-writer Ethan Coen, who are shooting their new movie, *The Hudsucker Proxy*, on a soundstage in Wilmington, North Carolina.

"Tom," says Joel quietly.

Technician Tom starts the pendulumlike balls and runs off the set. Paul Newman, sitting behind an enormous desk and looking sharp in a three-piece suit, barks into a phone as the balls click beside him. It's easy to imagine how weird this is going to look onscreen. Or possibly funny. Meanwhile, Tim Robbins, a pathetic flunky, makes his way toward Newman. He trembles and fidgets – Dorothy approaching the Wizard of Oz.

"Tom," says the first assistant director at the beginning of the next take. "On the balls?"

Between takes, Newman walks off the set to get some air, because there isn't any. With all the lights, it's unbelievably hot – 138 degrees on the catwalk above the set.

As midmorning drags into early afternoon, the crew breaks for lunch.

"You could've matted in the balls," one crew member remarks. Another agrees, "This whole scene could've been done optically."

It's ten months later, and the opticals – there are lots of them – are almost done. The Coen brothers are holed up in the Hotel Shangri-La, an unprepossessing hotel with a view of Santa Monica Bay. It's Fifties seaside Southern California. Tonight they are screening a print of *Hudsucker* that includes some of Warner Bros.' wishes – wishes that, by contract, they have to screen but do not have to accept. What's unusual here is not that the Coens have final cut – they always do – but that they're being so collaborative. To take one big step forward, they're taking one small step backward. The question is where all these steps will lead them.

The Coen brothers are art house darlings (see *Blood Simple, Raising Arizona, Miller's Crossing, Barton Fink*) who are making their first "mainstream" movie with mainstream money ($25 million) and mainstream stars (sort of). And there are some who wonder whether they are capable of making a commercial Hollywood movie. Even their friends.

"Joel used to always think that they could do a commercial movie pretty much whenever they wanted to," says Jim Jacks, who executive produced *Raising Arizona* for Circle Films. "So it'll be interesting to see if there's something in their personality slash style that prevents their movies from being all-out commercial movies."

The Coens are notorious personalities slash stylists. Newman, who has been around the block, calls them "real originals". He adds, "I've never had two directors. And I've never worked with two guys who had equal creative authority who didn't squabble."

"They are symbiotic," says Robbins, echoing what many say. "They are completely on the same wavelength and will finish each other's sentences. I've never seen them argue."

Jennifer Jason Leigh, who is in this film too, rhapsodizes about their smarts. "Their brains are amazing. You could just read that script aloud alone and laugh until you peed in your pants."

Odder still, they take turns answering the telephone.

We learn from Newman's phone conversations that he needs a patsy, a fall guy to run Hudsucker Industries into the ground so that it can be bought on the cheap by management – and there, conveniently, stands Robbins, who presents him with what looks like a moronic idea. Newman sticks a cigar in Robbins's mouth and invites him to sit in his own chair and put his feet up.

Newman: "Your friends. They called you a jerk, didn't they?"

Robbins demurs, shakes his head.

Newman: "Dope? Dipstick? Lamebrain? Shmo? . . . Not even behind your back?"

Robbins: "I was voted most likely to succeed."

Newman: "You're fired! Get your feet off my desk! Get out of my sight!"

Newman rips the cigar from Robbins's mouth and slams it on the desk. Robbins greets Newman's behavior with a marvelously disbelieving baby face, and in another inspired take bites down on the cigar. Half of it remains in his mouth. You can hear the tobacco tearing from 30 feet away. But that won't do, of course, because this cigar must remain intact, alight, so that it can set fire to some important documents lying on Newman's desk.

Says one onlooker, "I haven't heard 'dipstick' in years."

"It's not really wierd," insists the Coens' agent, Jim Berkus, of United Talent Agency. "It's warm, funny." Warm and funny are not words one would use to describe their earlier films. According to horror specialist Sam Raimi (*Army of Darkness*, *Darkman*), a longtime friend who co-wrote the script and is directing most of the second unit stuff, "Their movies have always been dark. Even *Raising Arizona*, which, after all, was about childnapping."

Barton Fink, their homage to creative constipation, earned them the Palme D'Or from the Cannes Film Festival and lots of ink from critics about what this – indeed all of their films – might "really" mean. They are bemused by this. One guy wrote a dissertation on *Miller's Crossing* and sent them a questionnaire.

"You make these stupid movies," says Ethan, "and then a year later you've got homework. It's really kind of alarming."

Ethan waits for the next setup, killing time by singing "With a Little Bit of Luck" from *My Fair Lady*. The Boys, as they are affectionately called, are going to need more than luck. According to Berkus, they're going to need money. They bought apartments in New York several years ago.

"Yeah," says Joel, "Berkus wants us to have mortgages. He would like nothing better than for us to be heavily in debt. He's an agent. He wants the money to keep coming in."

"On the other hand," says Ethan, "when we do something that he thinks is boneheaded, he goes, 'You're beautiful, guys. Never change.' "

They laugh.

The Coens resist the idea that *Hudsucker* is an attempt to cross over after the limited appeal of *Barton Fink*. Or that they're tired of tiny box office (their movies have either made a little money or virtually broken even). In fact, they wrote *Hudsucker*, or at least half of it, eight years ago with Sam Raimi.

"The reason we didn't make it when we wrote it," says Joel, "is we realised how expensive it was going to be; it had special effects and it was all done on stage sets. In fact, when we finally went looking for money, that was still true, until Joel stepped in."

The "Joel" he is referring to is none other than Joel Silver, a personality slash stylist in his own right and producer of the *Lethal Weapon* and *Die Hard* series. It was Berkus who had the bright idea of bringing him aboard to help secure financing and market the movie. Berkus says that when he first broached the notion, the Boys laughed in his face. Then he did a sell job, citing Silver's passion for their movies and downplaying his predilection for action beats and whammy charts. And Berkus had a few words for Silver too.

"I told Joel that you have to listen to them," says Berkus. "Joel said, 'Jim, I listen, I listen, I listen, and then I talk.' When they met, Joel went into a fifteen-minute rap about how honored he was to meet them and his vision of the movie, blah, blah, blah. The Boys started to laugh, and I said to Joel, 'Are you done listening?'"

Silver has a slightly different take on all of this. If he was talking, it was because he had something to say. And when he starts talking about producing successful movies, his voice assumes an almost pedagogic quality. He's the professor of success. "Here's the situation." he says. "People really don't read scripts in this town. They kind of just assess the players and assess the situation and analyse what it might make and crunch the numbers and then they make a decision. This movie just didn't come up right, so there wasn't anybody chomping at the bit. When I met with them, they were considering shelving the project and moving on to something else and coming back to it. But I really wanted to see the movie. They were surprisingly anxious to work with me, because they felt that what I had to offer them, they wanted. They like being quirky, artistic filmmakers, but they want to have their movie perform as well. It's kind of hard when you make a picture and no one really sees it."

"He likes to talk," says Ethan. "You can't object to being yammered at incessantly by somebody who's really a good talker."

Silver's entertainment value, though a plus, didn't put to rest their fears that he would meddle with the project. "We approached it with a certain trepidation," says the elder Coen. "Joel is legendary for being a difficult personality, but we didn't see any of that. You hear all this stuff about him, but from our point of view he did exactly what he said he was going to do."

That is to say, he got Warner Bros. and a slew of smaller companies, none of whom would foot the bill alone, to go in on the picture together. Otherwise, he kept his hands off the project. So the biggest difficulty in making this movie as far as the Boys were concerned was not Silver or the stars; it was the fact that they had to relinquish a certain

Norville Barnes (Tim Robbins), a Jimmy Stewart-type innocent, gets a pat on the back from predatory capitalist Sidney J. Mussberger (Paul Newman).

amount of control. The script called for all kinds of special effects and second-unit work, most of which had to be shot by other people. But at least in Raimi they had somebody they could trust. "I got to shoot all the fun stuff," Raimi says. "Drop a camera 240 feet. A Hula-Hoop rolling through the streets. A guy crashing through a window . . ." What's odd and charming and ultimately very Coen-like about the impish Raimi's efforts is that he wants to make this idiocy as realistic as possible.

And that's pretty much how the actors played it. Leigh, whose character is a fast-talking newspaper reporter trying to expose Robbins's proxy status, read bios and old fan magazines about such Thirties heroines as Jean Arthur, Rosalind Russell, and Katharine Hepburn, because these women brought a lot of themselves to their roles. And so does Leigh. In fact, so happy was she working with the Boys that, when her part was finished, she cried on the plane home. When apprised of this, the Coens, ever the sentimentalists, put their own spin on it.

"Ah," says Ethan, "she cries on the plane home from every movie."

And then there's Newman, not on the face of it the most likely recruit for a Coen brothers movie. A cynic might say that he was forced on the Boys because the moneymen felt the film needed star power.

True or no, Newman nonetheless plays a jerk, although he doesn't view it that way. "I think he's a hero," Newman says. "Every character every actor plays has to be the hero." And he sees nothing risky about playing a jerk for two guys noted for making a movie about writer's block. "It's an interesting script," he says, "and I don't have to worry about the financial end of things. What's the downside of this? That I'm booted out of the Hollywood fraternity and [become] unhirable? So?" He laughs. "And then what?"

Aside from being venturesome, Newman is self-deprecating. "Paul walked onto the set," says Ethan, "and he said it was the biggest he'd seen since *The Silver Chalice*." Newman was referring to his own legendary movie debut nearly 40 years ago, which was so bad that he actually took out an ad apologising for it.

The Coens might want to take out an ad of their own to dispute all the rumours about *Hudsucker* that have appeared in *Variety*. Like the ones about the "reshoots", which had the press speculating that the movie was in trouble. "First of all," says Joel patiently, "they weren't reshoots. They were a little bit of additional footage. We wanted to shoot a fight scene at the end of the movie. It was the product of something we discovered editing the movie, not previewing it. And the other thing is that we've done additional shooting on every movie we've ever made. In fact, probably less on this movie than any movie we've done before."

So will it work? Well, the Boys are actually testing this one to find out, something they've previously done only for *Raising Arizona*. Jim Jacks, who worked on that project, says the test was done after the film was locked. He wonders how much good testing a Coen brothers movie will do.

"I think that finally what their movies are is so deeply embedded in the movie's DNA that you'll never change it anyway," he says.

Apparently the Boys feel that the DNA on *Hudsucker* is in recognisably human form, unlike the usual bizarre stirrings of their cinematic unconscious.

"It's more of a straight comedy," says Ethan, "so it is more interesting and more informative to see with an audience than, say, something like *Barton Fink*."

"If there's a gag in the movie," says Joel, "and if people laugh, then the gag's working, but if they don't, it doesn't. And there's no reason why, in a lot of cases, it would be in there if it isn't working. It's there to get a laugh."

And if it doesn't work? "I know they're going back to a smaller movie on the next one," says Jacks. "They'll always be able to make those movies." "For a studio that makes 20 or 30 films a year, a Coen brothers picture is a great part of the mix," says Joe Roth, who ran Twentieth Century Fox when *Miller's Crossing* and *Barton Fink* were made there. "The success or failure box office-wise of one picture isn't going to change their future." Meanwhile, the Motion Picture Association of America has weighed in with its own assessment: PG.

"It's a Fifties movie," Joel says, laughing. "That's back before people swore."

With Newman once again screaming into the phone (he does a lot of that), a crew member torches the inside of a trash can and scoots out of camera range. The documents on Newman's desk are supposedly somewhere in there. Robbins, standing nearby, sticks a foot in the flames as if to extinguish them – and keeps it there, all the while hopping about the office. But before he can milk the hotfoot routine for all it's worth, the fire unceremoniously flickers out. The technicians confer. They didn't allow the Sterno or napalm or whatever it is that they're using in the trash can to heat up enough before sending him whirling around the room. So they light it again, Robbins steps in, and they wait. Robbins stares at his foot with an abstracted expression, as if it belonged to somebody else.

The camera rolls and off he goes, yelling "Oh my God, sir!" and doing a mad dance. He falls to the ground, and Newman turns around, screaming, "Up! Up! Off the floor! Nobody crawls at Hudsucker Industries!" He returns to his phone conversation. Robbins, meanwhile, disengages himself from the trash can, leaving his shoe still inside.

Cut. A technician douses the fire. They do the scene again. And again. On the fourth take, Robbins falls heavily and afterward limps off the set, wincing. The Coens follow him out the door.

Joel, looking at Robbins closely: "Are you all right?"

Robbins, being a trouper: "Yeah. I banged my knee. I can go again."

Joel, still studying him: "We don't have to go again. We've got it. We've got what we want." Then: "Unless you want to do something different."

Silence.

Ethan, thoughtfully: "Well, if we do go again, you can make it quieter, more apologetic . . . "

Never change, guys.

THE SPHINX
WITHOUT A RIDDLE

BY JOHN HARKNESS

There's a fine line between homage and rip-off. The Coen brothers' originality lies not in their stories, which are derived from any number of better-known sources, but in the sheer aplomb they bring to the film-making process, the relentless darkness of their humour and the ironic twists they give to familiar tales.

Blood Simple and *Miller's Crossing* are *film noir* plain but not simple, the latter owing so much to *The Glass Key* that it's a wonder the Hammett estate didn't sue for plagiarism. *Raising Arizona* functions simultaneously as a commentary on the baby-centric comedies of the mid-Eighties and a live-action realisation of a Road Runner cartoon. *Barton Fink* belongs both in the writers' nightmare school of Hollywood stories and as a concurrent remake of *The Tenant* and *Repulsion* – its Palm D'Or at Cannes came the year Polanski was president of the jury, though when I interviewed jury member Alan Parker shortly thereafter, he assured me that the decision had been unanimous.

The Coens' latest, *The Hudsucker Proxy*, predates *Blood Simple* as a project. Written by the Coens and their mentor Sam Raimi (*The Evil Dead*, *Darkman*), eventually someone managed to get hack genius Joel Silver, producer of *Lethal Weapon*s and *Predator*s, to put up $40 million to finance the production of this monstrous confluence of Frank Capra and Preston Sturges. This is the funniest thing about *The Hudsucker Proxy*.

Waring Hudsucker (Charles Durning) listens to his comptroller's financial report and then launches himself from the window of the 44th floor of the Hudsucker Building at the moment when Norville Barnes (Tim Robbins) arrives to begin his career in the mailroom. A graduate of the Muncie School of Business, Barnes has dreams of making it to the top of Hudsucker Industries, a plan that will be unwittingly assisted by the machinations of the evil Sidney J. Mussberger (Paul Newman). Barnes becomes the figurehead president of the company, and begins work on his invention, which he carries drawn on a carefully maintained, well-worn piece of paper in his shoe. The film charts Barnes' rise, fall and recovery, through the travails of bad press (Jennifer Jason Leigh as a tough-talking reporter with a heart of gold), accusations of fraud, and divine intervention,

From his infelicitous name to his physical clumsiness, Norville Barnes is a Preston Sturges hero trapped in a Frank Capra story, and never should that twain meet, especially not in a world that seems to have been created by Fritz Lang – the mechanistic monstrousness of the mailroom contrasted with the Bauhaus gigantism of the corporate offices perfectly matches the boss-labour split in *Metropolis*.

The difference between Capra and Sturges is that Capra has an authentic belief in the romanticism of pure individualism. His characters are genuinely heroic battlers against the grinding power of big money and big politics. It's a faith blind to its own darkest implications that untrammelled individualism is as much a piece of the capitalist monsters as it is of the heroes, the dividing line being that the capitalists' individualism is wholly self-interested.

Sturges, on the other hand, is a romantic wise-guy. He believes in love, but only in its more bizarre and tortured forms, as in Henry Fonda's obsession with Barbara Stanwyck's card-sharp in *The Lady Eve*, or Eddie Bracken's masochistic pursuit of Betty Hutton in *The Miracle of Morgan's Creek*. Sturges is too in love with the baroque possibilities of the English language to honour the simple decency of a Jimmy Stewart in *Mr Smith Goes to Washington*. The world created in his films is benign and harmless. His heroes do battle with their own limitations, rather than with the malevolent forces of darkness that range themselves against Capra's heroes. A Sturges hero would be eaten alive in Capra's world, which is why *Hudsucker*'s premise doesn't work. There isn't enough weird luck in the universe to save Norville Barnes from Sidney Mussberger, so the film's ending turns out to be more improbable than anything in either Sturges or Capra.

The Coens are quite different. People think their notorious press conferences and interviews, which consist of misdirected remarks and gnomic mumbles, are a put on, but really they work to hide the fact that the brothers don't believe in much of anything – they have enormous abilities, but are sphinxes without riddles. One suspects that Ethan's comment at the Cannes press conference for *Barton Fink* that their films are just frameworks on which they can hang cheap jokes was not a joke at all. There is an emptiness at the heart of their work which can be ignored when the films are entertaining, but which shows up dreadfully when they aren't.

One can easily see what the Coens are attempting here, with their extreme stylisation and willingness to reduce actors to single bit-players' mannerisms, but this misses the point. Directors in the Thirties and Forties used the stylised performances of the great bit players as a characterological shorthand, the way Renaissance dramatists could refer to the *commedia dell'arte* and everyone would know what they meant. But the leading players were not reduced to a single trick, the way the Coens shrivel Jennifer Jason Leigh into a caricature of Katherine Hepburn's drawl and one imperious gesture. (I think Jennifer Jason Leigh may be the most talented actress in American movies today, but all I could think while watching *The Hudsucker Proxy* was that she didn't enunciate well enough to be a plausible visitor from Planet Kate, and that, to echo Addison DeWitt, she simply wasn't tall enough to make the finger to the sky salute the Coens kept asking of her.)

The Coens' fondness for extreme stylisation often works. In *Blood Simple* and *Miller's Crossing*, their reduction of characters to trademark gestures and phrases is well suited to the hermetically sealed universe of *film noir*. *Raising Arizona*'s characters inhabit the same malevolently indifferent world as Wile E. Coyote, whom Nicolas Cage could play without resorting to a costume. The delirious self-absorption of the characters in *Barton Fink* emerges in their unique and completely differentiated mass of tics – it is entirely appropriate that the two least stylised players in the film would turn out to be John Goodman's serial killer and his victim, Judy Davis. *Barton Fink* can easily be seen as an opera in which everyone gets an aria, but they are all loath to sing duets.

In *The Hudsucker Proxy*, the Coens attempt to jam together two items that simply don't mix – a Thirties story and characters, and a Fifties setting. The styles of American film acting changed so much between the age of Gary Cooper and the age of James Dean and Marlon Brando that it's hard to realise that they were separated by only a couple of decades. The styles of urban everyman had changed, the style of supporting acting had changed, the style of dialogue had changed. The exterior assurance of the Thirties stars gave way to the tortured interior anguish of the Fifties Method mumblers. The first influx of New York writers, the Hechts and Perlmans and Parkers, all urban smarts, had given way to the seriousness of Inge and Williams, all anguish. The casual patter of comedies in the late Fifties is a drone, not the rat-a-tat of the old newspaper comedies. In addition, Thirties cinema has an intimacy that often disappears by the time the studios start filming on outdoor locations and trying to fill the Cinema-Scope frame. One can see why the Coens wanted a Thirties-style patter and a Fifties setting, for Barnes' invention is inextricably associated with the latter period, but big empty sets are not conducive to snappy dialogue, which is why there are so few laughs in *Lawrence of Arabia*.

Furthermore, the stylised acting of the Thirties and Forties comedies takes place around the realistic romantic leads. It humanises the beauty of the young Gary Cooper if his best friend is a baleful cynic like Walter Brennan. Even in Sturges' films, there is often a conventional leading man who exists as a still centre around whom and to whom things happen – Joel McCrea in *Sullivan's Travels*, Henry Fonda in *The Lady Eve*. Even in *The Miracle of Morgan's Creek*, the epic degradation of Eddie Bracken's character makes us sympathetic towards him – we never perceive him, as we do Norville Barnes, as some kind of geek savant.

Part of this comes from Tim Robbins' performance, though I don't think we can blame Robbins himself – the best performances in the Coens' films often seem to be ones that get away from the brothers' rigid conception (Goodman in *Barton Fink*, for example), and Robbins' broad mugging was probably asked for. We cannot blame an actor if his casting is a mistake from the outset. The hero is supposed to be a loveable little guy, and casting Tim Robbins as loveable or little is like casting Rip Torn as Gandhi. He towers over everyone else, and whatever Robbins' fine qualities as an actor, being loveable isn't one of them. Had he played this role earlier in his career, about the time when he was doing *Erik the Viking* and *Bull Durham*, he might have got away with it, but while Altman may have given him his two best roles – in *The Player* and *Short Cuts* – he also revealed

Feisty reporter Amy Archer (Jennifer Jason Leigh), who gets close to Norville in order to denounce him in her paper as an entrepeneurial imbecile.

that Robbins' great talent is an ability to inhabit the reptilian skins of men best described as cold-hearted bastards.

Capra was not an innocent film-maker, but he was a naive one, and there is no evidence that he ever doubted the peculiar American dream his films portrayed, or that he was anything but indifferent to the dark implications of his work: the way the "little people" are subject to manipulation at the hands of capitalist media and prone to lapse into mob violence and hysteria at the drop of a hat; the way his shining heroes are self-absorbed individualists as immune to compromise as any of the heroes of writer Ayn Rand – exemplified by the arch-individualist architect in *The Fountainhead*. It seems only too appropriate that Gary Cooper, who played Capra's small-time heroes Mr Deeds and John Doe, would later star as the overweening monumentalist in King Vidor's film adaptation of Rand's novel.

We live in an age so conscious of media manipulation and cinematic effects that it is difficult to make a film today that is not determinedly ironic about its own devices. Neo-Capra films such as Stephen Frears' *Accidental Hero* and Ivan Reitman's *Dave* cannot convince us of the reality of their worlds because the film-makers have lost that power of belief. Why else would *Accidental Hero* try so hard yet so futilely to evoke the Capra of the Thirties – its huge dissolve montages come straight out of *Meet John Doe*. The Capra films still function because of their extraordinary conviction and potent performances.

Capra's great films – *Meet John Doe* and *It's a Wonderful Life* – work because their dreams cannot contain their nightmares. The Coens' strengths lie in a stylisation that reduces or even eliminates the human presence from the frame, and a gallows humour they never shy away from. Their happy endings are ironic commentaries on the genres they subvert, and their world is composed only of nightmares.

DOUBLE VISION

BY JOHN NAUGHTON

Since their claret-soaked breakthrough in 1983 with the stylish thriller *Blood Simple*, Joel and Ethan Coen have been responsible for some of the most critically acclaimed movies, not to mention the most retina-stampingly memorable set pieces of the past decade: John Goodman rampaging down a fiery hotel corridor, shotgun pumping, in *Barton Fink*; Albert Finney shooting a hood, who then tommy-guns his own toes to the strains of "Danny Boy" in *Miller's Crossing*; a car screeching to a halt in front of a hostage tot in the childnapping comedy *Raising Arizona*; and, most recently, Tim Robbins sharing an inverted mid-air conversation with an angelic Charles Durning after falling from the 44th floor of a Manhattan skyscraper in their latest film *The Hudsucker Proxy*. So what new project has caused them to leave their native New York and bring their brilliant, ironic vision to West Hollywood on this sunny July morning? What is the brothers' latest *meisterwerk*?

"It's a Bud commercial," deadpans Joel.

"Budweiser have paid us an *awful* lot of money to do this," avers Ethan.

Even Rembrandt had to pay the rent and the Coen partnership (nominally, Joel directs and Ethan produces, but in reality the demarcation lines are much more blurred) has never had a wealthy patron. Instead they've existed in the murky hinterland somewhere between the independents and the studios, financing their low-budget movies initially through friends and acquaintances back in their hometown of Minneapolis, gradually increasing their spending as they moved closer to the studios, but always guaranteeing their artistic control by insisting on, and getting, final cut of their movies. At least, that was the situation until *The Hudsucker Proxy*.

The autonomy remained, but the budget soared to $25 million. And along with the loot came a big star, Paul Newman, and Joel Silver, legendary shoot-'em-up producer of the *Lethal Weapon* series. It was an unlikely scenario, unlikely enough to be source material for one of their own screenplays: two idealistic artists go to work with a Hollywood beast who chews them up and spits out an artistically compromised but hugely commercial film. Except it didn't work out like that, for life is not like the movies. The film sank like a cement block in the States, while Silver proved to be the proverbial pussycat.

"Joel's got this reputation for being a sort of Hollywood vulgarian," asserts the other Joel. "A producer of big, glass-shattering action movies. But his interests are actually much more wide-ranging than his press allows. He was great. He's a very funny guy, a great raconteur, and he knows what he's doing. If he's interested, we'll work with him again."

But there's no getting away from the fact that *The Hudsucker Proxy* – a comedy fable about big business and the hula-hoop – was a box-office flop. Not only is there no getting away from it, the brothers never even pretend otherwise. I suggest at one point that it may well do better in the UK, where the Coen sense of humour has always tickled a greater percentage of funny bones. With practised gallows humour Ethan smiles and replies, "It couldn't do any worse."

Lazy headline writers used to kick off features on Joel and Ethan Coen with the legend "Brothers From Another Planet", a wildly misleading description as they are anything but otherworldly. Pop your head into any trendy Stoke Newington cafe on a Saturday morning and you'll see their like, heads buried in the *Weekend Guardian*, one hand reaching out for the cappuccino, the other absentmindedly holding a cigarette.

Looking like a pair of perennial postgraduates, they grimace at the prospect of posing for a photo-session this early on a Monday morning (it probably wouldn't be any different at any other time). They stand uncomfortably while the lensman puts them through their paces on the roof of the Hollywood production office where they're currently based, first back to back, then trying to make them look into each other's eyes, a request which causes them both to crack up. Ethan (glasses, gingery beard, pink t-shirt, jeans and trainers) declares, "I don't think I can move any closer to Joel than this. He might be able to move to me, but I can't move any closer to him." Joel (glasses, black beard, ponytail, off-white t-shirt, denim jacket, black jeans, white sneakers) looks ineffably bored with the process and when the snapper enquires, "Do you guys always work together?", he rubs his eyes and musters an unenthusiastic "Uh-huh."

Fully aware that their less than dynamic approach to press interviews can be a drawback when it comes to giving members of the Fourth Estate material to mould, Joel recalls a great moment in journalism for the Brothers Uncharismatic. "The best interview we ever did was with a guy from *Details* magazine. We did it and then he went away and must have decided we were too boring, so he just made up the entire piece himself." "I have to say," interjects Ethan, "it was a big improvement."

Not only, as the snapper acutely observed, do these guys always work together, they seem to think together, laugh together, pause together and, with an adroitness reminiscent of the famous *Monty Python* sketch, finish off each other's sentences – together. Looking out through matching granny glasses, displaying a unity of thought and purpose redolent of the blond moppets in *The Midwich Cuckoos* and playing off each other's well-developed mutual sense of humour, these are no brothers from another planet.

This is the Coen Brothers: Eight Eyes, One Vision.

The Hudsucker Proxy has been around a long time. Set in New York in the late Fifties, it's a simple tale of a hapless sap, Norville Barnes (Tim Robbins), who is plucked from the bowels of the company mailroom by the conniving CEO, Sidney J. Mussburger (Paul Newman), to become chairman of Hudsucker Industries in an attempt to drive the firm into bankruptcy. The movie's been on the drawing board almost as long as the

Coen brothers have had a film career, or almost as long as they've been drawing breath, it might seem.

"There are certain movies that just won't die," sighs Joel as he sorts out the necessary coffee and ashtrays for the interview. "And this is one of them. *Blood Simple* was one of them: it lived forever, took us forever to finish it, forever to get it out to a distributor, and we talked about it for a year after it was done! And this is another one."

"Right after making *Blood Simple* we were actually in Los Angeles trying to sell it. We were sharing a house with Sam Raimi, who's an old friend of ours, and we started writing it then, the three of us, but we sort of put it aside when it became clear it was going to be a really expensive movie to make."

Raimi, director of the hugely successful *Evil Dead* trilogy, may seem an odd bedfellow for the Coens, but their relationship stretches back a long way, with Joel working as an assistant editor on *The Evil Dead* and Raimi co-authoring *The Hudsucker Proxy* screenplay and shooting second-unit footage (and, before the genesis of *Blood Simple*, the trio collaborated on the Raimi-directed *Crimewave*, a project the Coens now disown). As much as Frances McDormand, co-star of *Blood Simple* and Joel's wife, he's part of the family.

But while the movie's gestation period was prolonged, the artistic vision remained unchanged. In a 1985 interview the brothers spoke of a forthcoming project which "takes place in the late Fifties in a skyscraper and is about big business. The characters talk fast and wear sharp clothes." Which is pretty much how it remained. I suggest that it is their least ambiguous movie since *Blood Simple*.

"Yeah, that's right," they chorus in unison.

It's the stuff of banner headlines and rapidly revolving newspapers: Coen Brothers In Unambiguous Movie Shock. Their densely scripted, rigorously structured films have always attracted a highbrow following, accompanied by acres of newsprint devoted to the film's cryptic nuances. But, they argue, the film-buff dissection can almost distract from the simple pleasure of enjoying the film.

"In the case of this movie," reasons Ethan, "there was a lot of press here about how it was sort of a homage to these earlier movies, screwball comedies of the Thirties end Forties [most-cited reference points being the Ernest Lehman-scripted *Executive Suite* and an amalgamation of the work of Frank Capra and Preston Sturges]. And if you weren't familiar with all those movies you'd be missing something, you wouldn't "get" the movie in some sense, which is definitely not the case. It does sort of use the conventions of those movies, but it's not like anything could possibly be over anyone's head."

Joel picks up the thread. "In certain films we've done, where there is an ambiguity designed into the movie, it's frequently the case that the reviewer won't let it rest as being simply ambiguity. And the audience then feel that they're missing something, not understanding something, and have to analyse something into a concrete answer when in fact the movie itself is designed so that you should just be able to *watch* it and *enjoy* it.

"Those journalists have got a hard job," he continues in ironic vein. "They could say, This is a kind of funny movie and I laughed at it, and leave it at that, but they have to write a certain number of words, so they indulge in all sorts of things that will justify that number."

Tough gal meets dork: opposites attract when Amy plays with Norville's emotions.

Indeed, from Gabriel Byrne's floating hat in *Miller's Crossing* to the contents of John Goodman's box in *Barton Fink*, the brothers have had their symbolism thoroughly scrutinised.

"There were some pretty strange theories about what *Barton Fink* was about," says Ethan. "Particularly from the French . . ."

"What one would expect," chuckles Joel.

Nevertheless, it would be wrong to put all the blame on our *Cahiers Du Cinéma*-reading chums across the Channel, because the Coens do like to talk movies and are unafraid to venture into cerebral conversational areas which, like their films, some might consider almost pretentious. They do this with such gusto, however, that it's impossible to fault them. After all, they do love their movies. Listen, for example, as they explain how they hit upon the idea of the hula-hoop (when Norville Barnes takes over at Hudsucker, his solitary idea is the hula-hoop, which he weakly markets with the phrase, "You know . . . for kids." Naturally, it proves his salvation.)

"We had to come up with something that this guy was going to invent that on the face of it was ridiculous," explains Joel. "Something that would seem, by any sort of rational measure, to be doomed to failure, but something that on the other hand the audience already knew was going to be a phenomenal success."

"It all sort of came together as a ring in the script," extemporises Ethan. "The whole circle motif was built into the design of the movie, and that just made it seem more appropriate."

"What grew out of that was the design element which drives the movie," continues Joel, echoing his younger sibling's sentiments, "the tension between vertical lines and circles; you have these tall buildings, and then these circles everywhere which are echoed in the plot . . . in the structure of the movie itself. It starts with the end and circles back to the beginning, with a big flashback. The hula-hoop just seemed perfect."

Most people would be alerting the Pretentious Police by this point, but the brothers Coen are so disarmingly intellectual, yet straightforward, when talking about structure. Do continue.

Ethan: "When you get down to it, it's a very simple story with a rather banal moral to it. In that respect it is sort of anally constructed, because it's structured around principles of design. To a large extent it's what the movie's about."

Yes, but is it *funny*? The Coens could talk structure until the bovines are safely domiciled, and not surprisingly they've laboured under the label of postmodemism, like a kind of irony tag-team. Ashes to ashes, dust to dust, if Joel don't get you, then Ethan must. Are they now or have they ever been postmodemists?

"I'm not real sure," hesitates Ethan. "The honest answer is I'm not real clear on what postmodernism is."

Perhaps it means simply the knowing and repeated use of irony and distance.

"Well, that's definitely true, that's a characteristic of all our movies, the narrative tone and voices sort of step back from the stories. I'd accept that charge."

The other charges most commonly levelled at the Coens are that they haven't got a heart and condescend to their characters. Norville Barnes, the schlubb at the centre of *The Hudsucker Proxy*, is presented as Exhibit A by the prosecution.

"We have a lot of affection for our characters," Joel asserts emphatically. "Even the ones that are idiots! There's comedy in idiocy, just like there can be comedy in violence, but that doesn't necessarily mean you're condescending."

It's an accusation that obviously gets under their skin. "People get very uncomfortable when the main character in the movie is not sympathetic in a formula Hollywood way," complains Ethan, "and what's irritating about that is the implication that the only stories you can tell are stories about sympathetic characters, which is an absurd idea. It may actually have real implications for the box office and that's not necessarily absurd, [laughs] but the idea from any other point of view is crazy."

"The characters in some of our movies are intentionally unsympathetic," chimes in Joel. "Gabriel Byrne's character in *Miller's Crossing* is not supposed to be sympathetic, Barton is not supposed to be sympathetic. I was reading something recently about Alec Guinness doing *Bridge on the River Kwai* and he was asking David Lean about what sort of character he was supposed to be and David Lean said, 'Well the truth of the matter is that if you were at a dinner party with him, you'd find this guy a bloody bore.' And Guinness was very resistant to that idea, playing him as a bore. But he's not boring in the context of the movie."

Sighing with exasperation, he concludes, "Just doing that with a central character in a movie confuses people, and to a certain extent they think it's condescension that we're giving these people unsympathetic characteristics. Barton is in a lot of respects a shit, but it's not as if we're not interested in the audience having some access to him as a human being."

Perhaps it's the overtly cerebral approach to filmmaking which they embody, but, while they're always arthouse darlings, the Coens have yet to enjoy a box-office hit. *The Hudsucker Proxy*, despite its larger budget, has prolonged this trend. But they are not profligate and have a financial record which Joel defends vigorously.

"*Blood Simple* made money, *Raising Arizona* actually made a lot of money for the studio because it was produced for about five million dollars and grossed, just domestically, about 25. *Miller's Crossing* was not a profitable movie but only cost about eleven million dollars to produce, and *Barton Fink*, while it didn't make money domestically, did quite well overseas. You wouldn't call that a stellar box-office record, but it's not as if every movie we've made has lost money."

Ultimately, box-office blockbusters are not where the Coen Brothers are at. If one comes along, of course, they'd enjoy it, but for the time being they seem content to carry on making their lowish-budget movies, the next one possibly being "a sort of contemporary crime story, based on a true story, set in Minnesota".

Though they're happy to talk of success, failure and influences on *The Hudsucker Proxy* ("the architecture of Albert Speer, the design and scale of Terry Gilliam"), what, ultimately, seems to matter in their relationship is something observed by their former collaborator, *Addams Family* director Barry Sonnenfeld: "In the end, the only person Joel has to please is Ethan, and vice-versa."

"Fundamentally that's true," agrees Ethan. "We don't necessarily think about it that way, but I think at the end of the day we're pleasing ourselves. We've just been lucky in terms of the amount of control we've been able to keep over our productions, and I think that's really true of the way anyone would want to work."

FARGO

DO NOT MISS FARGO

BY GRAHAM FULLER

Joel and Ethan Coen's new film, *Fargo*, is a masterful black comedy based on true events, about desperate acts in a desert of white. In a snowbound Norwegian-American community in Minnesota, a nervy car salesman, Jerry Lundegaard (William H. Macy), hires two thugs – Steve Buscemi and Peter Stormare – to kidnap his wife (Kristin Rudrüd), his aim being to split the ransom put up by her father. It all goes wrong, and when the bodies start piling up, cheery, heavily pregnant backwoods police chief Marge Gunderson (Frances McDormand) gets on the case.

Fargo is the most unsettling film yet by the Coens, whose five previous features have established their taste for screwing with screwball comedy and making *film noir* funny. They write, produce, and direct their films together, although Joel (born in 1953) is the nominal director and Ethan (born in 1957) the nominal producer.

I wanted to know how a Coen brothers film gets made, so I trekked up to their Upper West Side Manhattan office in *Fargo*-like weather conditions to talk with them and with McDormand, who is Joel's real-life wife. During the interview, the laid-back Joel shared baby-minding duties with his and McDormand's adopted son, Pedro, while Ethan restlessly paced the room.

How do you guys write together?
JOEL COEN: It's loose and informal. We don't split things up, like one person does a scene and the other reworks it. We sit in a room together and talk each scene through, and we work without an outline; we just start from the beginning.
FRANCES McDORMAND: What really happens is that Joel lays on the couch and Ethan paces in a circle, and then after about an hour and a half, one of them goes "Uhhhh!" and they start writing.

Did you write the role of Marge Gunderson with Frances in mind?
JOEL: Yes.
FRANCES: Why?
ETHAN COEN: It's hard to say, because when you write a character for someone, it's not because the actor resembles that character: it's like you have a suit of clothes and you feel a certain actor's going to fit them.
FRANCES: Can you think of anybody else you would have cast if I hadn't been available?
ETHAN/JOEL: No.
JOEL: In fact, if someone we've written a part for can't do the movie, we'd just as soon not make it.
FRANCES: When I first read the script, do you remember if I said anything about Marge that influenced you at all?

JOEL & ETHAN COEN: BLOOD SIBLINGS

JOEL: Yeah, you said she should throw up because she's got morning sickness.

Once you were shooting, what did Frances bring to the film that wasn't in the script?
ETHAN: Everything. It's not Joel and I who create these characterisations in any real sense.
JOEL: It's 99.9 percent the actors. We might suggest they shade their performances one way or another, but that's all.
FRANCES: On *Fargo*, when Joel said, "Cut," after a take, the way he and Ethan laughed either meant it was good or it wasn't. When I worked with them on their first film, *Blood Simple*, I remember saying to Joel, "Don't try to articulate intellectually what the scene's about. Just tell me whether to breathe harder, breathe softer, talk louder, talk softer." It was the same on *Fargo*, except for that one scene – it's the last meeting between Marge and Jerry [Lundegaard] – when I went crazy and didn't know what to do.
ETHAN: The funny thing is that the scene really works.

[to FRANCES] Did you feel your performance was shaped by Joel and Ethan?
FRANCES: Only by the pregnancy pad I wore. [laughs] No. Actors tend to treat Joel and Ethan's scripts like theatrical pieces. They're laid out so well, you don't start messing with them.

As directors, is there a demarcation between what you two do?
JOEL: Not on the set. Our movies are definitely co-directed.

Barton Fink [1991] was surreal, **The Hudsucker Proxy** *[1994] baroque. With* **Fargo,** *did you want to get back to the spareness of* **Blood Simple?**
JOEL: Everything we've done in the past has been so self-consciously artificial. Because this was a reality-based story, it was an opportunity to do something at the opposite end of the spectrum, stylistically. *Fargo's* pictorial style is much more observational than our other films. We were also interested in doing a movie set in Minnesota, because it's where we grew up.

Fargo *is like a Frank Borzage or King Vidor movie in that it pits the interests of big business or ruthless entrepreneurs against the little man. The American Dream has gone sour for Jerry, and that's intensified by the bleak midwestern setting.*
JOEL: There's something interesting about the whole climate of business in that sort of setting. When we were raising money for *Blood Simple*, we did a certain amount of it in the Midwest. I remember having meetings with these hardened businessmen who would hang out in the local coffee shop and then put their parkas and galoshes on and slog out into this Siberian landscape, get in their cars, and fishtail off through the snow. They are personified by the character played by Harve Presnell [Jerry's father-in-law] in *Fargo*. Jerry's like a struggling version of that.

ETHAN: That specific Minnesota atmosphere was where the juice was for us. Maybe the characters do embody those grand themes you mentioned, but that question is independent of whether or not we're interested in them – and we're not.

FRANCES: See, that's the problem with talking to these guys. You can't get them on the grand themes.

The opening shot of the car coming up on the horizon in the snow sets a very disturbing mood.

JOEL: The whole idea of the car emerging ghostlike out of the snow – that whiteness and weirdness – was important to us. We talked with Roger Deakins [*Fargo's* cinematographer] about these landscapes, where you couldn't really see where the horizon was, where the ground melted into the sky. We put everything else aside and didn't shoot until we got that feeling. But it was nerve-racking.

What also struck me forcibly was the movie's lightness of tone. Considering there's a considerable body count by the end, this jaunty feeling leaves a strange aftertaste.

ETHAN: I think some people have a problem with that, but we don't, obviously. It's the juxtaposing of things that are amusing with things that aren't that keeps the film from being unrelentingly dark.

Do you cut your films together?

ETHAN/JOEL: Mmm-hmmm.

Frances, were you happy with the way they edited your performance?

FRANCES: Definitely. I tend not to make big changes when I work anyway, so I didn't really think they could mess up my performance too badly, although it's not like I haven't wanted to tell other directors how to edit my work.

FARGO

BY LEONARD KLADY

The slow unravelling of the perfect crime gone awry has long been an almost irresistible movie thriller theme. In *Fargo*, iconoclastic filmmakers Joel and Ethan Coen manage the precarious balancing act of respecting genre conventions and simultaneously pushing them to an almost surrealistic extreme. This darkly humorous yarn will strike a chord with sophisticated audiences and has the same domestic commercial crossover potential for Gramercy as *The Usual Suspects*, with international outlook strong as well.

Following the marketplace debacle of *The Hudsucker Proxy*, the new Coen brothers outing demonstrates an assurance viewing classic themes from a slightly askew perspective. Without demeaning its characters or mangling *policier* procedures, pic, which is based on true events of 1987, is very funny stuff.

Set-up involves Jerry Lundegaard (William H. Macy), a financially overextended Minneapolis car salesman. His fiscal desperation having reached the point of no return, he hires two lumbering ex-cons, Carl Showalter (Steve Buscemi) and Gaear Grimsrud (Peter Stormare), to kidnap his wife. He'll then secure the ransom money from his wealthy father-in-law (Harve Presnell), pay off the goons and get out of debt.

After abducting Jean Lundegaard, the duo head for a cabin in northern Minnesota. Along the way, they're stopped by a state trooper on a seemingly minor infraction, and the loquacious Carl attempts to talk his way out of the situation. Gaear simply pulls a gun and shoots the cop in the head. The fatality list that wintry night grows to include a man and his child who happen to pass by moments later.

The following morning, local police chief Marge Gunderson (Frances McDormand) wakes up with a triple homicide on her hands. Well into her second trimester, she pulls on her mukluks, drives to the crime scene and makes a first-class assessment of what transpired. It's not anything like the typical goings-on in Paul Bunyan country.

Despite the unexpected twists in the kidnap scheme, the conspirators proceed to the next stage in their plan – collecting the ransom – hoping that the random murders won't be connected to the primary activity. Meanwhile, Marge waddles through the available clues that will inextricably link the incidents.

The picture's disarming strength is its matter-of-fact progression along the two fronts of the main and incidental crimes.

Fargo is unquestionably blessed by its first-rate cast. Though McDormand, Macy and Buscemi have few scenes together, they work like an ensemble. The trio and Stormare go for a simple, naturalistic quality right down to the characters' clothing and the amusingly flat accent of the upper Midwestern U.S. There are also strong support turns from the too-long absent (from the screen) Harve Presnell, as Jerry's tough-as-nails father-in-law, and from Steve Park, who's touching as a former classmate of Marge's who effects a brief reunion.

That quality spills over into the tech area. The brothers work hard to convey the essence of direct, documentary-style filmmaking, and they create a masterful illusion. There's not a single conventional angle employed by director of photography Roger Deakins, and the complex narrative is aptly supported by virtually invisible transitions from editor Roderick Jaynes.

The film is absorbing less for plot machinations than for the people who populate the piece. Once we know the individuals, it's their personal interactions that prove striking and emotional – Marge's concern for her husband, a wildlife painter, or Jerry's explanation to his son about "mom's" disappearance. *Fargo* is a strikingly mature, unique entertainment that plays on many levels . . . all satisfying.

Police Chief Marge Gunderson (Frances McDormand), the very image of smalltown decency, courage, honesty – and pregnancy.

FARGO

BY TODD MCCARTHY

A title card at the beginning of the Coen brothers' snow-covered, bloodstained new crime comedy, *Fargo*, announces that the picture is based on a true story, while the end credits carry the familiar disclaimer that no similarity to actual persons is intended or should be inferred. The opposition of these two statements neatly illustrates the paradoxical nature of the film itself, which is at once both highly stylized, in the manner of all the Coen brothers' work, and super-realistic. While many moments seem cartoonishly condescending toward the corn-fed characters, the film is simultaneously so dead-on in its portrait of rural-Minnesota attitudes, quirks, and speech patterns that it also qualifies as a masterpiece of regional filmmaking.

Ethan and Joel display their Best Original Screenplay Oscars for Fargo, *with Joel's wife Frances McDormand holding her Academy Award for Best Actress.*

For the first time, the idiosyncratic Coens – bouncing back with a small-scale production after the commercial disaster of their big-budget Joel Silver extravaganza, *The Hudsucker Proxy* – have abandoned the realm of pure imagination for a narrative rooted in real events. Taking their cue from a nutty plot in which a Milquetoasty automobile salesman (played to mild-mannered perfection by David Mamet regular William H. Macy, looking like a ventriloquist's dummy) hires two thugs to kidnap his wife, the ransom for whom would bail him out of deep debt, the Coens have fashioned an immaculately constructed police procedural in which the lead investigator is the polar opposite of Frank Serpico, Popeye Doyle, and every other tough-guy cop to have achieved screen immortality. Strong-jawed, innately good-natured and seven months pregnant, Brainerd chief of police Marge Gunderson (Frances McDormand) initially seems as simple-minded as everyone else, waddling from place to place in her search for the perpetrators.

In other hands, the affably tenacious Chief Gunderson could have become the leading character in an agreeably offbeat TV series; instead, the Coens have her intersect *Twin Peaks* and *Blue Velvet* territory on the road to a blindingly white heart of darkness, even as she provides the film with its crucial redemptive grace. In an icy land where a crime of passion is unimaginable, one stupid man's greed sets off a chain reaction that leaves seven people dead. The Coens' extraordinarily bleak view of the human condition, comparable in its corrosive misanthropy to that of Stanley Kubrick, comes across more bluntly here than ever before because it is so cogently presented: People don't think before they act, they blithely ignore potential consequences of behaviour, and disregard even the most outrageous evidence of evil and malfeasance in their vehement desire to put the best face on things.

The Coens are unequaled among contemporary screenwriters in their ability to create memorable dialogue for aggressively ethnic characters, be they the Irish gangsters of *Miller's Crossing* or the Hollywood Jews of *Barton Fink*, and the cultural specificity of *Fargo* provides the terrain for a field day, of which they take rich advantage. No American film has ever been populated by characters who talk like this; their singsongy, eager-to-please chitchat contrasts with the succession of thoughtlessly amoral crimes, so that the pervasive sense of gruesome surrealism reaches dizzying heights.

Even the Coens' most sordid events are shot through with bitterly dark humour; *Fargo*, in its comic recapitulation of woefully misguided real-life deeds one-ups the spiky *To Die For* in its wayward hilarity. But every laugh, however genuine, shortly gives way to a rueful awareness of how shortsighted, stupid, and heartless the majority of the Coens' characters are, a grim assessment counterweighted only by the persistent goodness of Chief Gunderson.

The Coens have never achieved such balance in their work before, have never been able to so coherently harness and contain their diverse artistic impulses to the service of one story. By emerging out of their heads to tackle a nonfiction story, even something as bizarre as this case, by returning to their roots, however strange they are, the Coens have made their best film to date.

JOEL AND ETHAN COEN

BY PETER BISKIND

The Coen Brothers – writer-director Joel and writer-producer Ethan – have pulled off the ultimate balancing act. Despite having their movies financed and distributed by major studios, they have somehow managed to remain true independents, never giving up on their own fiercely idiosyncratic vision. From their startling *noir* debut, *Blood Simple*, to the sumptuous *Hudsucker Proxy*, all of the Coens' films have revealed their distinctive stamp: a determined rejection of commercial cliches; a cold yet flamboyant visual style; unforgiving characterisations conceived in a lush stew of crisp dialogue; the casting of remarkable character actors – John Turturro, M. Emmet Walsh, Steve Buscemi – who have since become neo-*noir* totems. (Though their movies are unique, the brothers themselves are at times indistinguishable; we had to ask for their help in order to identify who had said what on tape.) Their latest work, *Fargo*, is the true-life tale of a Minneapolis car dealer who arranges his wife's kidnapping in order to collect the ransom, and stars Frances McDormand as the pregnant cop trying to solve the case. It is a perfectly realised gem of a movie, deceptive in its modesty.

First, a burning question. You pepper your movies with in-jokes, like your so-called British editor, Roderick Jaynes, who supposedly wrote the introduction to the published scripts **Barton Fink** *&* **Miller's Crossing**. *He's obviously a fiction.*
JOEL: We sort of imagined him, just for the purpose of the introduction, as a bitter old English guy. Some television station in Sussex tried to look him up.
ETHAN: They weren't able to find him.
JOEL: They were horrified to learn that he didn't actually exist.
And the Joel Silver "interview" included with the **Hudsucker Proxy** *script?*
ETHAN: People also believed that one, which always surprised me.
You have a reputation for storyboarding so thoroughly and directing with such an iron hand that I imagine your films are relatively easy to put together.
JOEL: No, things always change while we're rehearsing and shooting. But having said that, we probably deviate less from the script than most people do.
ETHAN: Also, just in regard to storyboards – either we've become more relaxed or lazier, but if it's a really straightforward scene, we don't bother anymore.
It feels as if **Fargo** *was an effort to go back to basics – no stars, low budget, re-strained.* **The Hudsucker Proxy** *was such a big film; word was it cost $40 million. Is that true?*
JOEL: It cost $25 to $26 million. *Variety* said it was a $40 million movie. I have no idea where they get this stuff.
What did it gross?
ETHAN: Nothing. [Laughs] In the United States it was literally nothing. I mean –
JOEL: About three million dollars.

Three million dollars?

ETHAN: Yeah. Warner's lost a lot money. PolyGram, who had it overseas, probably broke even, at least.

JOEL: Still, Warner's investment was only thirteen million dollars, which was no big deal for them.

ETHAN: That's why they basically left us alone. They were more worried about their $40 and $60 million blockbusters.

JOEL: They were really good to us, actually.

How so?

JOEL: [Warner Bros. co-chairman] Terry Semel didn't repossess Ethan's car.

I've always felt you guys had an exemplary career, in that you've managed to make the movies you've wanted to make and did it within the system.

ETHAN: I think largely it's because the movies have been cheap.

JOEL: Other people make a $40 million movie as their second movie, and if that doesn't fly . . . We've kept the commercial expectations low. [Laughs] The fact of the matter is, the international film community is willing to finance movies that are a little bit out of the mainstream, as long as you're not spending tens and tens of millions of dollars on them, and we've always recognized that.

What was the biggest budget you'd had before **Hudsucker**?

JOEL: *Miller's Crossing*, which was about $10 million. *Hudsucker* was more than double that.

ETHAN: And triple what we had spent on the previous movie, *Barton Fink*.

What did **Barton Fink** *make?*

JOEL: Not much here, but overseas . . .

ETHAN: It did very well in Europe. Except for *Raising Arizona*, all of our movies have done better overseas.

Are you cult figures in Europe?

JOEL: I guess the answer is yes, to an extent. Ethan is a god in Liechtenstein.

Was the failure of **Hudsucker** *a traumatic event for you? Or was it more like, Oh, we'll just go back and do what we were doing?*

JOEL: Well, here's the thing: *Hudsucker* was a movie that required a fairly substantial budget, because the production dictated a certain style – big sets, special effects, that kind of thing. But on the other hand, if it had never happened, it wouldn't have upset us. We would have gone and done *Fargo* or something. So that's why I don't think it's quite accurate to say that we worked our way up to a big budget. It's nice to have that option if you want to. I guess we're lucky in that it doesn't bother us to make cheap movies.

ETHAN: We have a lot of half-written scripts and ideas for movies and some of them need money and some of them don't.

Yeah, but losing money for a studio never helps you, careerwise.

ETHAN: That's true, in the sense that it narrows your options. And that's certainly regrettable and it disappointed us.

JOEL & ETHAN COEN: BLOOD SIBLINGS

*You grew up in Minneapolis. Does **Fargo** have any autobiographical resonance?*

ETHAN: No, it doesn't, except that we're familiar with the people there, and sometimes the way we approach the writing of something is through the dialogue and the rhythm of the speech. That flat, Midwestern effect was what was interesting to us about this script.

JOEL: That sort of goes with the slate sky and flat snowscape. Everything is white, just an empty field of vision. One of the things we talked about with Roger Deakins, the director of photography, was the idea of not being able to see where the horizon line is, where the land ends and the sky begins. Originally, we were talking about doing shots that looked down from a high place that appeared to be almost the same as shots that looked up.

The script was based on a true incident?

JOEL: Yeah. We've always been interested in kidnapping. And we wanted to do something that was unlike the movies we had done in the past, which were all sort of self-consciously artificial. We wanted to try something based on a real story, and tell it in a way that was very pared down. That's the reason for a lot less camera movement and the one-shot scenes, to give it a more observational kind of style.

How close was the script to the actual event?

ETHAN: Pretty close.

Why have you always been interested in kidnapping?

JOEL: I don't know why. But we have. Like *Raising Arizona*. We also have a whole other script that is all about kidnapping.

*What is the significance of the Korean character in **Fargo** who wants an old-friends reunion with Marge [Frances McDormand], then pulls the wool over her eyes? His story doesn't go anywhere.*

ETHAN: That's the nice thing about doing this kind of movie. You can wander around and the audience doesn't expect the architecture that they expect from that made-up story. It can seem more random. We were sort of experimenting with naturalism.

JOEL: If you make it up, the characters have to have some big confrontation at the end. A lot of the movie is about what Marge sees, or what she can see, and it's just another strange thing that she runs into without expecting it.

It's part of her education. Things are not what they seem. Speaking of which, is Fran – like Marge – actually pregnant? Or is that Digital Domain?

JOEL: Yeah, it's a "Digital Domain" pregnancy.

ETHAN: That would have been a $49 million movie – "Sorry ma'am, but we've gotten your X rays back and it's only a digital pregnancy."

A question for all the Coenheads on the Internet: What is that Prince-like symbol, the smiley face on its side, in the end credits?

ETHAN: That was our storyboard artist, who played the guy who drives by in the car with the red parka. He asked us if he could have the credit. We also use a lot of names of people we grew up with, scattered throughout the movie, being paged on telephones. But that's mostly because we couldn't think of names that would be appropriate.

Some people will say that your attitude toward the characters is condescending. Everyone's a shmuck except for Marge.

JOEL: Well, we do hear that a lot – that we're poking fun at people in the Midwest or in Texas or in the Southwest or wherever the hell it is. I don't know what to say.

ETHAN: What *are* you gonna say, smart guy?

JOEL: It's a fundamental misperception, the charge of condescension. Because the only people who can really answer this is us, and we feel very affectionate toward all of these characters. You create them, and sometimes the more shmucky they are, the more you like them. It's a strange kind of –

ETHAN: You know what it is? It's connected to something else, which is that a lot of people feel uncomfortable with laughing at horrible situations. They think if you're laughing at a character, somehow you're condescending to them. And that also makes them uncomfortable.

JOEL: Right – "Am I permitted to find this funny?"

ETHAN: We don't give cues about how you're supposed to react. That's just boring Hollywood filmmaking, where you give clear cues for what everyone's supposed to be feeling and how everything's supposed to be taken.

JOEL: Our movies certainly do piss people off. You get weird reactions. The hostility always puzzles me, always seems a little shocking to me. I'll tell you what else puzzles me, while we are on the subject: the perception that our movies are parodies, which I have never understood. People will say, "This movie is a parody of a gangster movie," when it was never our intention to parody the genre.

They're not parodies in the sense that the Zucker-brothers movies, like **Airplane!**, *are parodies. But some people don't get your movies – don't feel in on the joke, don't understand them. Your movies make them feel stupid. Does that bother you?*

ETHAN: It is true that they don't know how to take them.

Why is that?

JOEL: I don't know. It's puzzling to me. I mean, on our own terms we are just trying to tell an interesting story with interesting characters, and beyond that there is nothing to understand. And yet, people don't know how to take them. That's a mystery to me.

What do you think people in your hometown will make of **Fargo?**

ETHAN: It'll probably be the same as anywhere else. The people who are inclined to be offended will be, no matter where they're from.

What's your collaborative method like?

JOEL: Well, you know, we just sit around a room and toss ideas back and forth.

ETHAN: Collaboration between writers on scripts falls generally into two camps. Ours is an ongoing, moment-to-moment collaboration, as opposed to, "You take this scene and I'll take that scene", splitting it up and then trying to put it together again.

JOEL & ETHAN COEN: BLOOD SIBLINGS

Do you ever have fights?

JOEL: Yeah, there are disagreements; they get argued out. There aren't fights. Not because we always agree or have the same point of view, but because the movies we do reflect both of our interests and points of view.

ETHAN: The reality is, most of the time *any* ideas are welcome. Just knowing what you are going to do next. I can't think of a time when we've both been so full of articulated ideas that we both came up with alternatives that we disagreed about.

How did it happen that Joel became the director, Ethan the producer? Ethan, have you ever wanted to direct?

ETHAN: Well, the truth is that we both direct.

JOEL: Yeah, our real working method is looser than the titles suggest.

ETHAN: It's just an extension of writing. We just keep talking and keep working out in detail what we've been talking about since we started writing.

So in what sense does Ethan produce?

ETHAN: Well, again, Joel share this. We both decide where we're going to go for the money.

JOEL: It's not like I say, "I have to have the crane", and Ethan says, "It's gonna be too much money." We're both aware of what the crane means in the financial sense.

So what do you guys make of the Quentin Tarantino phenomenon?

JOEL: I liked *Pulp Fiction*.

In a way, **Blood Simple** *kicked off the whole thing –* **Tarantino, The Usual Suspects, Things to Do in Denver When You're Dead.**

JOEL: *Blood Simple* came out of very specific things, like an affection for horror movies, which we were working on at the time. But we didn't want to do a horror movie, and we were also very drawn to *film noir*, but also to pulp fiction, like James M. Cain. It was those elements in our minds that sort of came together in the movie and made it whatever it is. *Usual Suspects* seems to be coming from somewhere else, some other tradition, in a way.

The guys who've really made it big, like Quentin and Spike Lee, revel in publicity.

JOEL: They are performers. Neither of us would ever be in one of our movies.

So what's your next picture?

ETHAN: We don't know actually. We've accumulated a lot of half-finished things. We'll either go back to one of those or write another. But we usually don't even start thinking about something until we've put the previous movie to bed. We can't chew gum and write at the same time.

HELL FREEZES OVER

BY LIZZIE FRANCKE

"**C**old" is a word the film-making Coen brothers know only too well: it's a frequent description of their ludic, ironic approach to cinema, and the detached precision with which they unravel their stories. *Blood Simple*, their 1983 debut, may have been set in an arid Texan landscape, where temperatures soared and ceiling fans and flies buzzed in the background, but it was a chilly twist on the standard contract-killer tale. Its array of lost characters short-fused in lurid fashion, while pale corpses stirred to life most unnaturally before becoming maggot-chow. 1990's *Miller's Crossing* was an excavation of the Thirties gangster genre (whether as construed in the black-and-white Warner Bros. movies or on the inky dark pages of James M. Cain and Dashiell Hammett). Cleverly plotted, it delighted to tease audiences with smart but often bafflingly abstract allusions: surely signs of an erudite but clinical sensibility at work? 1991's *Barton Fink*, set in Forties Hollywood, wound its story round that ultimate nightmare, the writer's block. It provided a glimpse of a clammy hell – which might not actually freeze over, but could at least nurture a substantial layer of mould. And in their

The wounded Gaear Grimsrud (Peter Stormare) crawls for it, with Police Chief Marge and a moral lecture on the futility of his crimes just a little way behind.

latest film, the elliptically titled *Fargo*, the coldness simply sweeps into the frame. The Minnesota-born brothers come home to the icy wastelands of the American north Midwest, with its Scandinavian influence. This vast *tabula rasa* of a blizzard-blasted landscape is the bleak backdrop to a story of a faked but botched kidnapping, apparently based on fact. As the prologue explains, "This is a true story. The events depicted in this film took place in Minnesota in 1987. At the request of the survivors, the names have been changed. Out of respect for the dead, the rest has been told exactly as it occurred." Except there's also the usual disclaimer: "No similarity to actual persons, living or dead, is intended or should be inferred." So snag yourself on that paradox, or leave it aside – the red roll-mop herring in the smorgasbord – as the Coens unfurl a defiantly moral tale. Jerry Lundegaard (William H, Macy, best known as Dr Morgenstern in *ER*) is a shiny-suited car salesman whose dangerously inept ideas about improving his finances lead to a high bodycount rather than a healthy bank account, after he hires Carl Showalter and Gaear Grimsrud (Steve Buscemi and Peter Stormare as a sadistic Abbott-and-Costello team) to abduct his wife Jean (Kristin Rudrüd). But while the usual mordant Coen humour is much in evidence, one can (perversely, amid all the snow) discern a thawing out. The brothers demonstrate a wry, teasing affection for the community that they grew up in, and *Fargo* is almost warm in its depiction of this Siberian-looking patch of the United States, with its strangely unlikely town–names (Brainerd). Nor is this just jesting play any longer. The film has a melancholic gravitas to it, enhanced by a rolling Carter Burwell score that gives Bernard Herrmann-style plaintiveness a Scandinavian lilt. Ethnically it is specific: so much so that audiences used to cinema's all-purpose Middle America may find the inhabitants of *Fargo* quite exotic, with their singing, Scand-inflected accents, punctuating all sentences with a "yah" or two (a genuine patois, if strange to foreign ears). But clearly these "Fargoese" are not just weird specimens to be scrutinised: the Coens' intricate sense of characterisation puts an eccentric spin on them. And by creating Marge Gunderson, the pregnant police chief who takes charge of the case (Frances McDormand – like Buscemi a Coen brothers regular – is married to Joel), they give the film its solid and wise core. With her portly husband Norm (John Carroll Lynch), a wildlife painter with his eyes on a postage-stamp contract, she is the calm centre in the violent storm that erupts.

MARGE, THE PREGNANT COP

JOEL: Everyone is bulked-up, moving in a particular way, bouncing off people. That sponginess is part of the regional flavour. Marge's pregnancy means she's doubly bulked-up. She's of the region, but is capable, which other characters aren't. She wears a funny hat and walks funny, but is not a clown. We wanted her as far away as possible from the cliché cop. Marge and Jerry are both very banal, like the interiors and landscape. But she is banal in a good way, a good person where he is evil. We wanted to give them everyday concerns. Being pregnant: you can't get more ordinary. In movies you may not see them, but there are all kinds of pregnant cops.

PSYCHOLOGY OF A CAR SALESMAN

JOEL: Jerry is a car salesman – just like the real man – but a lot comes from Ethan's experience buying a car five years ago.

ETHAN: This scene revolves round the TruCoat Jerry is trying to sell. It is almost a verbatim transcript of my experience. We were interested in the psychology of a person who constructs those pyramid financial schemes but can't project themselves a minute into the future or imagine the consequences.

JOEL: Part of his being a car salesman was his imperviousness, sitting in a cubicle all day screwing people who scream at him. He is neat and tidy, not as we envisioned him. We imagined him a sloven, uncomfortable in his body, a little overweight. Casting Bill we went in the other direction. He is very put together, but tight and repressed.

ETHAN: Bill refused to do a single scene without this inane pin on his suit, in token of five years' service to car dealership.

SWEDISH FOOD, MID-WEST LIFE

ETHAN: Food was particularly important for Marge. She is always eating in the scenes with Norm.

JOEL: In Minnesota you have all these smorgasbords. These Swedish-style eat-all-you can deals were very much part of our childhood. Marge is pregnant, so she's eating for a reason, but it is also that peculiarly Middle-American thing about mounds of food. She wants to catch the killer, but nothing gets in the way of lunch. John (Norm) is from Minnesota, as are all the subsidiary parts, so they were speaking in their own accents. The Tyrone Guthrie theatre is in Minneapolis, with a huge pool of very talented actors.

THE KIDNAP SCENE

JOEL: It occurred to me, in retrospect, that this is the second movie that we have done about kidnapping – and we have another one lined up that centres on another kidnapping. A kidnapping is pregnant with dramatic possibilities – the conflicts, the high stakes, all the obvious drama and melodramatic things that are good movie fodder. One of my all time favourite movies is Kurosawa's *High and Low*. It is probably the best kidnapping movie ever made, about a shoe salesman in Osaka whose son is supposed to be kidnapped but they get the chauffeur's son. I don't know why kidnappings are so fascinating but they are.

CARL THE MOTORMOUTH

JOEL: We wrote the part of Carl specifically for Steve (as we wrote the parts of Marge for Fran, and Grim for Peter) because somehow it was appropriate that amongst all these second-generation Scandinavians, we had a real Scandinavian. This is the fourth movie that we have done with Steve – unfortunately we have always just had little parts for him in the past. We are aware of his [psychotic] persona in other movies and wanted to push that in a specific direction. We wanted to write something substantial because he is so good. We first cast him in *Miller's Crossing* because we were looking for someone who could talk incredibly fast. Carl's part is the most verbal in *Fargo* – he is the motormouth and maybe it is connected to that.

Carl Showalter (Coens regular Steve Buscemi), a man who talks a good fight but finds himself fatally out of his depth.

BETWEEN SNOW AND SKY

JOEL: The key thing about the exteriors was that we couldn't see the line between the sky and the snow. Up angles would be very similar to down angles: we wanted to have this void, blank, featureless look in which we put certain graphic details.

ETHAN: Steve is burying the ransom-money which is never recovered. Again this detail comes from the fact that it is based on real life. And in real life things happen, objects of big dramatic concern just fall by the wayside. It was interesting not to have to do a story where it was architecturally pleasing, and there was a unified narrative, but where things can come and go as they do.

JOEL: This is one of the few jokes in the movie. There are a lot of laughs but this was a joke as a joke – the fact that at this moment he checked from side to side in this ridiculously large, featureless, empty landscape to see if anyone was looking.

CLOSER TO LIFE THAN THE CONVENTIONS OF CINEMA

BY MICHEL CIMENT AND HUBERT NIOGRET

Was **Fargo** *inspired by a news item, as the press dossier claims, or have you invented a false trail?*

JOEL COEN: Generally speaking the movie is based on a real event, but the details of the story and the characters are invented. It didn't interest us to make a documentary film and we undertook no research on the nature or details of the murders. But, by telling the public that we took our inspiration from reality, we knew they wouldn't see the movie as just an ordinary thriller.

Did that kidnapping (of a woman, organised by her husband) have many repercussions back in 1987?

ETHAN COEN: No. In fact, it's astonishing how things of that nature receive so little publicity. We heard about it through a friend who lived near to where the drama took place in Minnesota, which is also the state we originate from.

Why have you called the film **Fargo** *when the main action is situated in Brainerd, which is a town in Minnesota?*

JOEL: *Fargo* seemed a more evocative title to us than Brainerd, that's the reason.

ETHAN: It's literally the sound of the word that we liked. There's no hidden meaning.

JOEL: There's a Western connotation, with Wells Fargo, but we didn't intend that, it's just something people have picked up on.

You return in a certain way to the territory of your first films, **Blood Simple** *and* **Raising Arizona.**

JOEL: There are resemblances, but important differences as well. These three movies are set on a small scale. They're about criminality and kidnapping and are very specific in their geographical location. Frances McDormand plays in both *Fargo* and *Blood Simple*. But we've always considered *Blood Simple* as belonging to the tradition of melodramatic novelists like James M. Cain, with an additional horror-movie influence. In *Fargo* we attempted a very different stylistic approach, tackling the subject in a very dry manner. We also wanted the camera to tell the story as an observer. The construction is tied to the original true story, but we allowed ourselves more meanders and digressions.

Each incident didn't necessarily have to be at the service of the plot. We even took the liberty of not introducing the heroine, Inspector Gunderson, until the middle of the movie.

ETHAN: It was also a way of telling the audience not to expect a genre movie. It's different from *Blood Simple*.

What have you brought to the subject?

JOEL: There were two or three things that interested us in relation to that incident. First it happened within an era and a region we were familiar with, which we could explore. Then it concerned a kidnapping, a type of event which has always fascinated us. In fact, we have another very different script on a kidnapping that we'd like to film. And finally there was the possibility to shoot a criminal movie with characters far removed from the stereotypes of the genre.

ETHAN: It's probably a subject we wouldn't have dealt with outside of that context. When we begin to write, we try to imagine very specifically the world in which the story unfolds. The difference is that, up until now, these were purely fictional universes, while in *Fargo* we needed you to be able to smell the place. As we were from the region, it helped us to understand how it might play within that milieu.

In the credits, was the function of "accent adviser" a joke?

ETHAN: No, not at all. Most of the actors came from the region and they had no need of advice, but Frances McDormand, Bill Macy and Harve Presnell needed coaching so that their accents harmonised with the others.

JOEL: The people there speak in a very economic way, if not monosyllabic. That seems as exotic to other Americans as it does to you in Europe! In fact, the Scandinavian influence on the culture of that region, the rhythm of the sentences, the accent, are not at all familiar to the rest of America: it might as well have happened on the moon! New Yorkers have a general conception of the Midwest, but they ignore all of those cultural "pockets", those microsocieties with their idiosyncrasies and peculiarities.

ETHAN: When we were small, we weren't really conscious of that Scandinavian heritage that marked the region so strongly because we had no points of comparison. It was only on arrival in New York that we were astonished there weren't more, like Gustafsons or Sondergaards. All the exoticism and strangeness of that region comes from the Nordic character, from its politeness and reservation. There's something Japanese in that refusal to show the least emotion, in that resistance to saying no! One of the comic wellsprings of the story comes from the conflict between that constant avoidance of all confrontation and the murders gradually piling up.

JOEL: We didn't have to do much research into that manner of speech, those expressions, the cadences were all familiar to us. Our parents still live in that region, so we go back there regularly and we know its culture. After all, it formed us as people. But not having lived there for a long time, we've the feeling of being half-divorced from the environment in which we grew up.

The episode featuring Marge and her old friend from school is a digression from the very tight central narrative.

ETHAN: Someone pointed out that in that scene Frances plays very withdrawn, like an Oriental, while her Japanese friend is voluble and irrational like a "typical" American. By creating that digression we really wanted to draw a contrast.

JOEL: We wanted to give another point of view of Frances' character without it being related to the police enquiry. That's also what happens in the scenes with her husband.

ETHAN: Our intention was to show the story had a relationship to life rather than to fiction, setting us free to create a scene that had no relationship to the plot.

The Hudsucker Proxy *was without doubt your most "theatrical" film. This one, as a contrast, is probably the least.*

JOEL: We wanted to make a new start from a stylistic point of view, to make something radically different from our previous movies. And the impetus was the previous movie, which was the most stylised of all. But, curiously, by starting from real events, we've arrived at another form of "stylisation". The results are maybe not as different as we'd envisaged!

A little like Kubrick with **Dr Strangelove**, *you begin with a quasi-documentary presentation, then gradually, with a cold humour, everything becomes dislocated and absurd.*

ETHAN: That comes partly from the nature of the story itself. There's a shot composed at the beginning that's modified later in the film, as the characters lose control.

JOEL: It's implicit in the construction of the narrative. When a character suggests to you, in the first scene, how things are going to happen, you know full well it's going to unfold very differently. The reference to Kubrick has been made before, but I understand it more now. There's a very formal side to his approach, as well as a steady progression from the commonplace towards the baroque.

How do you manage not to fall into caricature, which could overwhelm your work at any time?

JOEL: I suppose it's partly intuition about the tone, and it particularly depends on the actors' capacity to know how far they can go. There is, for instance, with Frances a very authentic manner, very open in presenting her character. It prevents Marge from becoming a parody of herself. Frances was very conscious of the dangers of excess, with that mannerism of dragging out words at the very end of each sentence.

ETHAN: It was a constant process of adjustment on set between the actors and us. They gave us a wide range of behaviour and mannerisms that we constantly discussed throughout the shooting.

JOEL: We work a lot with *feeling*. It's difficult to express through words why Marge, in the movie, is not a caricature but a real, three-dimensional person.

ETHAN: All we know is that, when we wrote the script and when the actors interpreted their roles, none of us thought of the story as a comedy.

JOEL: And that helped to make the characters comical and credible at the same time. The comedy wouldn't have worked if it had been played as comedy, rather than with sincerity.

The relationship between Marge and her husband is also very strange.

JOEL: We were seduced during casting by the very direct acting and impassive face of John Caroll Lynch, who seemed to us perfectly suited to the tone of the movie.

ETHAN: He totally personifies how undemonstrative people are in that place. The relationship with his wife is based on the unsaid, but they succeed in communicating somehow.

The end resembles a pastiche of the classic Hollywood "happy ending", with the wife and husband in bed symbolising a return to order and normality.

JOEL: It's true that it's a return to normality, but we didn't intend for it to be a parody! There was an article in the *New York Times*, where the journalist asked why the people of Minnesota didn't like the ending when it all turned out so well for them!

The only question mark at the end concerns the money. But wasn't the money the main component of the plot?

JOEL: All the men in the movie are preoccupied by money.

ETHAN: At the same time we didn't want to be too specific, for instance, concerning the nature of the debt contracted by Jerry. It was sufficient to understand that that character was trapped by engaging in something which turned out badly. Elsewhere, during the whole movie, Jerry is a poor lost soul who can't stop improvising solutions to get out of the situations he's already gotten himself into. He never stops trying everything, brimming over with activity. He's almost admirable in that respect!

JOEL: What interested us from the start in the William Macy character was his absolute incapacity, even for one minute, to project himself into the future and evaluate the consequences of his decisions. There's something fascinating in that total absence of perspective. He's one of those people who construct a pyramid without thinking for a moment that it could collapse.

Did writing the script take much time?

ETHAN: We began it before shooting *The Hudsucker Proxy*, then returned to it; so it's difficult to evaluate the time it took us. Two years have passed. What's certain is that the writing was easy and relatively quick, particularly in comparison with other scripts like *Miller's Crossing*.

Was it established from the start that the kidnapped woman wouldn't have any physical presence?

JOEL: Absolutely. And even at a certain point in the story, it was clear for us she would cease to be a person to those who'd kidnapped her. Besides, it was no longer the actress Kristin Rudrüd playing the part, but a double with a hood on her head. So, we weren't interested in the victim! And, it didn't seem at any point that the husband himself was at all preoccupied with what could happen to her! Carl, one of the kidnappers, didn't even know her name!

Did you choose Steve Buscemi for the role before thinking of Peter Stormare as the other kidnapper?

ETHAN: In fact, we wrote both roles for those actors. Likewise for Marge played by Frances McDormand. Peter's an old friend of ours and it seemed interesting, given his Swedish origins, to give him this part. Of course, his character is an *outsider* in relation to the milieu, but at the same time he maintains ethnic bonds with it.

How do you work with your musical composer Carter Burwell?

JOEL: He's been our collaborator since we started. Usually, he looks at the movie from the outset, from end to end, then he composes sketches on the synthesizer to give us an idea of the direction in which he intends to work. Before creating his score, he plays us bits on the piano, and we reflect together on their relationship to certain sequences of the movie. Then he moves onto the next stage.

ETHAN: In the case of this movie, the central theme is based on some popular Scandinavian music that Carter found for us.

JOEL: We often work with him that way. For *Miller's Crossing* the music came from an Irish folk theme which he orchestrated and added to it bits of his own composition. For *Raising Arizona* he used American popular music, with Holly Hunter singing a tune. On the other hand, for *Blood Simple* and *Barton Fink* he wrote all the music, without external inspiration. With *The Hudsucker Proxy* it was different again, a mixture of original compositions by Carter and bits from Khachaturian.

ETHAN: When he's orchestrated his score we go into the studio with him for the recording. For the last two movies, he conducted the orchestra himself. As the movie's projected while he works, he can modify the score as he goes along. Our entire collaboration lasts a maximum of two or three months.

How long did the editing take you?

JOEL: Twelve weeks. Which is short for us because normally we take longer, as we don't begin editing while we're shooting.

JOEL & ETHAN COEN: BLOOD SIBLINGS

Did the photography pose any particular problems?

JOEL: It was simpler than for the other movies. We discussed it at length with Roger Deakins because we wanted to do a lot of shots without coverage. At the start we decided to have only fixed shots.

ETHAN: Then we realised that "purist" attitude was a little stupid.

JOEL: We made some adjustments by sometimes moving the camera, but in such a way that the audience doesn't notice. We didn't want to make the camerawork as stylised as we'd done in the past, because we didn't want to emphasise the action, to make it too dramatic or crazy.

ETHAN: Roger Deakins worked with a camera operator whereas before he's mainly been his own cameraman, including on the two movies he photographed for us. This time he didn't take everything in hand, although he often took control of the framing. On *Fargo* we'd had problems with the weather because we needed the snow, but the winter when we shot was particularly soft and dry. We had to work in Minneapolis with artificial snow. Then, as the snow hadn't yet fallen, we went to North Dakota for the end of the shoot, the big exterior scenes. We had what we wanted there: a covered sky, no direct sunlight, no line on the horizon, and a light that was neutral, diffused.

JOEL: These landscapes were really dramatic and oppressive. There were no mountains, no forests, only flat, desolate stretches of land. It's just what we wanted to convey on the screen.

Do you often put your eye to the camera?

JOEL: On the first movie we made with Roger Deakins, *Barton Fink*, we constantly looked in the viewfinder. On *Hudsucker Proxy*, less. And even less on *Fargo*. That's undoubtedly due to the material and the different visual approach to each movie, but also to the growing affinity with our cinematographer. He understood our intentions more and more and we trusted him more and more. When we work regularly with a collaborator, a kind of telepathic language is established. I also think Roger enjoys working with people like us who have an active interest in lighting, rather than with filmmakers who rely entirely on him.

There's a contradiction between the press package, which attributes the editing to you, and the credits, which list a certain Roderick Jaynes.

JOEL: When we assemble the movie ourselves, we use the pseudonym Roderick Jaynes. We prefer to lend a hand rather than be seated beside someone and tell them what to cut. It seems easier to us. Besides, we're both in the cutting room. When we work together we obviously don't get that feeling of isolation that others sometimes feel. On *Barton Fink* and *Blood Simple*, we were our own editor. On the other movies, we had an editor but we'd still be in the editing room whenever we could. If we've occasionally called in Tom Noble or Michael Miller, it's because the cutting had to begin during shooting.

Your films take place in New Orleans, New York, Hollywood, in the West and Midwest. It seems you like to explore the geography of America.

JOEL: We'd like to shoot elsewhere, but, strangely, the subjects that come to mind are always situated in America. That's what seems to attract us.

ETHAN: It always seems that the world in which our stories take place is connected to us, however remotely. In the case of *Fargo*, the bond was much tighter, of course.

JOEL: We need an intimate knowledge of the subject or at least an emotional relationship with it; at the same time, it only interests us if it's kind of exotic in some way! Minnesota, for example, we know very well, but not the characters who people *Fargo* and their type of behaviour. Or again, in the case of *Barton Fink* and *Miller's Crossing*, the exoticism comes from the temporal distance.

*What are your relationships with the characters in **Fargo** who, for the most part, are a little deficient?*

JOEL: We like all of them, perhaps most of all the simple ones!

ETHAN: One of the reasons for making them simple-minded was our desire to go against the Hollywood cliché of the bad guy as a super-professional who controls everything he does. In fact, in most cases criminals belong to the strata of society least equipped to face life, and that's the reason they're caught so often. In this sense too, our movie is closer to life than the conventions of cinema and genre movies.

JOEL: We're often asked how we inject comedy into the material. But it seems to us that it's present in life. Look at those people who recently blew up the World Trade Centre. They'd rented a van to prepare the explosion, and, once the job was finished, they returned to the rental agency to reclaim their deposit. The absurdity of that is, in itself, terribly funny.

What are your current projects?

ETHAN: At this moment we're preparing two scripts without knowing which will be finished first, or which will be financed first.

JOEL: One of them concerns another kidnapping, but in a very different manner. And the other's a kind of *film noir* about a barber in Northern California at the end of the Forties.

Translated by Paul Buck and Catherine Petit. Interview conducted in Cannes on 16 May 1996.

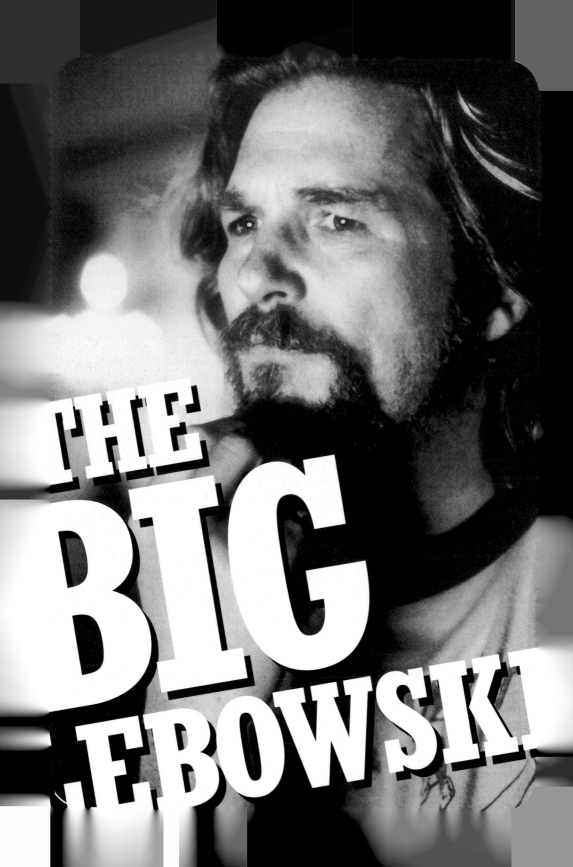

THE BIG LEBOWSKI

BY MIKE GOODRIDGE

The Coen brothers' follow-up to *Fargo* moves from wintry Minnesota to sun-baked LA, but it mines the same vein of American kitsch. Required viewing for the core crowd, it will leave the broader audience scratching their scalps. International response will mirror the domestic situation.

A millionaire in a wheelchair with a missing trophy wife, a ransom note attached to a lacquered toe, an estranged stepdaughter with a taste for slumming it, various gangs of brutes: into this *noir* landscape wanders not some Sam Spade but the Dude (Bridges), a good-for-nothing with a taste for white Russian cocktails and bowling. He is unexceptional in every way except for sharing the surname of the titular millionaire.

The Dude (Jeff Bridges – left) and Walter Sobchak (John Goodman) –
possibly L.A.'s two unlikeliest ever detective-heroes.

The satire is non-stop and multi-layered – in applying the finest filmmaking techniques and effects to the portrayal of the American bowling alley, the Coens are poking as much fun at studio portentousness – but it is unalloyed.

The Coen brothers' own particular genius lies in creating convincing yet improbable characters (Bridges' Dude is a match for Frances McDormand's Margie) but in this case the story is subservient to the images.

THE BROTHERS GRIM

BY ANDY LOWE

How do you cope with dual interviews?

ETHAN COEN: Fine. But we're much happier with the anal, film-geek types. It's also a lot easier in Europe with you guys. In the States, the mainstream press tend to poke around for . . . something else. They're not really interested in the two-way brother thing.

They want something scurrilous.

ETHAN: Yeah. Well, mostly, not even necessarily scurrilous. Something . . . warm and sweet normally makes them just as happy. But definitely something personal.

I'll try to stick to anal, textual film questions, then.

ETHAN: Okay. Good.

The bad guys in **The Big Lebowski** *are rather feeble German nihilist-pornographers. Why German? Why nihilist?*

JOEL COEN: Well, we're obviously not saying that all Germans are nihilists. We're saying that those particular Germans are nihilists. With John Goodman's character being so rabidly Jewish, it just sort of worked with that. And it also worked with the whole techno-pop thing. It was a function of the music we associated with the various characters. We are always looking to make characters geographically or sociologically or ethnically as specific as we possibly can. The more specific they are, the easier it is to develop them and make them more interesting for ourselves and for the audience. But people miss that, and they sometimes mistakenly extrapolate it into some grand statement about that region.

Your films do tend to get analysed to death. I found a tortuous breakdown of **Barton Fink** *on the Internet: the hotel represents Hell, John Goodman represents The Common Man, and the whole film is apparently a parable about the natural allure of fascism for The Common Man . . .*

ETHAN: Yeah. It's a weird impulse when people feel the need to read things as code – and very specific code, at that.

JOEL: We never, ever go into our films with anything like that in mind. There's never anything approaching that kind of specific intellectual breakdown. It's always a bunch of instinctive things that feel right, for whatever reason. A good example from *Barton Fink* is the two cops who come to interview Barton – if you watch it, one's kind of German and the other . . . well, we just wanted them to be representative of the Axis world powers at the time. It just seemed kind of amusing. It's a tease. All that stuff with Charlie – the "Heil Hitler!" business – sure, it's all there, but it's kind of a tease. We're definitely guilty of teasing.

ETHAN: America is extremely sensitive to ethnicity. A lot of people picked us up on the head of the studio in *Barton Fink* being Jewish. But . . . most studio heads *are* Jewish! What's the problem?

JOEL: There was a critic in the US who complained about that scene in *Miller's Crossing* where Bernie [John Turturro] is taken out into the woods and shot. He said that it was much too reminiscent of the genocide of the Jews in Europe. Well . . . I guess that's the risk you run by being so specific with your characters.

John Turturro can do them all, though. Italians, Jews, Mexicans . . .
JOEL: Yeah, John does get cast in a lot of those parts. He's very specifically ethnic, but it's very hard to tell . . . which one.

You've made your Texas, New York and Minnesota movies. Did you specifically want to make **The Big Lebowski** *your LA movie?*
ETHAN: Oh yeah. Definitely. It was conceived that way, in as much as all the characters are pretty much emblematic of Los Angeles – they're all types who seem like people you would meet there. But the LA thing is also connected to the fact that very consciously a Raymond Chandler thing – a sort of wandering intrigue which explores different parts of the city, through the characters.
JOEL: I've never had a chance to develop much of a relationship with LA. I'm always a tourist there. Happily, it is possible to make movies and not live in LA. But it was definitely Chandler's novels that inspired *The Big Lebowski* – in terms of its story and setting.

How familiar are you with the kind of people who inhabit your films? The earthy inhabitants of **Fargo** *are totally different from the more exotic characters who populate* **The Big Lebowski.**
ETHAN: Well, a couple of the characters in *The Big Lebowski* are, very loosely, inspired by real people. We know a guy who's a middle-aged hippy pothead, and another who's a Vietnam vet who's totally defined by, and obsessed with, the time he spent in Vietnam. We find it interesting for our characters to be products of the Sixties in some way, but set in the Nineties.

Did you have an urge to realise the cinematic potential of bowling?
ETHAN: Oh yeah. The guy who the Walter character is based on is an avid member of, and consequently obsessed with, an amateur softball league team in LA. But we changed it to bowling, because it's more interesting, visually. All of the stuff associated with bowling – y'know, the architecture, the machines, it's all sort of retro to the Fifties and Sixties. Classic bowling design era – you see it all over LA.

There's also a pre-set character type associated with bowling.
JOEL: Yeah. That fitted in well with the layabout Dude guy.
ETHAN: But you mean the slobby aspects of it, the male thing. Men getting together with their little leagues . . . and it is, in a strange way, kind of a buddy movie.

The English equivalent would be darts.
JOEL: Yeah. It's the same thing, really – big guys with their stomachs hanging out, drinking.
ETHAN: It's not really a physically taxing thing. You can be a slob and do it.

You give the impression that most of humanity is either moronic or mad, and both types come up in the two main **Big Lebowski** *characters.*
JOEL: Well, it's one thing making up stories, and quite another having a conception of the human race. One doesn't necessarily have anything to do with the other. But it is true, most of the characters in our movies are pretty unpleasant – losers or lunkheads, or both. But we're also very fond of those characters, because you don't usually see movies based around those kind of people. We're not interested in burly superhero types.

A big criticism that's been levelled at your pictures is that they're all technique and no heart.
ETHAN: Well, the process of writing a story is different from the business of how the characters behave or how they interact.
JOEL: *Lebowski* is a good example. The story, if you reduced it to the plot, would seem rather ridiculous or uninteresting. And it's the same with a lot of Chandler – the plots are there to drive the characters.

Why was **The Hudsucker Proxy** *such a flop?*
JOEL: I dunno, why was *Fargo* not a flop? Most people don't like *Hudsucker*, and I don't know the reason. It's as much of a mystery to me that people went to see *Fargo*, which was something we did thinking, ah, y'know, about three people will end up seeing it, but it'll be fun for us . . .

How do you work together? Is it essential that you produce and direct your own scripts? Would you consider developing someone else's script?
JOEL: We both re-write together, we're both out there on the set and in the editing room together. There are no creative tantrums. We just consider ourselves extremely lucky that, so far, we've been able to do our own scripts. It's not that we are philosophically opposed to the idea of working on someone else's material, but I think it would be difficult, because, for us, so much of the process starts with imagining the story. I think it would feel strange and very different to the modification process that we're used to. We just haven't found anything so far that's more interesting than what we've been writing or working on ourselves.

You seem to be very interested in crass, venal men who spend most of their time sitting behind desks. Do you have a lot of personal experience of these people?
JOEL: Yeah. That's true! No, we haven't had a lot of experience of them, but it is absolutely true that we're interested in crass, venal men behind desks. There's Sidney Mussberger in

Hudsucker, M. Emmet Walsh in *Blood Simple*, Jack Lipnick in *Barton Fink*, Arizona in *Raising Arizona* . . . I guess even Bill Macy in *Fargo* . . .

ETHAN: Waring Hudsucker – maybe. Although you can't really call it a desk. Maybe a threshold.

Is it true that you wait to make a film until your ideal cast is available?

JOEL: It was true with *Lebowski*, which was largely written before *Fargo*. We tried to get it together, and we held the Walter part for John Goodman until he'd finished with *Roseanne*. Jeff Bridges, too, although we didn't write only with him in mind. It varies. With *Fargo*, we wrote for Frances McDormand, Peter Stormare and Steve Buscemi.

What Hollywood films have you seen recently?

ETHAN: I liked *Starship Troopers*. Really funny. It was pretty bold that he went in on a $100 million movie with no stars.

JOEL: *Bound* was good. A lot of people said it was a "Coen brothers kind of movie". I don't know about that, but it was fun, I liked it.

ETHAN: *LA Confidential*. That was . . . okay.

Is mainstream Hollywood all out of ideas?

JOEL: Well, I think a lot of good, interesting movies still get made. It's just like any other aspect of popular entertainment – the majority of the stuff isn't going to be particularly good. It's the same with music, books . . . most of it is naturally going to be dull. Movies – especially Hollywood movies – are an easy American whipping boy, because it is true that most of it is shit. But it's not surprising. It's more a natural by-product of a healthy, extremely productive industry.

You took the Palme D'Or for **Barton Fink** *and the two Oscars for* **Fargo***. Does winning awards thrill you?*

JOEL: Well, 1996 was kind of a flukey year.

ETHAN: Yeah, they didn't have any other important movies to give the awards to that year.

JOEL: We have an odd relationship with Hollywood. We've never really felt marginalised from them, except through our own choice – we don't live in LA, we don't develop stuff through the studios. We've always had pretty cordial relationships with studios – y'know, they've distributed and financed our movies.

ETHAN: But that's the nature of this business. Box-office success, awards – it's all very capricious, and never quite what you'd expect. But you tend to snatch your moment of favour.

There was word of **Fargo** *being adapted into a television show. Is that happening? Are you involved in any way?*

ETHAN: Someone had the idea that it could be turned into a series of one-hour shows, and that Marge could solve a different case each episode. I think they filmed a pilot, directed by Kathy Bates.

JOEL: We weren't really involved. I can't say that we weren't happy that it died.

You're working on an Elmore Leonard novel – the Western, Cuba Librae.
ETHAN: Yeah. But only as a writing job, not to do the movie itself.

You worked with Sam Raimi (director of the Evil Dead films) on Crimewave and The Hudsucker Proxy. Do you have any plans to work with him again?
JOEL: No plans, but I'm sure it'll happen one day. Last I heard, Sam was making a movie in Minnesota. Hmm . . .

What's the atmosphere like on a Coen Brothers movie set? How are you to work for?
ETHAN: As with all movie sets, the atmosphere is mostly incredibly tedious. Elementally chaotic, maybe, but, to an observer, it would seem like nothing was going on. And, mostly, they'd be right. There's a lot of time spent doing really exciting things like setting up lighting.

JOEL: When the camera's running, you have to be very quiet and well-behaved. After the camera stops, you become a dictator. I think we're good to work for. It's more of a collegial kind of atmosphere. As you can imagine, given the fact that we do this together, we're essentially collaborative. We're just more comfortable working with people we're used to working with.

Can you think of a genre that you'll never get round to tackling? Sci-fi, perhaps?
JOEL: I'd like to do a Western.

ETHAN: I don't know much about sci-fi, so . . . I think outer space is maybe a little too sterilised, even for us. We thought of doing an American version of *The Odyssey*, with a guy escaping from a chain gang, finding his way home.

JOEL: That would be generically closer to what we've done a lot of. Y'know – a Southern hayseed movie.

So what's coming up next?
ETHAN: Our big thing at the moment is something set in California in the late Forties – we're working on the script now. It's basically the Bob Crane story. Bob Crane was the guy who played Hogan in *Hogan's Heroes*, which was a sitcom about American prisoners of war in Germany. Bob Crane was a guy who enjoyed playing the drums in topless bars, and watching and appearing in porn movies. He was murdered in Arizona years later, while being interviewed there by a guy who had installed lots of secret video equipment in order to tape himself in . . . certain sexual situations [Crane was bludgeoned repeatedly with a camera tripod and a video cable was tied round his neck]. I think it would be an interesting cautionary tale about Hollywood, sort of a companion piece to *Barton Fink*.

THE LOGIC OF SOFT DRUGS

BY MICHEL CIMENT AND HUBERT NIOGRET

Since **Raising Arizona,** *we've seen lots of twisted and eccentric characters in your films, but probably never in such great number as in* **The Big Lebowski!**

ETHAN COEN: That's true, you have the feeling you're attending a congress of misfits! Of all the participants, [John] Turturro is undoubtedly the strangest. I was just talking about that relationship with *Raising Arizona* with Joel yesterday. Perhaps it comes from all those secondary and tangential characters who drift in and out of the movie and are all bizarre in their own way.

One also has the idea that **The Big Lebowski** *is made in opposition to* **Fargo:** *an almost anarchic freedom facing a logical rigour, the heat of California after the coldness of Minnesota. You appear to take the same starting point situation, a kidnapping, then re-shuffle the cards.*

ETHAN: For us it was above and beyond all else a Californian story. We even drew loose inspiration from a Chandler plot outline. All his novels, or almost all, are situated in Los Angeles. We have to admit we like to do variations on a dramatic situation like kidnapping, which you can also find in *Raising Arizona*. You could also say that there's a certain logic in *The Big Lebowski*, but it'd be the logic induced by soft drugs!

JOEL COEN: The logic here is more episodic – like in a Chandler novel, the hero sets out to clear up a mystery and while doing so visits a lot of odd characters who spring up like Jack-in-the-boxes.

How did you construct that world populated with bizarre people?

ETHAN: We bore in mind Chandler's pattern, a story like *The Big Sleep*. We had a millionaire in Pasadena and, as so often with his novels, a mature and sophisticated woman, Maude, played by Julianne Moore, and a licentious and depraved girl, Bunny, played by Tara Reid. The main character is often involved in a romantic sub-plot with the first type of woman.

JOEL: But, of course, it's not a private eye movie. We wanted to use those conventions, but without being too literal.

ETHAN: We took models when they were convenient. For instance, in Chandler there are suave night-club owners like Jackie Treehorn, played by Ben Gazzara. He looks like Norris in *The Big Sleep*.

JOEL: Of course, one of the gags of the movie is that Jeff Bridges is involved in a private eye adventure, while he's the antithesis of that. His character, by the way, like

John Goodman's, is loosely inspired by real people. One is known by us, the other we heard about. Walter Sobchak [Goodman] is more of a composite of different people.

It's your second film set in Los Angeles. The first, **Barton Fink,** *evoked Hollywood, while this one has as its background a different kind of LA*

JOEL: We live in New York and we like LA, but we always feel like *outsiders* there. It's a fascinating enough place to entice us to shoot two movies there. In *The Big Lebowski* it's a more marginal Los Angeles – Venice Beach, the Valley, Pasadena – which, in people's minds, isn't really part of the city. The cultures in Los Angeles are more isolated from each other than in New York because of that huge surface spread. All of those sub-cultures are juxtaposed without really communicating. But, in fact, there's as much diversity as in New York.

ETHAN: The main difference lies in the characters. You wouldn't expect to meet the Dude or Walter in New York. First, they wear shorts! It's a totally informal city. You don't see the chief of police at any point, but he's probably wearing shorts too! The scene in the house with the guy who's a television scriptwriter, who's been inspired by a real-life event, couldn't be transported to a New York suburb and still stay in tune.

JOEL: The idle, laid-back, jobless character played by Jeff Bridges, who seems to live in slow motion, just seems typical to us of that local culture.

Bowling is in itself a subculture.

JOEL: It's pretty much an accident that it gained an important place in the story. One of the people who inspired Walter's character was part of an amateur softball team. We chose to make him into a bowling fanatic since that offered us more visual possibilities. The bowling culture was also important in reflecting that period at the end of the Fifties and the beginning of the Sixties. That suited the retro side of the movie, slightly anachronistic, which sent us back to a not-so-far away era, but one that was well and truly gone nevertheless. The action itself takes place at the beginning of the Nineties, but all the characters refer to the culture of thirty years ago, they are its aftermath and its mirror. Jeff Bridges is an aging hippie, John Goodman is defined by his Vietnam experience, while Maude (Julianne Moore) has for her blueprints the Sixties New York Fluxus artists like Yoko Ono before she met John Lennon, or Carol Schneeman, who literally threw herself into her projects for physical support. Maude owes her a lot! Ben Gazzara also echoes people like Hugh Hefner from that period. The difference from *Boogie Nights,* which represents the Seventies, or the new movie Todd Haynes has just shot, *Velvet Goldmine,* on rock stars like David Bowie in that same period, is that *The Big Lebowski* doesn't really take place in the past. It's a contemporary movie about what's become of people who were formed and defined by that earlier period.

Smokey (Jimmie Dale Gilmore – left) is warned by gun-toting Walter that he's entering a "world of pain", while the Dude and Donny (Steve Buscemi – centre) look on.

The voice-over of a character who we only see much later – which will also conclude the movie – is reminiscent of hearing popular legends of the Old West, as the narrator has a cowboy style.

ETHAN: In that specific case, I don't remember how the idea came to us. But we've always liked to create a certain distance that takes us away from reality by enclosing the story in a frame.

JOEL: The Stranger (Sam Elliott) is a little bit of an audience substitute. In the movie adaptations of Chandler it's the main character that speaks offscreen, but we didn't want to reproduce that though it obviously has echoes. It's as if someone was commenting on the plot from an all-seeing point of view. And at the same time rediscovering the old earthiness of a Mark Twain.

There's also a reference to Fargo via the girl with a Scandinavian name, Knudsen, who comes from Minnesota!

ETHAN: In fact, we'd more or less written that script before shooting *Fargo*. If there's a reference, it would actually be in reverse order, at least chronologically. We didn't specifically want to refer to *Fargo*, but it's true we'd been in Minnesota to check out the remote places that girl on the run might have come from.

Walter mirrors quite a few American archetypes: his memories of Vietnam, his violence, his relationship to women, his know-it-all claims . . .

ETHAN: And he's always right! That tough guy character presented great comic possibilities, above all if he was associated with the character of Jeff Bridges. They are obviously each other's stooges. Steve Buscemi wondered why his cretinous character made up a trio with those two! We thought about that: perhaps he's only there because he's the only one who can bowl well. For Walter, our model was one of our friends, a Vietnam veteran whose conversation always comes back to that war. There's also a bit of John Milius in that character: he's a great story-teller, but also a macho show-off, with the same concerns and the same obsessions.

Was the Dude the first protagonist you had in mind before writing the script?

ETHAN: The movie was conceived as pivoting around that relationship between the Dude and Walter. The idea sprang from the scenes between Barton Fink and Charlie Meadows, who was played by John Goodman. That's the reason why the bowling seemed an appropriate context: it's not that the sport isn't played by women, but they have their own teams. In bowling, there's a real segregation of the sexes. In *The Big Lebowski* you spend time exclusively in the company of men. The worlds of the private eye and the Western, which we refer to at the end of the movie, are also very masculine.

JOEL: The two women of the movie, Maude and Bunny, are minor characters and don't have big roles. This story is, in fact, that of a marriage, an odd couple formed by Jeff and John, their fluctuating relationship. There's often a *slow burn* in their confrontations, until John Goodman blows up.

The bowling scenes are very choreographed.

JOEL: The idea was to shoot those bowling rituals almost in slow motion. The credits sequence was conceived to make you enter that world and understand the importance of bowling to the movie.

There's a whole surrealist aspect in the visual ideas: the flying carpet, the naked man covered only with oak leaves, the beach party . . .

JOEL: The dreamlike sequences echo in one sense the hallucinations of the private eye in Chandler's novels. It's also to do with the marijuana consumption of the hero! For me that corresponds to Los Angeles, which is a more surreal place than New York. There's an Oriental side, a *1001 Arabian Nights* aspect to that city. You can't be more remote from a New York sensibility than in that beach party given by the pornographer. It's the world of the drugs consumer. And the sound of the bowling is also a narcotic for the Dude. In people's minds the hallucinatory psychedelic culture is associated with Southern California and San Francisco.

An image like that of the three red devils with their giant scissors, was it suggested by specific reminiscences?

JOEL: In a way we foreshadow that image with the picture showing scissors in a red field which hangs in Maude's loft.

ETHAN: We don't know specifically where we found our inspiration, but we knew the background had to be black. Nothing in particular influenced us. It was a synthesis of several ideas, including that of our costume designer Mary Zaphres. And, well, maybe Ingmar Bergman had something to do with it!

The choreography refers to Busby Berkeley.

JOEL: We always wanted to pay tribute to him, he's one of our heroes. He was an incredible choreographer who never worried about justifying his extravagance. His audacity and sense of freedom fascinate us. Frankly, it's very difficult to re-make that mixture of surprise and precision. We've even more admiration for him now after trying to imitate him!

ETHAN: Nobody can equal him because that would cost too much money. He had an abundance of resources and considerable rehearsal time to reach that state of perfection. We had 35 girls where he had 350.

Did you use a storyboard?

ETHAN: We were forced to for some shots that had to be composed on a computer, in particular where the Dude [Bridges] passes his head between the dancer's legs. It was very rigorous work.

The three nihilists are Germans. Do you think your movie could also be qualified as nihilistic? What is its moral point of view?

JOEL: Certainly not. For us, the nihilists are the bad guys, and, if there's a preferred moral position, it'd be that of Jeff Bridges, though it's difficult to define! In a curious way, you could say he has the moral code of the private eye. But, in his case, it's very fluid! What you can say with certainty is that the movie leads to a reconciliation between the Dude and Walter despite their difficult relationship. In a detective movie, there's a line of clear conduct, a much more solid spine, even if it's never explicit. That's not the case with the Dude.

ETHAN: It's also due to the fact that it's a comedy. In the detective movie, the protagonist leads a crusade after the death of his partner, for example, and he seeks the truth. He is a knight errant. The Dude wavers more at the surface of things. It's Walter who pushes him to undertake the venture, only to jeopardise it later.

As in a number of your films, the protagonist is like a prisoner in a revolving door from which he can't get out, and his life becomes a nightmare. But it's the first time you play on the confusion of identity where someone is mistaken for someone else.

ETHAN: That's not treated seriously, but it's true we were attracted by the idea that those two characters, the Dude and the Big Lebowski, who are so different, have meeting points.

JOEL: Here again, that nabob has been inspired by Chandler. You find him in *The Big Sleep*, and also in *The High Window*. He's a recurrent character, the domineering, all-powerful figure who becomes a catalyst. Chandler's novels cut across all the social classes of Los Angeles, and this character is at the top of the ladder. He represents Money. He appears in *Chinatown*, he's contributed to the town's construction. He symbolises an old order, which, in the end, you discover is all a sham.

You often mention Chandler. Are there any other crime writers you're attracted to?
JOEL: *Miller's Crossing* was certainly born from our desire to tell a story the Hammett way. But we also like James Cain a lot.

You add Jewish humour. But it's the first time you have had fun so openly with a Jewish character, Walter Sobchak.
ETHAN: It's true we've created Jewish characters before but we didn't make their Jewishness into a comic element.
JOEL: Our grandpa was very orthodox. He didn't drive his car on the Sabbath. I remember, as a child, that I found it weird he didn't want to light the cooker. That didn't seem such a big job to me! Our parents were religious, but not excessively so. When Grandpa paid us a visit during the Sabbath, my mother used subterfuges to make him believe we were obeying the law and refusing to do all that was forbidden. That's how we learned about acting!

The style of the photography in **Fargo** *is very clear-cut. How did you discuss the visual ideas for* **The Big Lebowski** *with Roger Deakins?*
JOEL: That's exactly the question Roger never stopped asking us, and I don't think we ever succeeded in answering it exactly! The difficulty for Roger was to juxtapose those stylised, dreamlike, abstract scenes with other very down-to-earth ones, like the place where the Dude lives, the scene at the end with the Stranger, not to mention the bowling alley. In that last case, the style of the photography was imposed by the fluorescent light on the ceiling. As always there's a link with the chromatic scheme and the design. Rick Heinrichs wanted very rich or very saturated colours, as you can see from the star-motifs on the far side of the bowling alley. The clothes also followed that style, as did Turturro's tights. That brings the movie closer to a studio work, as distinct from *Fargo*. Again, you can find the LA spirit in the colours, whether saturated or pastel, from the blue of the ocean to the blue of the sky.

The film opens on an aerial view of a landscape.
JOEL: We wanted to introduce the story with that panoramic view which goes hand in hand with the cowboy song, reminiscent of the pioneer spirit. The voice of the Stranger becomes a frame for the story. The original music, as with other elements of the movie, had to echo the retro sounds of the Sixties and early Seventies. There's a lot of tunes from

that period. There's also older classical music, like Mozart's *Requiem*, or Mussorgsky's *Pictures at an Exhibition*. There are sequences that we wrote with the music already in our head, like the latino song "Oye Como Va", for the sequence with Turturro.

ETHAN: In that case, it's the music that defines the character. It's the same for the cowboy played by Sam Elliott. Dylan's "The Man in Me" was chosen at the time of writing. As was "Lujon" by Henri Mancini for Ben Gazzara's character . . . The German nihilists are accompanied by techno-pop and Jeff Bridges by Creedence [Clearwater Revival]. So there's a musical signature for each of them.

Why shoot the film after **Fargo,** *when the script was written before?*
ETHAN: Because John Goodman was busy elsewhere. On top of that, while we hadn't an actor in mind for the Dude role during the writing of the script, we decided later to offer it to Jeff Bridges who was already working, shooting *Wild Bill* for Walter Hill. So it was for scheduling reasons that we shot it after *Fargo*.

Did the writing take longer than for other films?
JOEL: Not really. We write pretty fast, with the exception of *Miller's Crossing*, which took us much more time because we encountered difficulties in structuring the plot. Generally we work in stages. For instance, for *The Big Lebowski* we wrote 40 pages then let it rest for a while before resuming writing. That's fairly normal for our way of working. We have a project for which we've written a few dozen pages almost two years ago, and we'll soon be finishing that. It's not that we particularly like to work like that, but that's how it often happens. We encounter a problem at a certain stage, we pass to another project, then we come back to the first script. That way we've already accumulated pieces for several future movies.

Do they always revolve around a kidnapping?
ETHAN: Not always, but it's true that it comes up frequently in what we write. A screenplay we've half-written takes its inspiration from *The Odyssey*, which is also one of our favourite plot outlines. It's the story of a prisoner in a convict camp in the Southern States, during the Depression, who manages to escape and try to return home, going through different episodes in which he resorts to tricks like Ulysses. Curiously enough we've just finished a new script, commissioned this time for another director, which is an adaptation of an Elmore Leonard novel featuring a kidnapping!

Translated by Paul Buck and Catherine Petit. Interview conducted in Paris on 16 December 1997.

THE BIG LEBOWSKI

BY ROGER EBERT

The Coen brothers' *The Big Lebowski* is a genial, shambling comedy about a human train wreck, and should come with a warning like the one Mark Twain attached to *Huckleberry Finn*: 'Persons attempting to find a plot in it will be shot.' It's about a man named Jeff Lebowski, who calls himself the Dude, and is described by the narrator as 'the laziest man in Los Angeles County'. He lives only to go bowling, but is mistaken for a millionaire named the Big Lebowski, with dire consequences.

This is the first movie by Joel and Ethan Coen since *Fargo*. Few movies could equal that one, and this one doesn't – but it's weirdly engaging, like its hero. The Dude is played by Jeff Bridges with a goatee, a potbelly, a ponytail and a pair of Bermuda shorts so large they may have been borrowed from his best friend and bowling teammate, Walter Sobchak (John Goodman). Their other teammate is Donny (Steve Buscemi), who may not be very bright, but it's hard be sure since he never is allowed to complete a sentence.

Everybody knows somebody like the Dude – and so, rumour has it, do the Coen brothers. They based the character on a movie producer and distributor named Jeff Dowd, a familiar figure at film festivals, who is tall, large, shaggy and aboil with enthusiasm. Dowd is much more successful than Lebowski (he has played an important role in the Coens' careers as indie filmmakers), but no less a creature of the moment. Both dudes depend on improvisation and inspiration much more than organisation.

In spirit, *The Big Lebowski* resembles the Coens' *Raising Arizona*, with its large cast of peculiar characters and its strangely wonderful dialogue. Here, in a film set at the time of the Gulf War, are characters whose speech was shaped by earlier times: Vietnam (Walter), the flower power era (the Dude) and *Twilight Zone* (Donny). Their very notion of reality may be shaped by the limited ways they have to describe it. One of the pleasures of *Fargo* was the way the Coens listened carefully to how their characters spoke. Here, too, note that when the In & Out Burger shop is suggested for a rendezvous, the Dude supplies its address: That's the sort of precise information he would possess.

As the film opens, the Dude is visited by two enforcers for a porn king (Ben Gazzara) who is owed a lot of money by the Big Lebowski's wife. The goons of course have the wrong Lebowski, but before they figure that out, one already has urinated on the Dude's rug, causing deep enmity: 'That rug really tied the room together,' the Dude mourns. Walter, the Viet vet, leads the charge for revenge. Borrowing lines directly from President George Bush on TV, he vows that 'this aggression will not stand' and urges the Dude to 'draw a line in the sand'.

The Dude visits the other Lebowski (David Huddleston), leaves with one of his rugs, and soon finds himself enlisted in the millionaire's schemes. The rich Lebowski, in a wheelchair and gazing into a fireplace like Major Amberson in *The Magnificent Ambersons*, tells the Dude that his wife, Bunny (Tara Reid), has been kidnapped. He wants the Dude to deliver the ransom money. This plan is opposed by Maude (Julianne Moore), the Big Lebowski's

Jeff Bridges in The Big Lebowski's *dream sequence - homage to Philip Marlowe's hallucinations in* Murder, My Sweet *(1945) and to Busby Berkeley musicals.*

head, which happens often, and one of them involves a musical comedy sequence inspired by Busby Berkeley. (It includes the first point-of-view shot in history from inside a bowling ball.)

Some may complain *The Big Lebowski* rushes in all directions and never ends up anywhere. That isn't the film's flaw, but its style. The Dude, who smokes a lot of pot and guzzles White Russians made with half-and-half, starts every day filled with resolve, but his plans gradually dissolve into a haze of missed opportunities and missed intentions. Most people lead lives with a third act. The Dude lives days without evenings. The spirit is established right at the outset, when the narrator (Sam Elliott) starts out well enough, but eventually confesses he's lost his train of thought.

DOUBLE VISION

BY JONATHAN ROMNEY

The Coen brothers may not have the strangest film in Cannes this year [2000], but they can certainly boast the drollest promotional giveaway. It's a three-ounce tub of waxy, orange-coloured, sweetly-scented stuff labelled 'Dapper Dan Men's Pomade'. It carries the portrait of a rakishly coiffed George Clooney, looking determined and modelling a convincing facsimile of Clark Gable's moustache.

As promo novelties go, it makes a change from T-shirts and tote bags, and it relates more precisely to the advertised film than is usually the case. In the Coens' new film, *O Brother, Where Art Thou?*, Clooney's character Ulysses Everett McGill, an escapee from a southern chain gang, wouldn't go anywhere without a dab of Dapper Dan to sweeten his locks. His flight across the deep south is, you can imagine, rather more facetious than the Thirties chain gang movies that the Coens take as their model.

Minnesota-born brothers Joel and Ethan are known for liking their bit of fun, and, in their latest film, they haven't stinted themselves. *O Brother* is several films in one: a tale of three desperadoes on the lam in rural Mississippi; a blues and country musical; and, allegedly at least, a rewrite of Homer's *Odyssey*. Not that they've actually read *The Odyssey*, they admit. Fortunately, Ethan Coen says, one of the film's leads, Tim Blake Nelson, is a classicist. 'I wonder if he read it in Greek? I know he read it.' 'Yeah,' confirms Joel. 'Did he?' Ethan insists. 'I don't know if he read it in Greek,' says Joel. 'I know he read it.'

'Between the cast and us,' says Ethan, 'Tim Nelson is the only one who's actually read *The Odyssey.*' There's little point, then, kicking yourself if you can't place all the allusions. The Sirens are easy enough, a trio of singing Amazons doing their laundry in the Mississippi. And the Cyclops is John Goodman in an eyepatch.

Scylla and Charybdis I was less certain about. 'Scylla and Charybdis? Where were they?' puzzles Ethan. The whirlpool at the end, surely? 'Oh,' the brothers chorus, 'the whirlpool.' Ethan grins pensively. 'Oh, yeah, sure, Scylla and Charybdis.' Joel says, 'It's very, you know, selectively based on *The Odyssey.*' Interviewers often lament that with the Coens, there's no point even asking: they don't give anything away.

They have this reputation as tight-lipped enigmatic sorts who make enigmatic films. And yet the films pretty much speak for themselves; they are flawlessly accessible, even if you don't catch all the references to old movies and pulp paperbacks. The only thing that properly seems bizarre about the brothers' work is the breadth of their imagination: they specialise in pinpointing the kind of images and cultural references that are usually outside the remit of contemporary American cinema.

There's nothing that bizarre, if you think of it, about choosing to set a crime thriller in snowbound Minnesota, as the brothers did in *Fargo*, and having villains who relax by going to see Jose Feliciano in concert; it's just that it took the Coens to think of it. Every Coen film describes a world so thoroughly conceived that each one is its own fictional microclimate; in a sense the brothers don't really need to add much commentary. Hence, perhaps, the sense that when they give interviews, they are aware of the futility of the venture.

Here they are in Cannes again, sitting in the casino on top of the Carlton hotel, and although they have visited several times in the past (their *Barton Fink* won the Palme d'Or in 1991), they don't quite seem to belong. Older brother Joel looks as though he's done all the interviews he wants to in a lifetime, Ethan as though he's never done one in his life. Joel seems to have dressed for the part of the hot auteur in town and then lets it all get messed up over a rough morning: shoulder-length hair more scrupulously crimped than previously, in a black jacket that could be either very cheap or very expensive; both the beard and the low mutter are reminscent of Frank Zappa, and he keeps looking absently around the room as if he's wondering how long it is till lunch.

The friendlier Ethan, in a murky brown plaid shirt, with a scraggy beard and a faceful of freckles, constantly grins broadly, occasionally giving a wheezy laugh, and seems to be relishing various private jokes as if they've only just crossed his mind. Despite the grandiose title, *O Brother, Where Art Thou?* is as downhome and earthy a film as has come out of recent American cinema, although it lacks the lightness of touch of the Coens' best comedies.

It shares its title with the apochryphal movie planned by Joel McCrea's idealistic director in Preston Sturges' 1941 comedy *Sullivan's Travels*. Sullivan heads out across America to research his serious Steinbeckian hobo drama, only to conclude that it's a far nobler calling to make 'em laugh.

But the Coens' *O Brother* is not entirely the film that Sullivan would have made. 'It pretends to be a big important movie,' says Ethan. 'but the grandiosity is obviously a joke. It is what it is, it's a comedy. There is a chain-gang interlude in *Sullivan's Travels*, but that's it.' *O Brother* is another example of the Coens' partiality to period: *Miller's Crossing, Barton Fink* and *The Hudsucker Proxy* all explored past decades, and even their last film, *The Big Lebowski*, had a certain distance, being set in the early Nineties as opposed to 1998.

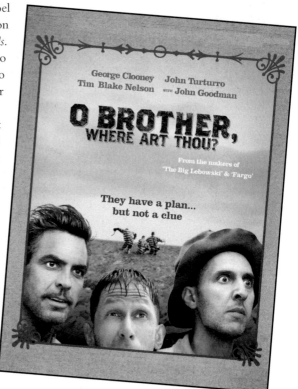

George Clooney   John Turturro
Tim Blake Nelson   with John Goodman

O BROTHER, WHERE ART THOU?

From the makers of
'The Big Lebowski' & 'Fargo'

They have a plan...
but not a clue

'We tend to do period stuff,' says Ethan, 'because it helps make it one step removed from boring everyday reality.' Their latest film carries a considerable weight of historical authenticity, not least in the soundtrack of vintage southern music – gospel, Delta blues and early country swing – assembled by singer-songwriter and one-time Dylan collaborator T-Bone Burnett.

One of the film's themes is the congruence of pre-war American pop with history and politics, as the errant jailbird trio encounter various real-life characters, among them gangster George 'Baby Face' Nelson and blues singer Tommy Johnson, who, like the better known Robert Johnson, was reputed to have sold his soul to the devil in exchange for blues prowess. Another real character is Texas governor Pappy O'Daniel, who would go electioneering accompanied by a 'stump band', a music show to whip up popular support. 'They'd draw the crowds,' explains Joel. 'People came to listen to the music and then they'd have to listen to the speech.'

The film's southern history, musical and political, looks detailed enough to have been thoroughly researched, but the Coens insist it wasn't. 'It's all stuff that to one extent or another we were aware of,' Joel says. 'It was all back there somewhere and filtered up into the script. We weren't going out and doing research and trying to apply it to a story, it's all much more haphazard. It wasn't like we were trying to create a realistic picture of the time

Three stooges on the lam: chain-gang escapees (l-r) Pete (John Turturro), Delmar (Tim Blake Nelson) and Everett (George Clooney) embark on a quirky odyssey.

and place so much as an imagined world where those things intersect – real people and made-up people.'

Both are keen that the film shouldn't be taken too seriously, even though for the first time (give or take the socialist convictions of their playwright Barton Fink, and the trendy crypto-fascists in *The Big Lebowski*) they seem to be focusing on political realities in *O Brother*. 'The political undercurrent of the movie,' says Joel, 'functions primarily for dramatic purposes, because the politics are frankly pretty primitive. The bad guys are racial bigots and KKK Grand Dragons, and the good guys are the heroes of the movie. So it's all kind of a story thing.'

Even so, the film pulls off something of a coup in managing to be more politically flippant than American comedies have managed since Mel Brooks's heyday. The scene where the heroes blithely wander into a torchlit KKK rally might, I suggest to the brothers, strike some viewers as being of questionable taste.

'Taste,' says Joel, 'has never been something we've worried about.' 'We're not big on taste,' agrees Ethan, his grin broadening even further. 'And actually, if you don't pander to undue sensitivities then it ends up usually not being much of a problem. In *The Big Lebowski*, we dumped the crippled guy out of the wheelchair, and no one seemed to mind that.' 'Everyone was saying, "You're going to get a huge amount of mail from disabled people about this." But it's all in the context of the story, and done by the John Goodman character who's clearly an idiot,' says Joel, and Ethan cracks up in laughter.

They are among the most film-literate of mainstream US directors – not indiscriminate movie-guzzlers of the Tarantino school, but scholars of a longer history whose films have referenced Warner Bros. gangster pics, Busby Berkeley musicals, and even William Faulkner's fraught Hollywood tenure as a hired script hand.

But the only time they directly used other films as a starting point, the brothers say, was in their 1994 film (probably their least-liked, unjustly so) *The Hudsucker Proxy*. 'We knew we were doing a sort of Capra-esque thing,' says Ethan, 'but even that was not a specific one of his movies, just the whole sort of just his thing, right?' They no longer consume films so tirelessly, they admit, largely the result of having children (Ethan has two; Joel has one, with his wife and occasional lead actress Frances McDormand). 'We don't watch them together a lot,' says Ethan, 'and neither of us watches as many as we used to. It's actually gotten more and more hit-and-miss – movies that I planned to see and never end up seeing.'

It is generally assumed that the Coens equally represent the presiding genius of their films, but while they share writing credits, Ethan is billed as producer and Joel as director. This means that in Cannes, each film is officially billed as 'un film de Joel Coen', although their own production notes specify, 'A Film by Joel Coen and Ethan Coen.' Confusingly, only Joel's photo appears in the *O Brother* press kit.

Of the two, it's Ethan who has explored outside ventures. He recently wrote *The Naked Man*, a film by the duo's regular storyboard artist J. Todd Anderson, about a character actor who moonlights as a pro wrestler. The film got a critical thumbs-down. 'I thought it was very funny,' Ethan says. 'I enjoyed it, and not just in a pride of ownership, 'cause it's really J. Todd's thing. It didn't get a theatrical release, for reasons I can understand. It's nobody's idea of a big audience mainstream movie.'

Amidst the mirth and the music, the Soggy Bottom Boys encounter Baby Face Nelson, the KKK, and pork-barrel politics in the Depression-era South.

More prominent was *Gates of Eden*, the short story collection that Ethan published in 1998. It is frustrating, in a way, because it suggests there's much more to his imagination and linguistic prowess than he is necessarily prepared to put into his movies. More striking than the dry squibs and Chandler parodies are the complex, concise character sketches, and the adolescent anecdotes which hint at the personally revealing movie the Coens have yet to make – although in all honesty, it's hard to imagine them coming up with a screen evocation of a synagogue-going Jewish upbringing in Sixties Minnesota.

The next Coen brothers film starts shooting in six weeks. Known as *The Barbershop Project*, it stars Frances McDormand and Billy Bob Thornton. 'It's set in a barbershop and is concerned with the minutiae of the barbering trade of the late Forties.' Is that why their distributor has been handing out Dapper Dan's pomade – as a teaser? 'It's just a coincidence,' says Joel. 'There's a lot of hair products in this next film.' 'Actually,' says Ethan, 'we use pomade in *Raising Arizona* as well, as a means of tracking the characters. It's a tired old gag.' I scan Joel's faintly slicked locks for traces of his own hair-care product. Would he personally recommend Dapper Dan? 'I take no responsibility for that pomade,' he says.

BROTHERS IN ARMS

BY JIM RIDLEY

Last summer, filmmakers Joel and Ethan Coen (*Raising Arizona*, *Fargo*) were in Nashville to find musicians for their latest film, *O Brother, Where Art Thou?* An episodic yarn that borrows from Homer's *Odyssey*, it stars George Clooney, John Turturro, and Tim Blake Nelson as escaped convicts on a seriocomic journey through 1930s Mississippi, a flight that includes brushes with bluesmen, bigots, gangsters, crooked politicians, and seductive sirens. (The title comes from Preston Sturges' *Sullivan's Travels*. It's the name of the movie Sturges' comedy-director hero Sullivan intends as his 'serious' picture about the struggles of the Depression.)

Before filming began, the Coens took the unusual step of recording the music first. For the movie's mix of blues, gospel, and bluegrass, the filmmakers and music producer T-Bone Burnett assembled a stellar lineup that includes Ralph Stanley, Norman Blake, Alison Krauss, Emmylou Harris, Gillian Welch, the Cox Family, and the Whites, and they recorded the music here last year. All those artists and more – plus the Coens themselves – will appear at a benefit show next Wednesday 24 May 2000 at the Ryman Auditorium, which will be recorded by documentarian D. A. Pennebaker for a concert film.

Soon, the Coens may have even more reason to celebrate. *O Brother, Where Art Thou?* screened last weekend to strong notices at the Cannes Film Festival, some of which mentioned the movie as a contender for the top prize, the Palme d'Or. If the Coens win, it would be their second Golden Palm (after 1991's *Barton Fink*). The movie itself will be released this fall. The *Scene* spoke to Joel and Ethan Coen last week from their home base of New York, where they're practicing their sibling harmonies for the Ryman stage.

How did you choose the music for the movie?

Joel: Well, actually, in the movie we used a sort of mixture of period recordings and rerecorded music. But the stuff that was redone and produced by T-Bone is all featured essentially live – it's music you see performed in the movie itself.

Ethan: It's not background, it's not working as underscoring, it's actually happening on camera.

Joel: In other words, it's in the context of the story. At one point, George Clooney sings and records a record that becomes a big hit, a song called 'I Am a Man of Constant Sorrow'. That's all part of the story, so it had to be a combination of prerecorded background instrumentals that the actors or musicians would sing live to on set, or prerecorded with the vocals and then lipsynched.

Which musicians actually appear in the movie?

Joel: The Cox Family, the Whites, Chris Thomas King. . .[John] Hartford was gonna be in it, but he was ill at the time we wanted to shoot his scene. The Fairfield Four are in the movie; they play gravediggers. They do a great version of 'You've Got to Walk that Lonesome Valley'. Most of Alison's band is in the movie.

Were there any artists you wanted specifically?

Joel: A lot of them were people that we knew and like and are fans of, like Alison and Emmylou and Gillian, and obviously we knew Ralph Stanley and John Hartford and all these guys. But they were actually brought in by T-Bone. At an early stage we sort of decided what music we wanted. Then T-Bone brought in a lot of different musicians and sort of collectively decided who was going to do what.

What was the selection process like?

Joel: Well, that was great, actually. At one point T-Bone basically had two days where he brought in lots of different people who all sort of played and sang together. And we got kind of a feeling for who was right. But it was a great experience, meeting all these people and hearing 'em play. It was unbelievable.

Ethan: Ralph [Stanley] coming in was kind of funny. You know, everyone's sort of hanging out and playing, picking, whatever, and then Ralph walked in. It was like they'd wheeled in one of the heads from Mount Rushmore. The whole room just kind of fell silent for a moment.

What are some of the most memorable songs in the finished film?

Ethan: There are a number of set-piece songs that are almost . . . not production numbers, because it isn't literally a musical, but have that kind of feel to them. One of the most notable ones is the Ralph Stanley thing, 'O Death'. Chris Thomas King [who plays a blues musician modelled on Robert Johnson] did a Skip James song, 'Hard Time Killing Floor Blues'. And there's the Jimmie Rodgers song . . .

Joel: . . . that Tim Nelson sings. It's really interesting, because he sings that live himself. He's not a trained singer, he's not a recording artist, he's an actor. But he's got this great country-western voice. He's going to sing in the concert, actually.

Ethan: It's this weird fantasy come true for Tim – he gets to stand on the stage of the Ryman and perform.

We heard something about a sirens' song . . . .

Joel: Oh, that's interesting! [The convicts] come upon these three women washing clothes in the river. That's Gillian, Alison, and Emmylou as the three voices. And they're singing this song which is from this old kind of black, bluesy lullaby from the period. Gillian wrote like four or five other verses for it.

She's actually in the movie, right?

Joel: Yeah, she is. She's trying to buy the hit record that Clooney has recorded, without any success.

If you have sirens involved, the **Odyssey** *parallels must hold pretty close.*
Joel and Ethan: (chortling) Yeah, well . . .
Ethan: We avail ourselves of it very selectively. There's the sirens; and the Cyclops, John Goodman, a one-eyed Bible salesman . . . .
Joel: Whenever it's convenient we trot out *The Odyssey.*
Ethan: But I don't want any of those *Odyssey* fans to go to the movie expecting, y'know . . .
Joel: 'Where's Laertes?' (laughter)
Ethan: 'Where's his dog?' (more laughter)

How seriously do you intend the reference to **Sullivan's Travels?** *Your movie sounds more like Sturges than the symbolic movie-within-a-movie that gives* **O Brother** *its title.*
Joel: In a way, that's true. There are things in it that are very reminiscent of *Sullivan's Travels,* but in a sense I would say 'reminiscent of' instead of rip-off. (laughs) In our minds, it was presumably the movie he would've made if he'd had the chance. The important movie. The one that takes on the big, important themes.
Ethan: And if he'd been steeped in Homeric literature and early country music. (laughter)

Aren't they the same thing?
Joel: Yeah, that's what T-Bone likes to say. They're both verbal traditions. Oral traditions.
Ethan: That's about as far as it goes, though.

What are you working on next?
Joel: We're doing a movie about a barber in Northern California in the early 1940s. (Pause, then accusingly:) I think I heard a little snicker there. I was in Texas a while ago, and I told that to Ann Richards, the former governor. She looked at me for about twenty seconds and said, 'I'm trying real hard to get excited about this.'
Ethan: There's more to it than Joel lets on. He actually is a barber, but he's interested in getting into dry cleaning.

While you're on stage at the Ryman, are you going to favour us with a tune? 'The Coen Brothers' does sound like an old-time hillbilly act.
Joel: Oh, yeah.
Ethan: Yeah, I'm bringing my washboard, and Joel's bringing his spoons. (Issues a laugh like a car alarm going off.) Wait for us, we're coming on last!

HI HONEY, I'M HOMER

BY PHILIP FRENCH

Invariably, some literary or cinematic source quirkily lurks beneath the original screenplays of the Coen brothers, Ethan and Joel. *Miller's Crossing*, for instance, is a conflation of Dashiel Hammett's *The Glass Key* and *Red Harvest*; the central character of *Barton Fink* is based on playwright Clifford Odets and the film's plot derives from *Deadline at Dawn*, a movie Odets scripted in 1946; their previous film, *The Big Lebowski*, reworks Chandler's *The Big Sleep*.

Their new movie, *O Brother, Where Art Thou?*, has several sources which are part of the film's meaning. On the surface, it's a picaresque comedy set in the Deep South in 1937 and stars George Clooney, John Turturro and Tim Blake Nelson as three convicts who escape from a Mississippi chain-gang. Clooney is the charming, loquacious shyster-lawyer Everett, with a Clark Gable moustache and the kind of flat cap and bib-front overalls Henry Fonda wore in *The Grapes of Wrath*. Turturro is Pete, a surly redneck with a mean streak. Nelson is kind-hearted Delmar, the simple-minded hick. They're a splendid comic trio.

Everett has smart-talked them into joining his quest to find the loot he's allegedly buried beneath a shack that will in four days time be submerged to create a dam. His real purpose, however, is to reach his ex-wife Penny (Holly Hunter) before she re-marries.

Along the way, they meet a black musician and cut a gramophone record at a remote radio station run by a blind manager. This bluegrass song makes them accidental radio stars, and they get involved in the re-election campaign of a corrupt state governor (Charles Durning), who's being challenged by an equally corrupt racist. As photographed by British cinematographer Roger Deakins, the bleached summer landscapes look a treat.

But the film announces at the start that it's based on *The Odyssey* and is prefaced by the opening lines of Robert Fitzgerald's translation: 'Sing in me, Muse, and through me tell the story of that man skilled in all ways of contending, the wanderer.'

Like Joyce's *Ulysses*, *O Brother* is a mock epic with a somewhat shorter time span than Homer's, and the classical allusions are fairly jocular. The Clooney character's full name is Ulysses Everett McGill; his wife Penny is, of course, Penelope, and on their journey the convicts meet a variety of Homeric figures. A blind railroad worker warning of trouble with cows is presumably Tiresias; the lotus eaters are Baptists having their past obliterated by full immersion in a swamp; three sirens lure the travellers and appear to destroy Pete; the Cyclops turns up as a massive, one-eyed preacher (John Goodman), who first robs them and is later confronted at a nocturnal Ku Klux Klan rally, a brilliantly choreographed sequence that moves from funny to frightening to fantastic.

In addition to Homer, the film wittily invokes twentieth-century American legends. Tommy Johnson, the musician the wanderers play with, is based on Robert Johnson, the black blues composer who allegedly sold his soul to the Devil. While being pursued by the

O Brother, Where Art Thou? *returned the Coens to the broad comedy of* Raising Arizona *and* Lebowski; *while* The Man Who Wasn't There *echoed the neo-*noir *of* Blood Simple *and* Fargo.

police, they're given a lift by a manic-depressive Baby Face Nelson, the gun-happy gangster who succeeded Dillinger as the FBI's Public Enemy Number One, though in fact (not that this is important) Nelson had been dead three years by 1937.

Hovering quietly ready for the film's climax is the epic of the Tennessee Valley Authority, Roosevelt's project to transform the rural South by providing cheap electricity, an event celebrated by grandiose poetic documentaries sponsored by the New Deal.

Most significantly, however, the Coens celebrate the ideas and films of the great Preston Sturges, who after a decade writing screenplays emerged as the writer-director of the political satire *The Great McGinty* in 1940.

The surname of their protagonist, McGill, is presumably intended to echo that of Sturges's anti-hero, McGinty, who threw in his lot with crooked politicians the way Clooney does. But a more important reference is to Sturges's dazzling meditation on his craft, *Sullivan's Travels*, in which a successful comedy director demands that he be allowed to make a film that 'teaches a moral lesson, has social insight.'

Sullivan's film is to be called *Oh Brother, Where Art Thou?*, but his exploratory odyssey through Depression America, which gets him sent to jail and put on a chain gang, convinces him that he's better employed combating human misery by making people laugh.

Moreover, Sullivan concludes: 'I never will have suffered enough to make *Oh Brother, Where Art Thou?* Besides it's already been done, they made it a couple of thousand years ago and I don't believe in remakes.'

Was Sullivan thinking of Homer when he said that? And are the Coens engaged in the delightfully postmodern activity of remaking a famous movie that never existed?

THE MAN WHO WASN'T THERE

BY GERALD PEARY

Many of my fellow journalists, in meeting up with the Coen brothers, Joel and Ethan, come away disappointed, or even disillusioned. Considering their smart, subversive, playful films like their *Raising Arizona*, *Fargo* or *The Big Lebowski*, we anticipate two happily verbal guys bubbling with fascinating things to say about their movies. But their *Brother Where Art Thou?* press conference at Cannes in 2000 was a typical Coens' showing: the duo smug and diffident, strangely disconnected from the Q&A. Their short-cut, frustratingly evasive answers made them appear tired of discussing their movie – although it was the world premiere!

In an interview for *Moving Pictures* magazine, the reporter, Damon Wise, challenged the Coens' stand-offish attitude. The Coens were unrepentant:

Ethan: 'You make the movie and journalists have to write about something . . . There it is. I don't know.'

Joel: 'What I think you are referring to is to the fact that we often resist the efforts of . . . people who are interviewing us to enlist us in that process ourselves. And we resist it not because we object to it but simply because it isn't something that particularily interests us.'

So I was braced – braced to get nothing! – at Cannes 2001, when a gathering of American journalists interviewed the leads and, again, the Coen brothers about *The Man Who Wasn't There*, their Billy Bob Thornton-starring homage to the hardboiled *noir* view of novelist James M. Cain.

First we got Thornton, an off-the-screen little guy in a Metallica t–shirt and anxious to talk . . . about how he adores his wife, Angelina Jolie. He leaned over the table to show the gathered fourth estate the vial of spouse-blood which hangs about his neck. 'For our anniversary, she gave me her will,' he said, proudly. 'She got us both burial spots in Arkansas next to my brother, who died in 1988.'

What about Thornton's character in this movie, small-town barber, Ed Crane? 'It's this guy and the guy in *A Simple Plan* who are closest to myself. I feel like "the man who wasn't there". I got my wife, my kids, my mom. I'm not interested in things outside the basement and the back yard. I always identify with John Lennon, who loved to stay home.

'I really don't care about commerciality. God knows if anyone will see this film. But I love these guys, the Coens, and their sense of humour. I agreed to do the film when Joel told me, "It's about a barber who wants to be a dry cleaner."

'I love all the Bogart movies, and Fred MacMurray in *Double Indemnity*. I think MacMurray is a great actor. For this movie, I didn't try to look like Bogart. I was thinking more about Frank Sinatra. When you get into that mood, you look like those guys. In real life, we're not in black-and-white, but somehow that feels more real in this movie, more

Doris Crane (Frances McDormand) stands trial in The Man Who Wasn't There*, with hotshot lawyer Freddy Riedenschneider (Tony Shalhoub).*

monochromatic. You can feel people sweating in black-and-white.'

Next up was Frances McDormand, wife of director Joel Coen, Oscar winner as the cornflakes Minnesota cop, Marge, in *Fargo*, and acclaimed as the protective mom in *Almost Famous*. 'Marge was the embodiment of all things an actress is supposed to be,' McDormand said, nostalgic for that once-in-a-lifetime part, 'and in *Almost Famous*, I felt voluptuous and free, very alive and jiggly and complex.' In marked contrast, she said of her *femme fatale*, Doris, in *The Man Who Wasn't There*, that 'the role was more technical than usual, me caring that my lipstick was right, the hair was perfect. The challenge was mostly the black-and-white. The movie is about Ed Crane, not Doris.'

What about the Coen brothers' communicativeness? McDormand, who is straight and open, shook her head, bemused. She knows, because the vacuum that journalists feel is also present on the set. Even for McDormand, being directed by her husband, Joel. 'Sometimes it's easier getting direction from Ethan,' she confided. 'He's more direct. Since *Blood Simple*, it's a huge improvement how they have dialogue with actors. Their not communicating was to the peril of certain performances.'

Are they really opening up? McDormand told us that *The Man Who Wasn't There* is a more personal project than earlier Coen brothers films.

Finally, the Coens: Joel, the taller one with the longer hair, director and co-writer; Ethan, producer and co-writer.

A journalist nudged them. 'Frances says this film is more personal. How is it personal?'

Ethan: 'I don't think it's more personal or less personal. There's nothing autobiographical.'

Joel: 'It's set in the 1940s, and that's not personal. These are stories which take us away from first-hand experience.'

The Coens at Cannes spill all! You've read it here first.

PICTURES THAT DO THE TALKING

BY ANDREW PULVER

There's a presence in the room; a ghostly, disembodied presence. Joel Coen, sitting unconcerned in an armchair, doesn't appear to feel it. Maybe it's just me, but isn't there normally two of them? 'I don't spend much time with Ethan outside of work,' says Joel, in a barely audible drawl. Where is Ethan? Joel mumbles something indistinct, but it doesn't seem right to press the question. Maybe they've had a row; maybe Ethan's mangled corpse is trussed up and stuffed in the ornate wooden chest under the window ledge. More urgently, will Joel be able to manage to complete a sentence on his own? Past evidence suggests it might be tricky.

If this isn't unsettling enough, there's more big news. Joel Coen has got rid of the pony tail. Throughout the Coen brothers' dazzling film-making career, Joel's haircut was something everyone just pretended they didn't see. No one talked about it. Now it's gone, no one will ever mention it again. Not that los hermanos Coen haven't made secret capital out of their appearance: a duo of skinny, unshaven four-eyes, looking like a couple of systems analysts who have got lost in the early 1970s on the way to the Jefferson Airplane freakout. Ethan has tended to sport a harmless frizzy mess, giving him a faintly rabbinical air. Joel's appalling pony tail was the best way to tell them apart. Well, I can report that he's cut it off. At 47, Joel Coen has graduated to a wavy, shoulder-length mop.

It turns out that brother Joel has been on a family holiday in Scotland with his wife – Fargo and Blood Simple star Frances McDormand – and adopted son Pedro, and Joel has headed to London for a back-slapping session with producers Working Title, and a private screening of the new Coen film The Man Who Wasn't There. He's also – with customary Coen reluctance – forcing himself to shill for his movie.

In fact, nobody could be less enthusiastic to talk about a Coen brothers movie than the Coens. Maybe it's all to the good that there's only one of them here. In tandem, the Coens are a tricky proposition. Most directors at least make the pretence that they like to chat about their work: they slog for endless months through the production, explaining their wants to all and sundry; jabbering to the media, you soon gather, is merely a continuation of the film-making process. Film directors tend also to be a little – to put it mildly – on the egocentric side. The Coens, in stark contrast, just don't seem to be interested. Arguably the most unconventional of mainstream American directors, they don't offer snarling hostility or even sullen wariness, just a helpless, unspoken consternation that they should have to talk about themselves and what they do.

But on his own, a single Coen brother does turn out to be a different animal. Without the other one with whom to trade in-jokes or exchange wondering glances, Coen solo is almost chatty, and prepared to acknowledge the nature of their relationship. How do they stand spending so much time with each other? 'Well, we work together, but it's limited to that. We spend the working day together, so at the end of that you never feel the need to say, "let's go out to dinner," you know what I mean? It's all kind of limited to work.'

Are your films simply the sum of two sibling personalities that are peculiarly perfectly meshed? 'No . . . it's difficult to explain. The work that we do together reflects the point at which our interests intersect. It's been eighteen years we've been working together, and it's a reflection of the point at which we're interested in the same things . . . That is to say, we're interested individually in different things, but that's not what gets worked at.' So you don't necessarily always run on the same track? 'It's always reflected in the work — in that it's a dialogue, it's an egging-on process, in that one person will suggest something and the other will respond to it or amplify it.'

So who actually does what? Do the credits, Joel as director, Ethan as producer, mean anything? 'No. We're both on the set; the movies are co-directed in every sense of the word. Actors often get paranoid before they start working with us — they're apprehensive that things'll be confusing. You know, that I'll say, "Slower," and he'll say, "Faster" . . .'

When did you realise you had a special affinity as a film-making team? 'It was really the point when we started writing together, when I was working as an assistant editor. We started writing scripts for other people, for people who were coming in to work on projects I was working on. It was that point we realised: this works out pretty well.'

Here Joel is referring to his own apprenticeship in the film industry: his first recorded job was, in 1980, to assistant-edit the debut of another tyro director, Sam Raimi. Raimi had the resource to raise money from family connections to finance his film — which became the savage comedy-horror classic *The Evil Dead*. Joel, a few years after studying film at New York university, was married at the time (this was well before he met McDormand, but the woman concerned wishes to retain her privacy). Meanwhile, Ethan, three years younger, had graduated from the philosophy department at Princeton (and written a paper on Wittgenstein), and joined his big brother in New York. It was there, as the Eighties dawned, that the writing began, often in collaboration with Raimi, who has co-scripting credits on *Crimewave* (which became his second movie in 1985) and *The Hudsucker Proxy* (which became the Coens' fifth, in 1994).

Inspired by Raimi's method of fundraising, the Coens took a third script, *Blood Simple*, back to Minneapolis to try and persuade friends and family to pony up. Another key member of the team, Barry Sonnenfeld, became their director of photography, and filmed a three-minute trailer for them in 1982. (Sonnenfeld has gone on to outdo all his former compadres as a big-budget director, squiring *The Addams Family*, *Get Shorty*, and *Men in Black* to massive success.) According to legend the Coens turned to the local branch of Hadassah, the American women's Zionist charity, who gave them a list of 100 wealthy Jewish philanthropists. Thus it was the brothers scraped together the $1.3m needed to get *Blood Simple* off the ground.

By later standards of low-budget, deferred-payment film-making, this sounds a lot, but in the early 1980s the independent film movement was in its infancy. This was well before template-setting shoestring productions such as *Stranger than Paradise* or *She's Gotta Have It* – let alone bargain-basement stuff like *El Mariachi* or *Clerks* – had made their appearance. In their adolescence, Ethan and Joel had messed around with Super 8 (titles are said to include *Ed . . . A Dog* and *The Banana Film*), but *Blood Simple* was the real deal. Looking back at the film now, all the Coen trademarks are there: an agglomeration of literary and cinematic references (with a heavy tilt to the hard-boiled school); idiosyncratic photography – including the now-immortal skip over a sleeping drunk as the camera tracks along a bar top – itself indebted to *The Evil Dead*'s cartoonish style; and studied acting performances that layer unfussy naturalism alongside high-key grotesque.

As barber Ed Crane, the eponymous 'man who wasn't there', Billy Bob Thornton's performance is a still-life portrait of stoical fatalism.

Their follow-up, *Raising Arizona*, set out along a different road entirely – so much so that it fell squarely into the wave of late Eighties baby comedies along with *Three Men and a Baby* (released the same year, 1987, as *Arizona*), and *She's Having a Baby* (1988). But the same stylistic tics that marked out *Blood Simple* are there, and the Coens' method was set. A chiselled script, actors that were required to fill out the dialogue but not improvise from it, and a new set of cultural baggage re-formed and re-tooled in the service of storytelling.

It's a method that has served them beautifully right through their career. The Coens are shortly to release their ninth movie, *The Man Who Wasn't There*. Rumour-mill aficionados may know of it as *The Barber Project*, the work-in-progress title that reflects the business occupation of its lead character, Ed Crane (played by Billy Bob Thornton). The title was changed shortly before its premiere at the Cannes film festival last May – to reflect, as the Coens said, Crane's emotional vacuum as well as a key element of its thriller plot. It's set in 1940s California (the same town in fact, Santa Rosa, as Hitchcock's 1943 noir *Shadow of a Doubt*), shot in a luminous black-and-white by the Coens' longtime cinematographer Roger Deakins, and, like *Blood Simple*, is infected with the spirit of pulp novelist James M. Cain, a key Coen touchstone. Thornton, stone-faced and laconic, is quite exceptional in his role as a barber who suspects his wife is cheating on him – so much so that, though it's a radically different performance from his trademark demon-haunted twitchiness, the Crane part fits him like a glove. It's a now established feature of the Coen modus operandi that they often tool their extraordinary characters with specific actors in mind, so was Thornton always the model?

It seems not. 'With this one,' says Joel, 'we wrote the part for Fran [McDormand, who plays Crane's wife Doris], and we wrote the part that Michael Badalucco plays [Ed's barber-shop partner Frank], but that was about it. We didn't know who was going to play the lead character. In that respect it was like *Fargo*: we wrote a part for Fran, we wrote a part for Steve Buscemi, but we didn't know who was going to play the part Bill Macy ended up with.

'But Billy Bob is someone we've known for a while, we haven't worked with before but we knew him, and . . . I don't know why he occurred to us, because he's not our image of the character. He's a southern guy from Arkansas, and Ed is not supposed to be that. But on the other hand, Billy Bob's such a transformative actor – both physically and in every other way – that we started to think that this would be rather interesting. And he certainly has the confidence to do this kind of character. Which, as an actor, you need to do it. Because Ed says very little, he's very still, and that would just drive most actors crazy. They'd be very insecure about it, thinking they weren't doing enough; we had a feeling that Billy Bob would understand.'

Was Cain – the literary progenitor of classic American *noir*, in the shape of *Double Indemnity*, *The Postman Always Rings Twice* and *Mildred Pierce* – as much of an influence on the film as it appears? 'Yes definitely. Cain was very much in our minds, because he was interested in crime stories that involved people in their everyday lives at work, and not about underworld figures. People who work in banks, or the insurance business, or restaurants . . . or the opera business, which was another obsession of his. In that respect, like the domestic melodrama that turns into a crime story, it owes a lot to Cain.

'But there are ways in which it's not *film noir*: for one thing, the main character couldn't be further from your conventional *film noir* hero, in terms of his obsessions and personality . . . but, it's got all that modern dread, that feeling of disassociation and paranoia about what's happening in the world about you. Also foreground in our thinking were science fiction films from the Fifties, all the postwar paranoia things. You get the pulpier, cheesier elements of American postwar culture, as reflected in men's magazines, and health movies you'd see in school, and science fiction movies you'd see about aliens, and civil defence movies, that kind of thing . . .'

By now, certain things are apparent. First, *The Man Who Wasn't There*, like every Coen film before it, readily lends itself to explication in terms of film and literary reference: a narrative line borrowed from here, a character from there, a camera move from somewhere else. Second, Joel can't stop saying 'we' or 'our'; even with his brother thousands of miles away, the sibling connection is a hard habit to break. Here's Joel talking about how *The Man Who Wasn't There* began to take shape: 'It's like a lot of the stuff we do: it starts in some form or other quite a while ago, but we very frequently will work on something for a while, we write a little bit of it, and then we come back to it much later. We probably first started thinking about it four or five years ago at least. It was pretty much finished by the time we started *O Brother*. But then George [Clooney] was available so we went ahead with that. Frequently, the order in which you do movies is dictated by when certain actors you want to work with are available to do them, and so the whole thing comes together.'

It's a tantalising thought, the Coens and their scripts. You can't get rid of the feeling that in some bulging bottom drawer lies a stack of unseen treasures waiting for their chance to get in front of the camera. It's happened before; *The Hudsucker Proxy* lay unused for a decade, written in the early 1980s with Raimi before *Blood Simple* had even begun filming. While *Blood Simple* was waiting for release, the three of them knocked off *Crimewave*, which became Raimi's second film a year later. A few years ago Ethan wrote a script about a wrestler-superhero called *The Naked Man*. (That became a feature film directed by their storyboard artist J. Todd Anderson.) They have completed an adaptation of *Cuba Libre*, an Elmore Leonard novel about a bank-robbing cowboy set in the 1890s. They did a draft (presumably rewritten again by someone else) for a still-to-be-shot film called *Intolerable Cruelty* that's been hanging around Hollywood for years. They've talked cryptically about something they've written 'for Ed Harris'.

As film history records, the Coens had to wait until special-effects technology had advanced to realise *Hudsucker*'s expensive fantasy sequences – and to command the budget to cover them. (This, at $25m, wasn't achieved until the mid-1990s, with the help of the unlikeliest of partners, action-movie superproducer Joel *Die Hard* Silver.) And despite all they've achieved, the brothers have just run slap-bang into the same barrier; their next project, an adaptation of James Dickey's *To the White Sea*, starring Brad Pitt and with a budget of $60m, has lost its backing from 20th Century Fox. The story of a US airman attempting to make his way home after crash-landing in Japan during the second world war, it ran into problems after Fox apparently baulked at the Coens' decision to film on location in Hokkaido.

What would be the Coens' biggest film to date is by no means dead yet, but reinforces Joel's wariness about getting involved with the big boys. 'You know, the ease with which we finance projects is completely dependent on what the budget of the movie is, and who's in it, I guess, more than who we are or what we've done. For a certain price it's easy for us to get things financed because now we're established ... you know, let us play in our corner of the sandbox so long as no one gets threatened or hurt. It's hard for someone to lose money so long as the movies are done very cheaply. But when the movie gets up above a certain amount of money it gets more difficult, more dependent on other factors. *To the White Sea* is quite a bit more expensive and very difficult subject matter.'

The turning-point, from a financial point of view, was undoubtedly the success of *Fargo*; up until then, they had thoroughly boxed themselves in to a high-prestige-but-low-money ghetto, imprisoned by the increasingly modest box-office figures of *Miller's Crossing*, *Barton Fink* and *Hudsucker*, none of which took more than $10m in their home country. And this despite the solid backing they obtained from British outfit Working Title, who came on board the Coen operation to help fund *Hudsucker*, and have stuck with them ever since.

"Maybe Doris will be there," Ed hopes of what lies beyond this world. "And maybe I can tell her all those things they don't have words for here." His closing lines demarcate the existential distance between them.

Despite the Cannes Palme d'Or they won for *Barton Fink* in 1991, the particularly depressing results for *Hudsucker* (released in 1994, cost $25m, took $2.8m in the US) meant that, like it or not, they had to think small. Against all expectations, *Fargo* – set in and around their home town of Minneapolis – at less than a third of the budget, took ten times their previous film, won two Oscars, and suddenly elevated the Coens to the front rank of American independent film-makers. Hence the flurry of activity since; you sense the brothers are making up for lost time, as well as striking while the iron is hot, and the light is green. Hence also the Coens' regular attendance at Cannes; European admiration has kept them afloat financially as well as critically, and they're grateful for it.

Since *Fargo*, the Coens have given the world *The Big Lebowski*, *O Brother, Where Art Thou?* and now *The Man Who Wasn't There*, each with their own pool of background reading, film technique and one-liners. They are, the French would agree, the consummate *auteurs*, their freaky-deaky brotherliness only serving to accentuate the idiosyncrasy of their films. But, strange to say, it's hard to believe the Coens have really developed as film-makers – other than in expanding the reading list. Where, you might ask, is the heart? You might ask, but you won't get an answer.

If the Coens are consistent about anything, it's the almost total self-effacement, authorially speaking, as regards their highly wrought films. Each seems independent of the others and of the people that made them. Joel is defensive on the point. 'I just see it as moving from story to story. There's no development, except that you try to do something a little different each time, different at least from what you did just previous to it so you keep the exercise interesting to yourself.'

If the Coens stand for anything, perhaps, it's a persistent desire to stand up for classical film-making. 'We still cut on film and not on computer. It's to do with idiosyncratic things about what kind of screen I want to look at all day. I like handling the film, too; how I learned how to edit was on flatbed editing machines and Moviolas, all the dinosaurs of the trade.' Since the industry has pretty much converted wholesale to computer editing, Joel is letting old habits die hard. That's also what makes the Coens' editing pseudonym – Roderick Jaynes, a mythical crusty old buffer from the British film old school, who was actually nominated for an Oscar for *Fargo* – a joke of such powerful longevity.

It's a principle that also extends into the shoot: no mucky DV cameras for them. 'The actual craft of movie making is part of what we're interested in,' he says. 'I'm not that interested in digital film-making because there's something . . .' Here he pauses to think. 'The technology's evolving and some day all movies will be made like that, but right now I don't find the results it yields are at the same level as shooting on film.' *The Man Who Wasn't There*, he says, was shot on colour stock, then printed on high-contrast black and white title stock. 'That's basically because no one in the last 40 years has developed new black and white film, so you can't find high-speed, fine-grade black and white stock. No one shoots it any more.' In contrast to their seemingly Luddite attitude to cinema technology, the Coens have quietly absorbed a lot of fancy computer-generated effects into their movies (principally *Hudsucker*), and even pioneered a particular software application by colour timing *O Brother* on computer to give the movie its washed-out sepia-photograph look. 'You just take what you need,' says Joel, tittering.

However much of an inscrutable face the Coens like to present to the world, their long-term success has seen the spawning of a quiet but persistent spin-off industry. Books have come along – most notably *The Making of The Big Lebowski* by William Preston Robertson – which have built a picture of their detail-obsessed working methods. They can be glimpsed in the background of *Down from the Mountain*, a Pennebaker and Hegedus documentary about the 'old time mountain style' bluegrass performers featured on the soundtrack of *O Brother, Where Art Thou?* Most significant of all, maybe, brother Ethan committed a collection of short stories to print last year, complementing the occasional articles that the Coens have issued to various magazines and published screenplays over the years.

It's through these writings that the avid fan can glean the kind of details that turn the Coens into human beings. In Robertson's book, for instance, the Coens' creative process is gone through in great detail; it also reveals that this most lolloping of Coen films is by far their most personal, in the sense that the two lead characters are based directly on acquaintances of theirs. A real life stoner, Jeff Dowd – aka the Pope of Dope –

metamorphosed into Jeff Lebowski; another bunch of friends (including he-man director and gun nut John Milius) contributed key aspects of John Goodman's Walter Sobchak.

All this is well documented; what's less often noted is the way the Coens' heavily orthodox Jewish upbringing has found its way into the character. Sobchak is forever quoting Zionist founding father Theodore Herzl – 'if you will it, Dude, it is no dream' – or shoehorning in references to his supposed Jewish background ('I told that kraut a fucking thousand times I don't roll on shabbas'). Turn if you will to Ethan's short story 'I Killed Phil Shapiro' in the *Gates of Eden* collection: there you will find, with the pungency of true authenticity, an account of a trip to a summer camp in Wisconsin – Camp Herzl. 'The camp director, Rabbi Sam,' writes Ethan, 'was a dark slender man with a yarmulke and hairy legs and a tall gnarled intensity. He spoke a few words of welcome in which figured the phrase "If You Will It, It Is No Dream."' It all clicks into focus, like those corny binocular shots in 1970s thrillers. Joel, as ever, is having none of it. 'Yeah, people sometimes want to feel like the stories have a direct relationship to your own life, or people that you know, or some continuing story which is a continuing reflection of your concern. Some film-makers work that way, very effectively. It's just not at all the way we approach the – whatever you want to call it – storytelling, or whatever it is. The stories are constructed out of what is interesting to us at the time, and different elements that we're interested in from things that we've read or seen or experienced and, ah . . . yeah . . .' He trails off.

But this stuff must come from somewhere? Reluctantly, Joel gives in. 'Yeah, we grew up in the Minneapolis suburbs, with a fairly religious upbringing. A lot of the Jewish references in *The Big Lebowski* come from things we heard over and over again in synagogues.' You don't strike me as religious now. 'No.' He giggles. 'It was just a big part of who we were growing up. We went to Hebrew school from second grade, five days a week after school. For a while there they were really drilling it into us. My mother comes from a pretty orthodox family, so it came from her mostly; my father not so much, though he was a fairly willing accomplice.'

Joel, however, grows fidgety fast under this line of questioning. He's even less interested in talking about anything to do with McDormand ('Fran's been there from the very beginning, from the first day of the first movie'). So it's bit of a shock that he suddenly becomes animated on the subject of his social life – after I ask him if he's ever had anything to do with Woody Allen, a film-maker of whom the Coens are a kind of bizarre inversion. 'I've never met him, but I saw him once in an elevator. He was slouched in a corner with a hat pulled over his face so no one would recognise him. It's funny, as a film director, you don't meet other directors at all often. In New York you can live your life in the film business and, if you choose, have nothing to do with other people involved in the same business. That's one of the nice things about New York – it's not a company town like L.A. It's actors who meet lots of film directors, because they go from movie to movie. So most of the directors I know are people I've met through Fran. I'm very good friends with John Boorman, for example, because of Fran doing a movie, *Beyond Rangoon*, with him. That's the way it works.'

After that small insight into the *auteur* film-makers' dinner-party circuit, Joel shuts up. He can go now, and he does.

THE MAN WHO WASN'T THERE

BY PETER BRADSHAW

'**D**idja ever think about hair?' asks the Barber, played by Billy Bob Thornton, snipping away at a chipmunk-favoured, comic-book-reading little boy, the crown of whose head he has turned into a hypnotic blond whorl. 'How it's a part of us? How it keeps on coming, and we just cut it off and throw it away?' His colleague tells him to cut it out: his weird intense talk is going to scare the kid. But the Barber persists. 'I'm gonna throw this hair away now and mingle it with common house dirt,' he says wonderingly, quietly, apparently on the verge of some kind of breakdown. But then, with an infinitesimally dismissive wince, the Barber waves the thought away and replaces his ever-present cigarette: 'Skip it.'

All of the power, the understatement and the profound enigma of Billy Bob Thornton's magnificent performance is contained in that brilliantly controlled and modulated scene, difficult though it is to single that out or anything else. This movie is quite simply the Coen brothers' masterpiece, and Thornton's brooding presence as the Barber, Ed Crane, is a stunning achievement. He is reticent, watchful, neither ingenuous nor jaded, but toughly stoic; he's quietly cynical and even desperate yet with a strong strain of decency, even quaintness: his strongest oath is 'Heavens to Betsy!'

Ed Crane's Americanness runs through him like a stick of rock. He has hardly any dialogue, but dominates the movie through his rumbling, tenor voiceover: he is indeed there but not there. This is a classic performance from Thornton, displaying the kind of maturity and technical mastery that we hardly dared hope for from this actor. His Ed Crane forms a kind of triangle with Henry Fonda in *The Wrong Man* and Gary Cooper in *High Noon*: a paradigm of virile, yet faintly baffled American ordinariness.

The work is a thriller in the style of James M. Cain, set in suburban California in 1949 and obviously influenced by the movies of the period, yet somehow transmitting the atmospheric crackle of a strange tale from *The Twilight Zone*. It is the story of how self-effacing Ed Crane, in yearning for a better station in life than that of the humble barber, with his smock and scissors, succeeds only in getting mixed up in the adulterous affair being conducted by his wife Doris, played by Frances McDormand, and her boss Big Dave (James Gandolfini), leading to blackmail, bloodshed, and the shadow of the electric chair.

The Man Who Wasn't There is shot in black-and-white by the Coens' long-standing cinematographer Roger Deakins, with superbly observed locations and sets: exquisitely lit, designed and furnished. As in so many of the Coens' films, an entire universe is summoned up, partly recognisable as our own, and yet different, a quirky variant on real life with its very own fixtures, fittings and brand names. Doris and Big Dave work in a department store with the jocose name of Nirdlinger's, whose creepy mannequins and hulking display cabinets are shown in the empty store at night. Ed Crane reads pulp magazines with names like *Stalwart, Muscle Power* and *Salute*. Yet in one shot he's also frowning over *Life* magazine, whose cover advertises an arresting article: 'Evelyn Waugh: Catholics in the US'. In a previous scene we've seen Ed and Doris attending church on a Tuesday night for the charity bingo session: a secular High Mass for the semi-believers.

Frances McDormand is the second compelling reason to see this film, the querulous wife who married our dourly taciturn Ed after a courtship of just two weeks, and on being asked if they should get to know each other more, simply replied: 'Does it get better?'

Ed is to reveal, glumly, that he and Doris 'have not performed the sex act for many years', yet somehow their relationship is saturated with a gamey erotic perfume, like the ones she gets from Nirdlinger's with her staff discount. She lounges in the bath, asking languidly for a drag of his cigarette and getting him to shave her legs, which he does humbly, unhesitatingly: an uxorious moment of displaced sexuality which is recalled in the movie's final, devastating scene.

With extraordinary clarity and economy, Joel and Ethan Coen present scenes from a marriage as fascinatingly fraught as anything in the cinema. All the time, Thornton's face looms over everything, a one-man Mount Rushmore of disquiet. Later on, Ed's pushy lawyer is to describe him as a piece of modern art, and that indeed is what he is, a piece of art, one moreover that the camera loves: his face is a composite of planes and lines, crags and wrinkles, defined by the crows' feet that fan out as he squints into the sun, or to filter out the cigarette smoke.

What a stunning, mesmeric movie this is. I can only hope that on Oscar night the Academy are not so cauterised with dumbness and cliché that they cannot recognise its originality and playful brilliance. *Noir* is the catch-all term given to movies like this – yet the Coens achieve their greatest, most disturbing moments in fierce sunlight, in the outdoors and in the dazzling white light of the final sequence. So I propose a new genre for this film – *noir-blanc*, a seriocomic masterpiece which transforms the quotidian ordinariness of waking lives. It is the best American film of the year.

INTOLERABLE CRUELTY

BY JEAN OPPENHEIMER

The Coen brothers had a golden opportunity to make a darkly humorous, deliciously clever battle of the sexes, and they let it slip through their fingers. Instead, the duo behind such irreverent and perverse comedies as *Fargo* and *Raising Arizona* settled for a broad farce that is long on manic, cartoonish behaviour and short on intelligence and wit. Given the palpable chemistry that exists between stars George Clooney and Catherine Zeta-Jones, this proves doubly disappointing.

A public accustomed to broad, undemanding Hollywood comedies filled with sitcom characters and buffoonish situations may react more kindly. Considering the star wattage here and the fact that audiences are starved for a good romantic comedy, Universal can expect a modest hit.

Clooney plays ace divorce attorney Miles Massey, whose killer charm and underhanded tactics have won more cases for more clients than any matrimonial lawyer in all of Los Angeles, Beverly Hills included. But after years of nothing but success, Massey has gotten bored. Something is missing from his life. At the very least, he needs a new challenge.

Enter Marylin Rexroth (the devastatingly gorgeous Zeta-Jones), about-to-be ex-wife of Massey's client Rex Rexroth (Edward Hermann). Thanks to caught-in-the-act photographs by private eye Gus Petch (Cedric the Entertainer), Marylin has an ironclad case. Or so she thinks. Massey uncovers some dirt on her, and she ends up with zip.

Surprisingly, Marylin doesn't seem to hold a grudge against Massey. She even goes to him to write a pre-nup for her next, very hasty marriage to oil billionaire Howard Doyle (Billy Bob Thornton). Massey, who was smitten with the elegant, unflappable Marylin the moment he laid eyes on her – an attraction cemented when they trade Shakespearean barbs over dinner (the film's only example of witty repartee) – tries to dissuade her from the marriage, which she clearly means to abandon at the earliest, legally permissible moment.

He fails, but when the inevitable happens and she leaves Doyle, Miles is waiting, and the two run off to get married. It turns out that the clever Marylin has a few tricks up her tastefully tailored sleeve, however, and Massey, truly and hopelessly in love for the first time in his life, is hung out to dry. He vows his own revenge, and soon the two are engaged in their own rehash of *Prizzi's Honor*.

Clooney has the potential to be another Cary Grant, and perhaps, given the right script and direction, he could succeed – think of Grant and Irene Dunne in one of the great romantic comedies of all time, *The Awful Truth* – but here he becomes increasingly bug-eyed and goofy as the movie wears on, as if he is playing Miles as another version of his character in the Coens' *O Brother, Where Art Thou?* The script doesn't help. Aside from a couple of very funny lines, the dialogue is undistinguished, lacking the zing and wit that made the likes of Preston Sturges and Noel Coward such a delight.

Alpha male meets femme fatale. *Ultra-smooth divorce lawyer Miles Massey (George Clooney) meets his match in Marylin Rexroth (Catherine Zeta-Jones), from* Intolerable Cruelty.

Known for much blacker and more perverse humour than that exhibited here, director Joel Coen and producer Ethan Coen (who share screenwriting credit with Robert Ramsey and Matthew Stone) can be forgiven for trying a more conventional type of film, but it's disappointing to think they meant it to be quite this broad and generic. The stereotypical slapstick of the opening scene, in which a TV hack played by Geoffrey Rush catches his wife with the brawny but brainless pool guy, is lazy and witless. Hermann as Marylin's ex and Paul Adelstein as Massey's worshipful associate are an embarrassment.

Amazingly, the audience at the Venice International Film Festival laughed through much of the movie. Maybe viewers no longer require a sharp script or incisive humour. George Cukor, Howard Hawks and Billy Wilder must be turning over in their graves.

INTOLERABLE CRUELTY

BY DAVID ROONEY

Proving he's the closest thing to Cary Grant in contempo cinema, George Clooney effortlessly radiates mischievous charm in *Intolerable Cruelty*, a thoroughly entertaining comedy about love, lawyers and fat divorce settlements. While a slight imbalance in the romantic formula stops it just short of truly soaring, the crackling dialogue and buoyant wordplay make this a delightful throwback to classic screwball comedies. More mainstream and conventional than anything Joel and Ethan Coen have done in the past, yet not without the brothers' trademark wit, this should top *O Brother, Where Art Thou?* to become their most commercial entry to date.

Universal premiered the pungent comedy at the Venice Film Festival as a work-in-progress, with some further tinkering reportedly still to come prior to the fall release. Clooney said at the Venice press conference – which the Coens skipped due to shooting commitments on their next project – that a couple more new scenes have been shot,

Intolerable Cruelty makes fun of the pre-nuptial agreements of the rich and famous – laughing at the Beverly Hills lifestyle while bringing the Coens closer to mainstream Hollywood.

Aspiring to the vintage screwball comedies of Howard Hawks or George Cukor, Intolerable Cruelty *features Catherine Zeta-Jones as a Katharine Hepburn figure – adding modern sex appeal to her charm and sophistication.*

which may be included. However, aside from some minor tweaks to the sound mix and dialogue levels, the film appears ready to roll as is.

Clooney plays Miles Massey, a wildly successful Los Angeles divorce attorney feeling the incipient itch of boredom and midlife crisis. Miles' ability to win cases regardless of the evidence stacked against his clients is illustrated when Bonnie Donaly (Stacey Travis) retains his services and bleeds dry her TV producer husband, Donovan (Geoffrey Rush), despite his having caught her entertaining a pool cleaner (Jack Kyle) in a house with no pool.

Similarly daunting evidence weighs against philandering real estate developer Rex Rexroth (Edward Hermann), who hires Miles to represent him when his wife, Marylin (Catherine Zeta-Jones), obtains a video of her husband and a floozy bouncing around a motel room. While Miles is far from immune to knockout Marylin's ice-cool charms, he turns the tables on her in court, presenting a surprise witness (Jonathan Hadary) who exposes her as a gold-digger who set out to marry a wealthy fool. As a result, Marylin comes away with nothing.

Licking her wounds and plotting revenge, Marylin resurfaces in Miles' office with her future husband, oil tycoon Howard Doyle (Billy Bob Thornton), and insists on signing the famously impenetrable 'Massey pre-nup' as proof her love is unsullied by material concerns. Taking a hint subtly planted by Marylin, Howard destroys the contract during their wedding as a gesture of his love, allowing his bride to take him to the cleaners.

Six months later when she reappears, the mutual attraction between Marylin and Miles is stronger than ever, and she sinks her claws into him with an unhappy-rich-girl act. But Miles gets wise to her conniving, prompting an increasingly ruthless series of deceptions and counter-tactics.

Remarkably sustained and consistently funny, the film often recalls classic comedies of union and divorce like *The Awful Truth* and *Mr. and Mrs. Smith*, or the attraction-animosity of *Bringing Up Baby*. The precision-tooled screenplay by the Coens, Robert Ramsey and Matthew Stone sparkles with clever dialogue, dark humour and some hilarious comic set pieces.

One scene in particular, involving asthmatic hit man Wheezy Joe (Irwin Keyes), seems destined to become a classic in the Coens pantheon. The script also has real bite in its observations about the vultures of Beverly Hills, whether they be amoral lawyers or Botox-pumped career divorcees.

As always with the filmmakers, there's a colourful gallery of peripheral figures, superbly cast with gifted character actors. A pony-tailed, California-bronzed Rush perfectly sets the slightly manic comic tone in the terrific opening sequence; Thornton's timing and delivery are razor-sharp as the verbose Texan dolt; Cedric the Entertainer scores some big laughs as an overzealous private detective who specialises in nailing adulterers; Hadary is a riot as the fey hotel concierge; and Paul Adelstein is enormously appealing as Miles' blindly loyal, sentimental associate.

The script's one weakness – though not a crippling one – lies in the development of Marylin. Zeta-Jones looks spectacular and plays the calculating beauty with flawless poise and authority. But the character is so venal and self-serving that she lacks the warmth and heart to be fully convincing when her deeper feelings for Miles kick in. On one hand, this keeps the audience guessing about whether she's on the level or still scheming, but on the other, it slightly undermines the romantic comedy.

But this is really Clooney's film, and as he did in *O Brother, Where Art Thou?*, the actor again shows his comic sensibility and the Coens' are a genial match. In a running joke that echoes Clooney's endless hair concerns in that earlier film, Miles' dazzling capped teeth are his main obsession here. Slick and unscrupulous but never for a moment seeming without a soul, Miles is all about easy confidence and control, fast talk and an ultra-smooth manner. But Clooney balances just enough emotional openness to be believable when the lawyer drops his smart cynicism.

Appropriately, for this kind of star-driven vehicle, regular Coen cinematographer Roger Deakins goes for a crisp, glossy look and rich colours, matched with stylish costumes, handsome production design and upscale Los Angeles locations that reflect the well-heeled characters. Musically, the film makes amusing use of Simon and Garfunkel tunes, but perhaps under-utilises Carter Burwell's jaunty score.

AFTERWORD

BY PAUL A. WOODS

THE TITLES

Intolerable Cruelty. The Ladykillers. Romance and Cigarettes.

THE PITCHES

A mainstream Hollywood romantic comedy, with a twist of Coenesque dark humour, harking back to the screwball comedies of the 1930s/40s and featuring an A-list cast.

A very loose adaptation of one of the darker Ealing comedies of the 1950s, contemporised to the present day and the Deep South.

According to *Variety*, "a cross between the stylised 1981 Steve Martin musical *Pennies from Heaven* and *The Honeymooners*."

THE INSPIRATION

The Coens were about to go into pre-production on *To the White Sea*, adapted from the novel by *Deliverance* author James Dickey. Scheduled to star Brad Pitt as a WWII pilot shot down over Japan, the brothers took the helm on the basis that they discard the already existing screenplay and prepare their own. On the heels of the commercial failure of their brilliant *The Man Who Wasn't There*, it might have been their most audacious film yet: the story followed B-29 gunner and Alaskan hunter Muldrow as he undertakes an odyssey to the desolate island of Hokkaido off the northern coast of Japan. Featuring virtually no dialogue and much violence, the $55 million budget and location filming made some of the backers, who included 20th Century Fox, back out at the eleventh hour.

When *To the White Sea* 'went down the old drainerino', as Joel so Dude-ishly puts it, the brothers' immediate recourse was to head for a safer commercial option. Their screenplay for *Intolerable Cruelty* was already placed with Universal Pictures, having been written back in 1994. An altogether more conventional work about a *femme fatale* seducing a Beverly Hills attorney with a view to making his life hell, for the first time it wasn't an original Coens screenplay – the first draft being by screenwriters Robert Ramsey and Matthew Stone.

While the mixed critical response to *Intolerable Cruelty* suggests it may please the mainstream audience more than long-term Coen-heads, the brothers have ducked the issue by going into production on their next film while it previews at the 2003 Venice Film Festival. *The Ladykillers* follows their current trend by being based upon an already existing screenplay, that of the 1955 British comedy directed by Alexander McKendrick. But that's where the resemblance ends. While the premise of a gang of incompetent thieves trying (and failing) to murder their old landlady stays the same, the screenplay promises a range of gleefully Coenesque characters: from landlady Mrs Marva Munson, a devout old black woman who talks to her dead husband and complains to the sheriff's office about "hippity-

Brothers on a roll: laconic Joel and chirpy Ethan direct the Hollywood A-listers on their most commercial film to date.

hop", and her charming linguist boarder, Prof. Goldthwait Higginson Dorr (really the gang leader), to Lump Hudson, a hulking failed football player, 'a goon, an ape, a physical brute' who acts as the gang's muscle.

The mooted *Romance and Cigarettes* goes one further in not being a Coen screenplay at all. Written by Coens stalwart John Turturro, this musical, set in his hometown of Bensonhurst, Brooklyn, is said to follow the melancholic style of *Pennies from Heaven*, the US version of TV playwright Dennis Potter's Depression-era tragedy with songs. It sounds like the empathy with Turturro and his material may make for a quirky triumph, if not a grand folly.

THE CASTING

After a twenty-year career, the Coen brothers can truly be said to have 'arrived' as A-list directors with an A-list cast. *Intolerable Cruelty*, of course, features Clooney in the lead, purportedly seeking to repeat the good time he had on *O Brother, Where Art Thou?*, while his gorgeous tormentor is played by ex-pat Brit Catherine Zeta-Jones, still reaping accolades for *Traffic* (2001). Eccentric character roles are also occupied, in time-honoured style, by such distinct figures as Cedric the Entertainer and Billy Bob Thornton. *The Ladykillers* stays up in the big league, casting Tom Hanks as the gang leader while Marlon Wayans makes a stylistic and ethnic substitute for original Brit gang members like the young Herbert Lom and Peter Sellers. And, if *Romance and Cigarettes* goes ahead, the Coens are scheduled to bring us an all-singing, all-dancing James Gandolfini, Susan Sarandon, Kate Winslet and Christopher Walken.

As Joel acknowledges, "We do tend to work with bigger stars now." After Clooney, the trend continues with Tom Hanks in The Ladykillers.

THE MOVIES

Now that the first couple of Coen films that don't originate from their own source material are in the pipeline (overlooking Sam Raimi's co-authorship of *The Hudsucker Proxy* and Homer's posthumous contribution to *O Brother*), we'll just have to see what consitutes a Joel and Ethan Coen movie in the mid-2000's. Quibbles already abound as to vhether *Intolerable Cruelty* is a Coen brothers movie or a mainstream movie with the odd Coen touch. Other adapted screenplays are on hold: *Cuba Libre*, their adaptation of Elmore Leonard's historical action novel, is apparently "just a writing job"; *Fun with Dick and Jane*, their take on the 1977 Jane Fonda-George Segal bank-robbery caper, was to be a directorial project for old buddy Barry Sonnenfeld, until their former director of photography pulled out.

Meanwhile, however, the leaked script of *The Ladykillers* promises much character idioysyncrasy in the time-honoured style: a professorial expert on dead languages, who's planning to rob a riverboat and kill his landlady, leading a gang that includes a Grizzly Adams-alike explosives expert suffering from irritable bowel syndrome and a Vietnamese general who runs a doughnut shop in Mississippi.

Whatever the respective merits of this new wave of Coens films, it's safe to echo Joel's appropriated quote: "What's the Raymond Chandler line? 'All good art is entertainment and anyone who says differently is a stuffed shirt and juvenile at the art of living.'"

FILMOGRAPHY

BLOOD SIMPLE

RAY	John Getz
ABBY	Frances McDormand
MARTY	Dan Hedaya
VISSER (PRIVATE DETECTIVE)	
	M. Emmet Walsh
MEURICE	Samm–Art Williams
DEBRA	Deborah Neumann
LANDLADY	Raquel Gavia
MAN FROM LUBBOCK	Van Brooks
MR GARCIA	Senor Marco
OLD CRACKER	William Creamer
STRIP BAR EXHORTER	Loren Bivens
STRIP BAR SENATOR	Bob McAdams
STRIPPER	Shannon Sedwick
GIRL ON OVERLOOK	Nancy Finger
RADIO EVANGELIST	
	Rev. William Preston Robertson

Casting: Julie Hughes and Barry Moss
Music: Carter Burwell
Production Designer: Jane Musky
Editors: Roderick Jaynes, Don Wiegmann
Director of Photography: Barry Sonnenfeld
Associate Producer: Mark Silverman
Executive Producer: Daniel F. Bacaner
Producer: Ethan Coen
Written by Joel Coen and Ethan Coen
Directed by Joel Coen
97 minutes, 1984 (River Road Productions)

CRIMEWAVE

HELENE TREND	Louise Lasser
FARON CRUSH	Paul L. Smith
ARTHUR CODDISH	Brion James
NANCY	Sheree J. Wilson
ERNEST TREND	Edward R. Pressman
RENALDO "THE HEEL"	Bruce Campbell
VIC AJAX	Reed Birney

Music: Arlon Ober
Editors: Michael Kelly and Kathie Weaver
Director of Photography: Robert Primes
Executive Producers: Edward R. Pressman,
Irvin Shapiro
Producers: Robert Tapert, Bruce Campbell
Written by Ethan Coen, Joel Coen and Sam Raimi
Directed by Sam Raimi
86 minutes, 1985 (Renaissance Pictures)

RAISING ARIZONA

H. I. MCDUNNOUGH	Nicolas Cage
ED	Holly Hunter
NATHAN ARIZONA, SR.	Trey Wilson
GALE	John Goodman
EVELLE	William Forsythe
GLEN	Sam McMurray
DOT	Frances McDormand
LEONARD SMALLS	Randall "Tex" Cobb
NATHAN JR.	T. J. Kuhn
FLORENCE ARIZONA	
	Lynne Dumin Kitei
PRISON COUNSELLOR	Peter Benedek
NICE OLD GROCERY MAN	
	Charles "Lew" Smith
YOUNGER FBI AGENT	Warren Keith
OLDER FBI AGENT	Henry Kendrick
EAR-BENDING CELLMATE	
	Sidney Dawson
PAROLE BOARD CHAIRMAN	
	Richard Blake
PAROLE BOARD MEMBERS	
	Troy Nabors, Mary Seibel
MACHINE SHOP EARBENDER	
	M. Emmet Walsh

and the voice of William Preston Robertson
Casting: Donna Isaacson and John Lyons
Music: Carter Burwell
Production Designer: Jane Musky
Editor: Michael R. Miller
Director of Photography: Barry Sonnenfeld
Associate Producer: Deborah Reinisch
Executive Producer: James Jacks
Producers: Ethan Coen, Mark Silverman
Written by Ethan Coen and Joel Coen
Directed by Joel Coen.
94 minutes, 1987 (Circle Films, Inc.)

MILLER'S CROSSING

TOM REAGAN	Gabriel Byrne
VERNA	Marcia Gay Harden
BERNIE BERNBAUM	John Turturro
JOHNNY CASPAR	Jon Polito
EDDIE DANE	J. E. Freeman
LEO	Albert Finney
FRANKIE	Mike Starr
TIC-TAC	Al Mancini
MAYOR DALE LEVANDER	Richard Woods
O'DOOLE	Thomas Toner
MINK	Steve Buscemi
CLARENCE "DROP" JOHNSON	
	Charles "Lew" Smith
TAD	Olek Krupa
ADOLPH	Michael Jeter
TERRY	Lanny Flaherty
MRS CASPAR	Jeanette Kontomitras

JOHNNY CASPAR, JR.
Louis Charles Mounicou III
LANDLADY   Hilda McLean
GUNMEN IN LEO'S HOUSE
Monte Starr/Don Picard
RUG DANIELS   Salvatore H. Tornabene
CASPAR'S DRIVER   Michael Badalucco
HITMEN AT VERNA'S   Charles Gurning/
Dave Drinkx
MAN WITH PIPE BOMB Jack David Harris
SNICKERING GUNMAN   Sam Raimi
BOXERS   Joey Ancona/Bill Raye
and the voice of William Preston Robertson
Casting: Donna Isaacson and John Lyons
Original Music: Carter Burwell
Production Designer: Dennis Gassner
Editor: Michael Miller
Director of Photography: Barry Sonnenfeld
Associate Producer: Graham Place
Executive Producer: Ben Barenholtz
Producers: Ethan Coen, Mark Silverman
Written by   Joel Coen and Ethan Coen
Directed by   Joel Coen
115 minutes, 1990 (Circle Films, Inc.)

BARTON FINK
BARTON FINK   John Turturro
CHARLIE MEADOWS   John Goodman
AUDREY TAYLOR   Judy Davis
JACK LIPNICK   Michael Lerner
W. P. MAYHEW   John Mahoney
BEN GEISLER   Tony Shalhoub
LOU BREEZE   Jon Polito
CHET   Steve Buscemi
GARLAND STANDFORD David Warrilow
DETECTIVE MASTRIONOTTI
Richard Portnow
DETECTIVE DEUTSCH
Christopher Murney
and the voice of William Preston Robertson
Casting: Donna Isaacson and John Lyons
Music: Carter Burwell
Production Designer: Dennis Gassner
Editors: Roderick Jaynes, Michael Barenbaum
Director of Photography: Roger Deakins
Executive Producers: Ben Barenholtz / Ted Pedas /
Jim Pedas / Bill Durkin
Producers: Ethan Coen, Graham Place
Written by   Ethan Coen and Joel Coen
Directed by   Joel Coen
116 minutes, 1991 (Circle Films, Inc.)

THE HUDSUCKER PROXY
NORVILLE BARNES   Tim Robbins
AMY ARCHER   Jennifer Jason Leigh
SIDNEY J. MUSSBERGER   Paul Newman
WARING HUDSUCKER   Charles Durning
CHIEF   John Mahoney
BUZZ   Jim True

MOSES   William Cobbs
SMITTY   Bruce Campbell
LOU   Joe Grifasi
BENNY   John Seitz
BEATNIK BARMAN   Steve Buscemi
VIC TENETTA   Peter Gallagher
Casting: Donna Isaacson and John Lyons
Music: Carter Burwell
Production Designer: Dennis Gassner
Editor: Thom Noble
Second Unit Director: Sam Raimi
Director of Photography: Roger Deakins
Executive Producers: Eric Fellner, Tim Bevan
Producers: Ethan Coen, Graham Place
Written by   Ethan Coen, Joel Coen and Sam Raimi
Directed by   Joel Coen
111 minutes, 1994 (Silver Pictures, in association
with Working Title Films)

FARGO
MARGE GUNDERSON
Frances McDormand
CARL SHOWALTER   Steve Buscemi
JERRY LUNDEGAARD William H. Macy
GAEAR GRIMSRUD   Peter Stormare
WADE GUSTAFSON   Harve Presnell
NORM GUNDERSON John Carroll Lynch
JEAN LUNDEGAARD   Kristin Rudrud
SHEP PROUDFOOT   Steven Reevis
MIKE YANAGANITA   Steve Park
SCOTTY LUNDEGAARD   Tony Denman
REILLY DIFFENBACH   Warren Keith
STATE TROOPER   James Gaulke
JOSE FELICIANO   Himself
Casting: John Lyons
Music: Carter Burwell
Production Designer: Rick Heinrichs
Editors: Roderick Jaynes, Tricia Cooke
Director of Photography: Roger Deakins
Line Producer: John Cameron
Executive Producers: Tim Bevan, Eric Fellner
Producer: Ethan Coen
Written by   Ethan Coen and Joel Coen
Directed by   Joel Coen
97 minutes, 1996 (Working Title Films)

THE BIG LEBOWSKI
THE DUDE   Jeff Bridges
WALTER SOBCHAK   John Goodman
MAUDE LEBOWSKI   Julianne Moore
DONNY   Steve Buscemi
THE BIG LEBOWSKI   David Huddleston
BRANDT   Philip Seymour Hoffman
BUNNY LEBOWSKI   Tara Reid
TREEHORN THUGS   Philip Moon/Mark
Pellegrino
NIHILISTS Peter Stormare/Flea/Torsten Voges
SMOKEY   Jimmie Dale Gilmore
DUDE'S LANDLORD   Jack Kehler

JESUS QUINTANA	John Turturro
QUINTANA'S PARTNER	James G. Hoosier
KNOX HARRINGTON	David Thewlis
THE STRANGER	Sam Elliott
JACKIE TREEHORN	Ben Gazzara
MALIBU POLICE CHIEF	Leon Russom
PRIVATE SNOOP	Jon Polito
NIHILIST WOMAN	Aimee Mann
SADDAM	Jerry Haleva
Casting:	John Lyons
Original Music:	Carter Burwell
Production Designer:	Rick Heinrichs
Editors:	Roderick Jaynes, Tricia Cooke
Director of Photography:	Roger Deakins
Line Producer:	John Cameron
Executive Producers:	Tim Bevan, Eric Fellner
Producers:	Ethan Coen, John Cameron
Written by	Ethan Coen and Joel Coen
Directed by	Joel Coen

127 minutes, 1998 (Working Title Films)

O BROTHER, WHERE ART THOU?

ULYSSES EVERETT MCGILL	George Clooney
DELMAR O'DONNEL	Tim Blake Nelson
PETE	John Turturro
BIG DAN TEAGUE	John Goodman
GEORGE "BABY FACE" NELSON	
	Michael Badalucco
GOVERNOR OF MISSISSIPPI	
	Charles Durning
DOBRO PLAYER	Jerry Douglas
HOMER STOKES	Wayne Duvall
PENNY MCGILL WHARVEY	Holly Hunter
SIRENS	Mia Tate/Christy Taylor/Musetta Vander
Music:	Carter Burwell and Chris Thomas King
Second Unit Director:	Jonathan McGarry
Production Designer:	Dennis Gassner
Director of Photography:	Roger Deakins
Associate Producer:	Robert Graf
Executive Producers:	Tim Bevan, Eric Fellner
Producer:	Ethan Coen

Written by Ethan Coen, Joel Coen and Homer (from his poem *The Odyssey*)

Directed by Joel Coen

106 mins, 2000 (Working Title Films, in association with Buena Vista Pictures)

THE MAN WHO WASN'T THERE

EDWARD "ED" CRANE	Billy Bob Thornton
DORIS CRANE	Frances McDormand
FRANK	Michael Badalucco
DAVID "BIG DAVE" BREWSTER	James Gandolfini
ANNE NIRDLINGER	Katherine Borowitz
CREIGHTON TOLLIVER	Jon Polito
RACHEL "BIRDY" ABUNDAS	Scarlett Johansson
WALTER ABUNDAS	Richard Jenkins

FREDDY RIEDENSCHNEIDER	Tony Shalhoub
PERSKY	Christopher Kriesa
KREBS	Brian Haley
BURNS	Jack McGee
THE NEW MAN	Gregg Binkley
DIEDRICKSON	Alan Fudge
MEDIUM	Lilyan Chauvin
JACQUES CARCANOGUES	Adam Alexi-Malle
Casting:	Ellen Chenoweth
Original Music:	Carter Burwell
Non-Original Music:	Wolfgang Amadeus Mozart/Ludwig van Beethoven
Production Designer:	Dennis Gassner
Editors:	Roderick Jaynes, Tricia Cooke
Director of Photography:	Roger Deakins
Associate Producer:	Robert Graf
Executive Producers:	Tim Bevan, Eric Fellner
Producers:	Ethan Coen, John Cameron
Written by	Ethan Coen and Joel Coen
Directed by	Joel Coen

110 mins, 2001 (Good Machine/The KL Line/Working Title Films, in association with USA Films)

INTOLERABLE CRUELTY

MILES MASSEY	George Clooney
MARYLIN REXROTH	Catherine Zeta-Jones
DONOVAN DONNELLY	Geoffrey Rush
GUS PETCH	Cedric the Entertainer
REX REXROTH	Edward Herrmann
FREDDY BENDER	Richard Jenkins
HOWARD DOYLE	Billy Bob Thornton
WRIGLEY	Paul Adelstein
SARA SORKIN	Julia Duffy
Casting:	Ellen Chenoweth, Rachel Tenner
Original Music:	Carter Burwell
Production Designer:	Leslie McDonald
Editor:	Roderick Jaynes
Director of Photography:	Roger Deakins
Associate Producer:	Robert Graf
Executive Producers:	Sean Daniel, James Jacks
Producers:	Ethan Coen, John Cameron, Grant Heslov

Story by Robert Ramsey and Matthew Stone, John Romano
Written by Robert Ramsey and Matthew Stone, Ethan Coen and Joel Coen

Directed by Joel Coen

100 mins, 2003 (Alphaville Films/Imagine Entertainment/The KL Line, in association with Universal Pictures)

THE LADYKILLERS

PROFESSOR GOLDTHWAIT HIGGINSON DORR	
	Tom Hanks
GAWAIN MACSAM	Marlon Wayans
MRS. MARVA MUNSON	Irma P. Hall
LUMP HUDSON	Ryan Hurst
THE SHERIFF	George Wallace
Producer:	Ethan Coen

Written by Ethan Coen and Joel Coen, based on the original screenplay *The Ladykillers* by William Rose

Directed by Joel Coen

for release in 2004 (Buena Vista Pictures)